Fortune's Foal

A True Tale of Courage, Hope, and Unbreakable Bonds

Anita Bell

Tarampa Studios
a Division of Bleetie & Co Pty Ltd

International & National Library
Cataloguing-in-Publication Data

Bell, Anita
Fortune's Foal: A True Tale of Courage.
Hope and Unbreakable Bonds
COPYRIGHT © 2024, Bleetie & Co Pty Ltd

Format: Paperback
ISBN 13: 978-1-7635325-3-3
   1. Young Adult Non-Fiction
   2. Pets
   3. Horses

ALL RIGHTS RESERVED:
Part of this story was previously published as:
"Fortune's Foal: A True Story of a City Girl and
a Little Horse Who Made History Together" by Anita Bell
COPYRIGHT © 2013, Bleetie & Co Pty Ltd

Executive Director & Author; Anita Bell
Australian Business Number: 97 098 664 389

Cover art: © Anita Bell 2024
All photos: © Anita Bell 1984

Extract from *Potties Horse Dictionary* (by Methuen) reprinted
under Fair Use of Copyright for Educational Purposes.

Without limiting the rights under copyright above, no part of this publication may be reproduced, stored in or introduced into a retrieval system or transmitted in any form, or by any means (electronic, mechanical, photocopying, recording or otherwise) without the prior written consent of the copyright owner and/or author.

Foreword by Dr Norbert Gaulton, School of Veterinary Science
Queensland

Being a veterinarian is not an easy job. Animals cannot talk, so we rely on the owners for the history of the current condition and for the ongoing treatment once a diagnosis is made. During my 25-year career in private practice I had many clients who were compliant with prescribed treatments and nursing care for their animals, however none as diligent as Anita.

After my first meeting with her, I thought, "This is an amazing young girl". She was so positive about Lucky's treatment and the thought of his not recovering did not seem to have entered her mind.

Tetanus is a serious, and preventable, disease which is usually fatal. I can remember saying to her at the time "It will be the nursing care which will pull him through, not the veterinary medicines".

Her dedication to Lucky's care was outstanding. I am proud to have known her for so long.

Thank you, Anita, for making my job easier ...without your persistence I would have not known Lucky for all of those years.

All the best.
Norbert

Contents

1. Black Friday 1
2. Just a City Girl with a Country Heart, and Too Many Pets Already ... 3
3. The Thing That Changed Everything 13
4. Historically Horrific Happenstances 21
5. Meeting Lucky 29
6. Fortune Played Me Like a Fiddle. 33
7. Bidder Number 26 39
8. Scraping It Up 47
9. Racing That Deadline 53
10. Beg, Grovel, Beseech, Implore, Entreat… 61
11. Thus Began The Saga of the Return Journey 65
12. To Catch a Horse Thief 75
13. Out of the Frying Pan… 81
14. The More the Merrier, I Hoped 89
15. Night of the Raving Lunatics 95
16. Option C; by Bitter Experience 103
17. Legalities of Life 111
18. Fright of the April Fools 123
19. Change of Scenery 129
20. The Desperate Search for a Driver 135
21. Dawn of the Ordeal 143
22. The Epic Quest for a New Vet 151
23. Consent for Two Lethal Injections 159
24. Meeting Norbert 169
25. Back to Blackwood 179

26. For as Long as it Takes	193
27. Emotional Rollercoaster (Day 2)	201
28. End of the Marathon (Days 3 & 4)	211
29. Dead Again	217
30. The Sling	233
31. Dawn of the Prowler (Day 5)	243
32. Resignation (Days 4 to 6)	249
33. Day Five	257
34. The Littlest Soldier	263
35. Warm Horse Tea (Days 7 & 8)	271
36. Power Naps, Power Nightmares	275
37. Dark Moment of the Soul	283
38. The Sound of Joy	289
39. Frosty Road to Recovery (Days 10, 11 and 12)	299
40. One Final Turn of Fate	303
Appendix I: Recipes for a Sweet Finale	307
Our 'Never Fail' Chocolate Cake	307
Anzac Biscuits (or charred chunks)	308
Appendix II: Extract from *Pottie's Horse Dictionary*	309
My Personal Notes to this Extract:	310
Dedications (& Pat-hooeeys)	311
Lucky on his 13th & 26th Birthdays:	313
About the Author	315

ANITA BELL

1. Black Friday

January, 13th 1984

The storm hit our little valley near Rosewood hard that night. It seemed like the cruelest weather for giving birth, especially for a horse who feared lightning. The mare was skinny after surviving the last few years of severe drought and extreme heat, and the deadliest bushfire season for a century. Now the Big Wet was finally taking its turn, whipping her brown hide with a vengeance.

Alone in the large expanse of an abandoned mining paddock, with only the discarded mounds of coal rubble as shelter against the icy wind, she laid down and strained to give life. Rain and hail pelted her, while inside the foal turned, forcing her to rise again and churn circles around her chosen birthing spot until his little front hooves moved up into position, below his nose.

At eighteen years of age, the mare had experience as well as instinct and intelligence. But eighteen for a horse is sixty-three in human years. A real grandma, giving birth again.

Her thirteenth foal would be her last.

She dropped to her knees in time for the next contraction. Rolling down on her side and stretching out her neck and stomach in the mud, she took rests as often as possible – working through the pain - until morning.

When the man in the yellow plastic raincoat came to fetch her, he found her standing squarely over her tiny newborn.

Her feet remained splayed wide apart around him, sheltering the little chestnut as best she could.

Tying a rope around her neck, the man tugged and led

her away, back through the tangle of rusted wires in their fence.

She nickered for her little colt to follow, and as he rose on spindly legs, he stumbled and trotted after them, leaving only his small hoof prints to mark the start of his story in the mud behind them.

… 13 days later…
On the other side Ipswich city…

I slept peacefully in my own bedroom on the second floor of our home; surrounded by sketches of horses and ponies, dating back to my first stickman in kindergarten.

Many also had inspirational quotes I'd been collecting since primary school… like one above my bed, from a coloring book, with Bugs Bunny in pink crayon, warning;

In my book, Doc, humans are only as good as they treat animals.

I didn't realize it yet, but it was a lesson I was about to learn in the harshest way.

2. Just a City Girl with a Country Heart, and Too Many Pets Already

7:13am
Splat!

A bird crashed into my bedroom window.

More regular than my Bugs Bunny alarm clock, which was supposed to wake me each morning at 7:45 with an inspirational or insightful quote to help get my day going, that silly bird crashed every morning at dawn. And it had been crashing for months – ever since my parents raised our little timber house in the suburbs to build brick walls underneath for an office, bathroom and lounge area for my dad's backyard mechanical business.

Close to the city, our suburb sat in the U-bend of a brown river that often smelled like a sewer, but the soil was dark and rich, so the lawns were lush and the gardens colourful. Everywhere except *our* yard, where my father had concreted the middle third for customer parking. That left only a small area right at the back for an old swing set, my dad's fruit trees and a patch of lawn that often grew as high as my ankles.

On my window ledge, the bird shook himself. He had bright blue wings, but he couldn't have been very bright in the head if he couldn't remember our house was taller now amongst the leafy trees.

'Hi Bruiser,' I said, but he only shook himself and flew off again, same ritual as always, leaving me to cancel my alarm before it went off. No quote from Bugs today, but Thursday's quote was only a reminder to be kind to animals, and I already had that ingrained on a molecular level.

I threw back my covers, stood up in bed and leapt for my door, racing my Siamese kitten Muffy out to the kitchen. She loved to play "tiger under my bed", hiding and attacking my ankles if I tried to rise out of bed like a normal slow, sleepy human.

'Grr-ow-ow-ow!' Doggo complained, as only a sheep-dog can. As a cross between a border collie and Australian kelpie – where both of my dog's parents had been high energy champions, bred for their instincts in "policing" large flocks of sheep outside the city - our Doggo was often bored, so he'd appointed himself as our family police dog, and always tried to break up any disputes or boisterous play before anyone got hurt. Usually me.

Asleep under the dining table until we disturbed him, Doggo raced out and chased my heels too, herding me past the open bedroom doors to my younger brother and sister's rooms, and past a row of inspirational quotes on wall hangings that were meant to remind us all how to behave or set goals, without my parents needing to nag us every day while they were busy with the business.

Not that my pets ever lent me much time to ponder over such things – except maybe in the loo, where we'd all glued up so many famous inspirational quotes that I'd painted a label for the back of the door in neat calligraphy that said; *The Little White Throne Room's Great Wall of Wisdom.*

Yet I didn't have time for a pit-stop there either. Or the chance. As I raced past the bathroom, I tackled Muffy at the same time as she tackled me, and we tumbled onto the floor together in the hall outside my parent's bedroom, laughing and playfully hissing at each other, while our other four Siamese kittens all raced out from each bedroom, keen to join in our mad morning ritual.

'Anita's up,' said my dad without needing to look. He

simply groaned as he rolled over in bed.

I headed for the kitchen, keen to enjoy my very first public holiday. My first since graduating highschool, at least. Sixteen years old, and I'd already scored my first job – even if it was only as a casual "check-out chick" at my local supermarket. I'd been grabbing every possible shift and working overtime all month, trying to save up enough to move out of the city.

Yet my pay was so low, after deducting my regular expenses and weekly board and lodging fees to stay living at home with my parents, my surplus savings rarely surmounted five dollars. So my first public holiday as an "employee" seemed sweeter than ever. But I couldn't get busy with fun yet.

My #1 Rule: *Never feed myself until after I'd fed my pets.*

That way, I'd never forget. I doubt they'd let me, but on that particular morning, I'd also scheduled an additional task with a vet down on the riverbank at the end of my street, where I kept my two largest pets; Apache and Snow - a pair of hardy Australian stock horses that I'd bought and cared for by myself since I was 12.

Fiction, you might think, or exaggeration, but the truth is; I'd been begging my parents for a horse ever since I outgrew riding our dog, so by the time I turned 10, my dad gave in – sort of – and said I could get one, provided I could save up enough and find somewhere to care for it all by myself.

'There's no room in a city for a horse,' he'd warned me. 'You'll have to save up and buy a farm in the country.'

But like any cheeky daughter, since he hadn't said no, exactly, I took it as permission to find a way in the meantime. So I did.

It only took me two years of starving at school, secretly hoarding my lunch money and working chores for neighbours up and down the street. During this time, I also discovered that most of the houses along the river had lush grassy banks that had been going to waste. It seemed like the perfect place to "make a paddock" by simply hammering in a border of steel pickets and hanging up a few strands of wire - which were all surprisingly cheap, provided I didn't count all the bandages for my cuts and banged fingers. I'll confess; hammers and I are life enemies.

Lucky for me, our neighbours were keen on the idea of fresh manure for their gardens or pony rides for their kids. Even old Mr Nosey and Mrs Parker – my nicknames for the two most annoying gossips who lived at opposite ends of our street and always seemed to keep their beady eyes on me.

Mr Parker had a lawn that he kept insanely neat by mowing, then trimming the edges with scissors three times a week – I kid you *not* - while Mrs Parker had an explosion of wild floral shrubs, which mesh wire fences could barely contain. *He* always sat at his window, watching for kids who'd commit the crime of walking across his precious green footpath, leaving crushed-grass footprints that could last up to a minute, while *she* scowled at me every day for over a decade after I committed the heinous crime of plucking a blue daisy from an overhang on my way home from kindergarten.

Most of our other neighbours seemed sane enough – except maybe the gorgeous international swimsuit model who jogged across Mr Parker's footpath one day, got abused for it, and then did it again the next morning, wearing jogging shoes with football spikes for maximum grip.

We also had a butcher, a baker and a wedding dress maker who were always friendly on the rare occasions I saw them, but most of our neighbours kept to themselves so much that I didn't even know what they looked like. So approaching the three who lived furthest from me along the river for the first time felt really scary.

Simply knocking solved that worry.

They turned out to be ordinary working families who never asked for a single day's rent from me for use of their grassy banks, because controlling the grass also meant minimizing the habitat for the world's deadliest brown snakes, as well as the more aggressive red-bellied blacks. They even let me keep a hose on a tap outside so I could fill an old bath tub every morning with fresh clean water, so my horses didn't have to drink from that foul river. Later, after heavy rain, we'd also learn that constant grazing could compact the soil and save the slope from erosion, and then after that, *everyone* along the river wanted my horses for a few days each week.

However, at the time I went shopping for my *first* horse, all I'd cared about was making a nice home for Snow; an old grey mare with a long scar down her pretty face from where a previous owner had beaten her with the back of an axe. He'd been jailed for it, but that couldn't heal all the damage he'd done to her. He'd also whipped scars into her neck and shoulders, and blinded her left eye with a cigarette – so she'd been very shy of smoke and humans, and nearly impossible to catch until she met me.

I smelled like warm bread, and offered her the whole bag that I'd brought with me. I'd never ridden a horse before, so I had no intensions of it at that stage. I didn't own a halter or bridle at that stage either, and nor did her rescuers, but he had a rope, which she feared. He told me I'd need to get it around her neck, and sit on her, or leave and never come back.

Challenge accepted. I wrapped the rope around me so it looked like a belt, and sat in the grass, humming lullabies to myself. I managed to entice her up to me, with a curious look on her face, and in exchange for a little patience and kindness, the old mare discovered that she loved bread. I fed her small bites in exchange for pats... and for sniffing the rope... and within an hour, she let me ride her around bareback with nothing more than the rope noose around her slender neck.

'Wow, she *likes* you,' said the plump engineer who'd rescued her first. He looked surprised. 'She hasn't let anyone on her back in the whole four years she's been healing here with us. Nice and fat now, but she was skin and bone when we found her. And if it wasn't for the fact that we have to move overseas, we wouldn't be selling her at all.'

He smiled at me, and explained how he didn't want to sell to *me* especially. For starters, I was only 12 years old, and I'd arrived on my pushbike, so far out of town, with no sign of my parents.

'I'm worried,' he admitted after a ten minute quiz session about it.

'But they work long hours,' I explained. 'They can't get here until after dark and then it's too late!'

'We need someone *responsible*,' he replied kindly. '... somebody who owns a large paddock and can guarantee a safe home for her, for life. And for her son too, because they're inseparable.'

I didn't know what he meant, at first, because the only other horse they had was fully grown and big enough to take care of himself. 'He protects her from wandering dogs,' said the engineer. After everything Snow had been through, I could hardly argue, so I simply hugged her while I explained how much I'd done so far in preparing a lush, shady paddock for her.

Her rescuers didn't believe me at first, so I gave them my parent's phone number. I even invited the engineer to see the riverbank for himself, and when he did, he not only changed his mind about selling to me, he also dropped Snowy's price to a mere $50 so I could afford both horses at once!

Too naïve to know how dangerous a traumatised mare could be usually, I felt totally at ease with her, and it seemed that she sensed that in me, because she never gave me the slightest trouble. Except when it came time to load her into a hired trailer. It stank of disinfectant and must have reminded her of all the pain she'd been through after being beaten. But Apache marched straight in, even though he'd never even seen a horse trailer before, and then Snowy walked up too, despite our total lack of skill. Like me, her rescuers knew more about dogs than horses. They owned a kennel and bred Rottweilers as a hobby, and they hadn't really been interested in riding her anyway. They'd only wanted to help her heal and give her a safe home as a lawnmower for all the grassy spaces between their puppy pens.

They'd also tended to her wounds and begun feeding her back to health, not knowing she'd been in foal. Still skin and bone when Apache appeared after the first week with them, she'd had no milk for him, so the engineer and his wife had been forced to raise the foal initially by bottle, and to keep him warm at night in a box under their kitchen table, just as they did for any orphaned puppies.

That also explained how Apache came to be house trained, even though he grew so big he had to duck to get through doorways. We never invited him inside after he came to live with me in the city, but there was that *one* day when dad closed the gate to customers and let the horses graze on the only grass in our back yard while we all went shopping, and the muddy tracks that we found later told a funny story. Confirmed by neighbours, who'd been attracted by the commotion; Apache had thundered up the back steps, around the kitchen stove, past the TV and out down the stairs again – chasing a very frightened burglar all the way.

Raised with Rottweilers, he'd learned how to be a guard dog, but he also grew into a big strong horse with a cool head for danger. He saved my life twice before I'd even left highschool.

The first time, we'd been holidaying out of town on a large farm for my first and last time at a pony club camp. We'd spent the day learning how to herd cattle. All of the other horses had been yarded for the night, and some were bickering, asserting their dominance, so I kept my two horses close to my tent in a pen that I made by tying a line of ropes and reins around four trees. On dusk, the herd of cattle came down from the hills for water, and as I came out of my tent, one of the cranky young bulls startled and attacked me. Apache reacted so fast, I barely had time to blink. He jumped the ropes and took the goring in his belly, keeping himself between me and the bull while he fought it and chased it away.

Back in the city, he'd been well healed a year later when I rode him to the corner shop three blocks away to buy bread and milk. We'd paused beside a brick fence where six friendly puppies often trotted out to greet us… when a red car raced around the corner, careening out of control.

It headed straight for us

I froze in horror.

Apache's head shot straight up in alarm, and then everything seemed to happen in slow motion. He seemed quite calm and casual as he looked around, and then leapt sideways over the brick fence into the yard with the pups. Until then I had no idea that a horse could jump sideways, but he not only did it, he also avoided the pups and shifted his weight back a step in a way that caught me from falling. The car smashed into the fence where we'd been, knocking out a brick that struck my knee, yet the driver failed to stop. He just hit the accelerator again and sped away.

Apache snorted as life came back to normal speed, and when I looked down, I saw all six puppies standing underneath us, staring up as if to ask; how the heck did we materialise on their side of the fence?

'What did you do?' shouted their owner as he ran out from his house, shaking his fist at me. 'Get off my property!'

Apache reared up, defensively.

'It wasn't me!' I pointed at the fresh deep ruts in his footpath, and then I gave him a description of the driver and car, including the number plate. It's only then that I noticed a new a sign on the man's gate that said; *Pups for sale.*

'Hey, dad!' I pleaded as soon as I got home. 'Have you seen that white house at the corner with the sign on the gate?'

'No, and neither have you,' he replied, not bothering to withdraw his greasy grin very far from the engine of a black Mercedes. 'You've got too many pets already.'

Famous last words.

That's what the gossips would be calling it.

Image: Apache and Snow grazing the footpath outside one of their vacant allotments by the river in East Ipswich.

It doesn't look it from this angle, but the main street of the city is SO close! It's just a short ride around that corner in the background, turning right, then left across the railway... then keep riding for about the same distance on the other side.

Also, please excuse the poor quality of these "vintage" photos. My cheap little pocket camera could only capture memories with a modest 240p resolution, (a mere 0.1 megapixels by today's standards). So while they cannot dazzle us with sharpness, they make me feel nostalgic with their authentic charm. I think they also help to preserve this genuine glimpse into the past, unaltered by digital touch-ups, aside from the arrow and text overlay.

3. The Thing That Changed Everything

Walt Disney,
father of all Disney cartoons,
once said;

*The way to get started is to
quit talking and begin doing.*

My morning routines always started that way,
except if you count talking to animals.

Like on *Thursday, 26th of January;*

Innocently, I finished playing with my pets in the kitchen, filled 5 bowls of kibbles for the cats, plus one for the dog and stored the leftovers from the dog's big tin of meat in the fridge. As I closed the door, one of my magnets with inspirational quotes reminded me to get my butt into gear.

'Thanks, Mr Disney.' I patted a kiss onto his magnet and bolted for my pushbike, needing to beat the vet to the river paddock, so I could put halters on Apache and Snow before they recognised him.

That dreaded time had come around again for my horses to get their annual inoculations against tetanus and strangles; two of the deadliest, most painful and common ways for horses to die.

I hated the idea of giving needles to my horses myself, despite the hefty call-out fee from my cranky old vet. I called him the vet-o-matic, because he could suck money out of my pocket better than any vacuum cleaner. Prime example; charging double time for all after-hours visits, even though Sundays and Thursday evenings were the only times he serviced my area.

'Triple time on public holidays,' he'd warned me, but only *after* I'd booked him for my day off that week. I had no other choice. At the time, he was the only horse-vet I knew.

We didn't own a proper horse truck or trailer, and my dad was always busy with cars for customers, so we could hardly take the horses 30 kilometres out to a more professional clinic. As a new driver myself, I'd done my first six weeks on L-plates and could drive alone, without a supervisor under those old rules, but my learner's licence still only permitted me to drive "Tina;" my little old blue Ford Cortina sedan, which also meant that renting a truck or trailer was off the option list for me too.

I would often jog down to the river to check my horses, but that morning I also needed to make fence repairs near the water, so before leaving the garage, I looped a new roll of fencing wire around my bike's handle-bars and shoved a pair of wire-pliers into my jeans pocket.

I could have driven Tina. She had a generous trunk – big enough for two bales of hay – but it seemed like a waste of expensive fuel.

Reluctantly, I also packed my bike's pink carry basket with a thing I called "It;" a cranky chain about half as long as my arm, with savage metal teeth for tightening wire fences and which never *ever* co-operated in getting a job done without a big fight. "It" turned every two minute job of tightening fence wire into half an hour of war, and even though I always won, I'd often come away with fresh scratches on my hands and arms. "It" even snapped and hooked my face one time, leaving me with a long thin scar near my left eye.

Keen to get there, I also loaded the rack on the rear of

my bike, as usual, with two "biscuits" of lucerne hay; that's two sections of clover-like dried grass-hay, about the size and shape of a pillow. But since my horses hated the vet as much as I did, I loaded extra treats too; a small ice-cream container each, full of rolled oats (the human breakfast cereal variety), bread scraps and equal shares of the vegetable peelings from last night's dinner - in this case, potatoes, pumpkin and snow peas.

I must have looked crazy with my bike loaded up like that, but I didn't care, even though I had to ride past the house of the cutest guy in the area. I often carried my saddle on the back of my bike as well, and that was trickier, since I still had to carry the hay and feed buckets every day.

Weird sights often greeted me on the way to the river too, and that day seemed no different. I saw a cat chasing a stray dog from its yard, a man in a window getting fitted for a bridal gown – just the dressmaker's skinny husband cheerfully playing the role of manikin - and a pair of young girls dressed as piglets being unloaded from their twins pram by their single mother, who'd just moved into one of the newly built houses.

'... and can we see the horsies again tomorrow?' asked one of the piglets – making it easy to guess where they'd been for their morning walk.

'I like the big white horsie,' said the other. 'I'm nearly as tall as her knee, aren't I Mummy?'

I smiled and waved as I rode by on my bike, content to know that my four-legged friends had gained another family of fans in the neighbourhood. Or so I thought.

At the river, the vet-o-matic arrived late, as usual, and began his annual check-ups with Snowy first, who tolerated him only because she trusted me.

'How old is this mare?' he asked as he inspected her

teeth.

'Can't you tell?' The shapes, angles and amount of wear on each tooth were all supposed to make ages obvious for experts. It also seemed strange to me that he couldn't remember from the last three years, or at least know from his records.

'It's harder to tell their age after they turn twenty one,' he said. 'It also depends on how hard she's lived.'

'She was 26 when I bought her,' I explained, 'and I've owned her for nearly four years.'

'"Twenty *six*?" he laughed. 'You *paid* for a twenty-six year old horse?'

'Hey, she only cost me fifty dollars, and she's got tons of life left in her. She can bolt from stop to a gallop in one leap, even in wet weather, and she can slam on her brakes, do skidding turns and she can even trot backwards!'

'I wasn't talking about her training. I meant they should have paid *you*, Pet…'

It seemed so bizarre; a vet calling me *Pet,* and yet that was one of the few things that I liked about him. He treated people like animals. The only downside; he treated animals like animals too.

'Most horses only live into their mid-twenties,' he explained. 'Or less if they've had a hard life, like this mare, obviously. Did you know that she's blind in this eye?'

He pointed to her left eye; the most important eye for a riding horse, since that's the side they're trained to watch for riders getting on and off.

'So?' I snapped defensively. 'She can still gallop a straight line.'

'But I'll bet she shies at anything that pops into sight unexpectedly.'

'Then you'd lose that bet. As long as I'm with her, she's not scared of anything.'

'Sorry, Pet. It's getting well past time to gather wood for her bonfire. Or maybe you know somebody who owns a backhoe? You're going to need it to get rid of her body soon enough.'

'Why?'… I panicked. 'Is she sick?'

'Not at the moment. Her heart sounds strong enough for two actually, but she's already reached that age when it could fail her any day.'

Shocked into silence, I realised I'd been living in denial for four blissful years. I much preferred to cling to the rarer stories about horses living well into their thirties and forties. I felt like he'd slapped me in the face with the cold fact that there'd come a day, fairly soon according to him, when I'd find her dead in the paddock. And as much as I hated that idea, it worried me even more that her son would be there to watch her go down, and be left standing all alone in his world.

Another horrible thought; that it would break Apache's heart as much as mine. I knew her death would herald the start of extra pain for him; having to live the most part of every day and night alone from then on. And as a very sociable animal who'd never been alone in his whole life, I suspected it might even kill him from pining. Of course, I'd continue to spend quality time with him at least twice a day, as usual, but now that I was out of high school and working at the supermarket in the neighbouring suburb, the most I could be with him was roughly 2 to 5 hours per day, and none of it during the darkest, loneliest moments in the dead of night.

That's when it hit me. I needed to start looking around for a third horse to keep him company when the time came. And not just any horse. It would have to be one that I could trial for a few weeks first, to ensure they all got along happily in the meantime. I'd heard that many mares could be bitchy to each other, so the *last* thing I wanted was a new mare who'd fight with Snow and maybe drive her even closer to the grave.

Miserably, I paid the vet, fixed the fence and made it home in time for breakfast with the rest of my family. I could barely hide my tears, so while they prepared a cheery visit to my grandparents in a nearby country town, I glumly opened the newspaper.

The classifieds often abounded with livestock for sale, mostly racehorses that couldn't make the grade at the local tracks.

I didn't want to waste anyone's time by going out to try horses that I had no intention of buying. And my heart was already too full to fall in love on first sight, as I had with my first two. But I forced myself to keep looking. Then I saw it;

Australia Day Horse Auction; Yamanto.

I glanced past it automatically at first, because the concept of an auction scared me. I'd seen movies with people who'd accidentally bought huge expensive houses or cars by accident when the auctioneer accepted their bid, even though they'd really only been swatting a fly or winking at a friend. The big horse auctions also had a bad reputation as dumping stations for "rubbish horses and doggers," suited only for dog food, usually, because they were sick, injured or spoiled by bad owners. However sales on a public holiday were rare, so I wondered if they might be different; perhaps intended to attract people who worked 9-to-5 through the week. I also wondered if they'd offer a mix of higher quality horses for sale.

The idea of an auction still scared me, because I feared falling foul of a "horse swindler." There was absolutely no way I could afford to pay for a new horse just yet, no matter how much I needed one. And as much as I loved the ability to get extra pay from overtime shifts at the shop, I couldn't see any long term career as a check-out girl, so I'd already applied for a job as a junior payroll clerk in a government department – which meant I'd soon be taking a huge drop in pay for two years. Or, so I hoped.

Cash only, the ad declared in the largest font.

Oddly, that felt reassuring, because with only five dollars in my wallet and barely ten in my savings account (after repairing the fence and fuelling my car), I knew nobody could wring payment for horse out of me under *any* circumstances, no matter how clever they were as a scam artist.

Bidding starts: 10am Sharp.

The noisy ticking clock over my Mum's stove showed the current time as 8:13am. Yamanto was barely ten minutes' drive away – or less if I caught all the green lights. So I had plenty of time to look around at horses, learn which breeds were available locally, and I'd still be able to get away before the auction even began.

That settled it.

In that one brief silent moment between tick and tock on my mum's noisy clock, I realised I'd be perfectly safe. I had no money, no desire, no pressure and no suitable vehicle to bring a horse home - giving me absolutely no way, no how and no chance of being suckered into buying just any old horse that day.

ANITA BELL

4. Historically Horrific Happenstances

Dwight (Ike) Eisenhower,
the 34th American President,
once said;

*History is not written
by Chance, but by Choice.*

Yet for me that day,
chance kept over-writing my choices.

My family set off for their sunny day in Rosewood with my grandparents, and then the storm clouds closed in, over me. The skies let loose with torrential rain, yet I still chose to go outside in it. The only cheery blue left in sight was the paint on my little old Cortina.

As the car radio came on automatically, I learned that storm cells stretched all the way to New Zealand, where the poor wretches were copping the very worst of it. Historic flash flooding had just put Invercargill Airport under three meters of water, and washed thousands of valuable farm animals out to sea, so compared to them, I had it easy. Little more than slick roads and full drains to avoid as a novice driver.

I passed two fatal accidents along the way, and normally would have taken that as a bad omen and turned back, but the idea of Snow dropping dead any day, leaving Apache alone needlessly... that still haunted me.

Arriving at the sale-yards seemed like a small victory by

itself. Less bleak too, because the rain eased up to a fine drizzle just as I switched off my engine. But as I stepped out and my favourite white sneaker found a muddy puddle, I realised that the sale-yards weren't anything like I'd expected.

I'd imagined a bitumen carpark and a large industrial shed with steel yards and concrete floors that would enable the pens to be hosed out easily and kept clean for the next batch of animals coming in. I'd also imagined a separate building for bidders to do their business in comfort after their morning inspections, and I'd imagined all the sellers waiting patiently somewhere else akin to the lounge area for my dad's customers. Much like the movies I'd seen.

Instead I found myself in a large grassy paddock where stones had been brought in and packed down to make a road and to prevent the biggest livestock trucks from churning up the most trafficked areas. Yet one of the 18-wheelers had bogged up to the axles. The yards themselves were also bigger than I'd expected, covering at least five acres. Many of the timber railings seemed new but the posts looked to be as old as my grandfather, with one section roped off as derelict - and no concrete anywhere, except for a small strip at the window of a caravan labeled *office*, where a small line of gruff men laughed and joked with the crusty middle-aged blonde, who seemed to be the receptionist.

A whip cracked, a horse screamed, and a chorus of whinnies responded. I startled; at the horrific ring of fear in the scream that triggered it. Until that moment, I had no idea that a horse could scream at all, yet there's no other way to describe it.

Nearing the yards, I began to see the nearest horses and their pitiful predicament, for a city with no room for a kid's pony, these auctioneers had managed to cram in hundreds. I saw far more breeds than the thoroughbreds that raced locally. Trucked in from outer areas, obviously, but ankle deep in thick smelly mud, there wasn't an animal anywhere that seemed calm, let alone happy to be there - not even the three fit stock horses that were safe enough under saddle with the stockmen who used them to herd and sort the others.

Situated high on a hill; I'd expected the auction yards to be well drained, but the pens and public paths had churned up with the kind of deep, sloppy swamp gruel that looks and stinks like chunky diarrhea. And me, in my best sneakers.

It didn't matter how clean and well presented the horses might have been before they arrived either. It took barely ten steps for them to be ankle-deep and splashed all over with muck.

The horses hated it. The buyers hated it. But if I couldn't stiffen up and smile at passersby, then I would have cried – especially near the foal pens, where the poor little critters had been separated from their mothers and were calling out, terrified, as if their worlds were coming to an end.

In one case it did. A lanky black colt charged the fence, desperate to escape, but his head slipped and jammed between rails, and as he fell back, the weight of his own body broke his neck. Poor little thing. The yard men dragged him out with a rope and left him to go cold in the filth – and that only made it worse for all the foals around him, since they could still see him, and smell him through the rails.

It upset me a lot too; enough to ask one of the mounted stockmen if they could cover his body, or take him away, out of the drizzling rain.

'Don't waste your pity on him, luv. Poor little mite. His worries are over.'

I waited until he turned his back and then spat after him.

I hated how some men could become so hardened and uncaring. I didn't understand how much some of them really did care, I'm ashamed to say, but I'd soon learn.

I passed by the other pens, offering pats and kind words of comfort to those who'd take it. Stepping around the worst of the mud, and climbing along the rails near all the boggiest gates, I made my way up and down the rows, getting a good look at all the horses and ponies, and noticing a few that might be interesting enough to stay and watch to see how much they'd sell for - just to get a rough idea of market value. I still expected the best horses to be sold from their homes privately, but I also had those movies in my head warning me that things could get rowdy, and that some buyers could get pushy in a physical way, so the only safe place for a timid, trouble-dodging teenaged girl to watch was from a distance. Unfortunately for me, I have lousy eyesight that lenses can't fix, so I needed to find a fairly safe midpoint so I could see just enough details.

So staying behind the auctioneer and his 5 helpers, I tried to keep a low profile, hoping that even if they did turn around and spot me blinking or swiping rain from my eyes, they'd realise that I wasn't in the right place to make a bid. I just assumed they only looked for bids from the crowd in front of them.

From the higher positions on the rails as I scrambled around the muddiest corners, I also noticed that most of the private buyers who drove in, promptly drove out again without stopping. I feared that would leave a sale-yard full of horses, where the only buyers would be agents for the local meat works, and maybe a few horse traders. All counted flesh and bone the same way; in columns of a profit or loss book.

As a horse lover amongst meatworks buyers, I felt like a spy in enemy territory. I couldn't tell who were the private citizens and who were the professional "hitmen," since all buyers had a bidding card, but only some of them kept them in sight, in their pockets, hands or hats. I couldn't tell the buyers from the sellers either, except by their body language.

The main cluster of eleven buyers with bidding cards visible looked like old stockmen, roughly fifty to eighty years old. I brushed passed them and overheard them organising who'd be bidding on each pen, so they could all buy cheaply without bidding too much against each other. Clever for buyers. Nasty for sellers. They seemed to poison the whole "emotional environment" so much that all the nearest horses shied away from them, except for one quiet pen in the middle row of the grid. Pen number 13-13. Current contents; two mares, two foals and one fat female pig.

I spotted two little children in that pen too – a boy and girl aged about six and eight, riding a big muddy bay mare. Bareback. Under an umbrella. In rain that showered over us again.

All the neighbouring horses seemed afraid of those noisy flapping umbrellas. I also knew that my own horses had been a little shy of the first one they'd ever seen too, mostly because of that weird sound of rain against plastic. Yet this mare and the grey mare which shared the pen must have been exceptionally quiet and trusting, since they didn't seem the slightest bit worried by anything.

Their foals *did*. The grey mare had a large black filly foal, while the bay had a spindly young chestnut colt, and both babies seemed so terrified by all of the other frightened horses that they hugged tightly against their mother's sides like barnacles, while the pig cowered tightly in the furthest corner and tried desperately not to get trampled.

Then I noticed the only control the kids had of the bay

mare was a single rope tied into a noose which they'd looped around her nose. It stayed on despite gravity because the mare remained so well behaved that she only required a slight tension from their small hands to keep it in place.

Skinny with a pot belly, the bay had the shape of a mare who'd been used mainly as a breeder without all the proper nutrients. Snowy had the same shape at first, but with proper care I knew that could be fixed, so I stopped for a closer look. I couldn't help myself. After the death of the black colt, I needed to see people who really cared about animals.

No harm in looking, right?

I assumed the two kids were testing her out, in the hope of buying her – until I noticed their faces, and realised they were both sobbing.

I glanced around, in search of a parent, but saw nobody who looked the slightest bit interested in watching over them.

'What's wrong?' I asked, feeling a motherly urge that I'd never felt before. 'Are you scared? Because there's no need to be. She's as safe as any horse I've ever seen.'

'We know. She's ours!' cried the girl. She leaned forward and hugged the mare snugly around the neck. 'We have to say goodbye now.'

'Why?' I asked aghast. The mare looked big enough to carry a full grown rider, and well behaved enough to handle any task required of her, so it seemed hardly likely those two kids would ever outgrow her. At their size, they would have looked small on Shetland ponies. 'What did she do wrong to make your parents want to sell her?'

'They don't *want* to sell her,' sobbed the girl. 'We *have* to. The bank made us sell our farm and now we have to move to the city.'

'I live in the city, and I keep my horses on a river bank.'

'Our farm is bankrupt,' explained the six year old boy — using that banking word that no child should need to know. 'We already sold all our cows and tractors, but the bank is making us sell everything. Dad has gone home with the truck to bring the next load full of horses.'

'Next load?' I asked, horrified. 'You mean you have *more* quiet horses like this?'

'Two hundred and four,' said the girl. 'Not counting their foals. Mum breeds them and sells the yearlings, so in a good year we usually make hundreds of thousands. Before the drought, we were rich.'

It certainly sounded like it to me. If I kept working full time all year, my pay would barely break over seven thousand.

'They're really very clever stock horses. Dad often sells them overseas, but the bushfires burned down a lot of our fences and hay sheds, and they're too expensive to fix, and now the bank says that our place isn't worth as much as our loan, so they want to own it too. Greedy scum suckers.'

I nearly laughed in surprise, hearing a little girl use language like that, but she seemed so tragically earnest, I could only nod silently in agreement.

The pig stayed in its muddy corner, looking as sad as any pig could be. With so much mud, I expected it should be partying, but then I realised it reflected the mood of the kids.

'Look,' said the boy as he scrambled across onto the bare back of the grey mare without his feet touching the ground.

I couldn't tell what shade of grey she might be under so much mud.

'She's bomb proof too,' he said proudly.

He steered her by leaning a tuft of her mane from side to side – the same trick I'd taught both Apache and Snow.

The girl dropped the noose of her rope on the bay mare's

neck and showed how she could steer with only a tuft of her mane too.

'This is Penny,' she said, introducing me to the bay.

'And this is Tuppence,' said the boy. 'Dad said they're both named after small English coins but that's just a joke really, because they're both worth a fortune.'

He brought the grey mare to a halt using only a slight tug on the small tuft of her mane, then squirmed around backwards, and hugged her rump so he could lean over her to point out the foals to me. 'The black filly is Blacky,' he said, pointing to her, 'and the little colt is Lucky.'

I almost laughed. The chestnut colt seemed anything but Lucky. Slimy foul mud dripped from every part of him, including his long eye lashes.

5. Meeting Lucky

In Ancient Rome, during the reign of Augustus, there was a poet called Publius Ovidius Naso, now known famously in English as "Ovid", who once said;

Luck affects everything.

Dude, you weren't kidding.

I stared at the tiny filthy colt for far longer than I should have.

'Lucky?' I asked as I glanced from the foal to the kids. 'How on Earth did he earn *that* name?'

'He was born thirteen days ago, on Friday 13th in the wrong paddock,' explained the girl. 'The fence broke and Penny escaped into the old coal mine next door. Lucky she did, because the milking cow that stayed in her paddock got killed by lightning. Then two days later, he escaped a pair of savage dogs. Some new neighbours from the city let them loose every night after work, because they think their mutts are cute and harmless. Instead, they always come over to our place, killing chickens and pigs. We tried telling them to keep them fenced up, but they wouldn't believe us.'

'Yesterday, the dogs came over and chased the horses,' added the boy, but he sniffled, too upset to continue, so his sister explained the rest.

'The colt got separated from Penny when she was trying to protect him and he ran into the dam. The dog ran in trying to drown the foal - until our stallion ran in and killed it. Lucky that Big Boy was running with the mares that night, because he's normally locked up in his own paddock. But it was his last chance to be with all his girlfriends, so Dad let him run free with the mares. Another mare killed the other dog, because she had a foal to protect too, but she got so badly hurt that Dad had to send her to heaven early for her Pegasus wings.'

The bay mare nudged my hand gently and I patted her nose. 'Hello, Miss Penny,' I whispered. 'They tell me you're a brave old lady.' She had a few grey hairs around her eyes which made her look older than Snowy.

'She's not old!' the boy said, as if I'd offended him. 'She's only eighteen, They both are. I heard some people telling my dad that's old for a horse, but it's not really. She's still got years of life in her. Do you want to ride her to see for yourself?'

'Oh, no thanks,' I said and backed up a step. 'I can see how good they all are from here.'

'Please buy them?' pleaded the girl. 'The only other person who's looked at them so far is that scary big man from the meatworks.' She pointed past me, and I wondered how such young kids could recognise someone from the knackery – until I saw a tall, fearsome man with a beard and tattoos staining down his neck and arms. He wore the logo for the local meat works emblazoned across the back of his raincoat.

As I watched him, I noticed that I wasn't entirely alone in looking at him with dislike. A little old lady in a daisy patterned raincoat saw his shirt too, and shook her crooked finger at him. She looked almost comical in her bright pink rain hat and matching mud boots, standing up to him like that. Only half his height, she lectured him for sending so many horses to the glue factory, when synthetic glues were now possible.

'Mind your own business,' he complained. 'It's just a job,

lady. Somebody has to do it, and much better that it's me than someone who'll flog them all the way.'

Old Miss Daisy Raincoat huffed at him and trudged towards me next, sinking almost knee deep in her mud boots. She paused beside me, listening to the kids explaining about the ages of the two foals and how quiet and playful they could be when they weren't being terrified by all the commotion of the sale-yards. The sturdy little black filly had just turned six months old, while the bay's twiggy little chestnut colt was only 13 days old. Not even a whole fortnight! In all the wet weather, his umbilical cord hadn't dried enough yet to fall off. I could still see it hanging under his tummy, shriveled up to about the length of my pinkie finger, and dripping mud – which meant a high risk for infection, because the soft blood-soaked tissue could serve as a highway for germs into his body.

'Please buy them,' the kids pleaded again. 'Or they'll be killed for dog food or glue. And do you know what they do with the foals?'

I sighed, really wishing I could help, but I couldn't even scratch my chin for fear of raising their hopes. I didn't have enough cash to buy a lead-rope, let alone a horse for the other end of it. *Five bucks in my pocket, ten in the bank, and that's it* I reminded myself. Yet I could see that these poor kids loved their horses as much as I loved mine. It nearly broke my heart watching them.

I thought about how much it would hurt me, being forced to sell any of my pets, or worse; *all* of them. How would I cope?

I stared at the mud, which had oozed up around my ankles, and wondered how many of the other six hundred horses had similar stories. I didn't care about my favourite sneakers anymore, even though they were ruined forever.

The more I thought about it, the more useless I felt. Rain

drenched my hair, making me feel even more miserable. By the end of the month, nearly all of these little herds around me would be dead and canned - just in time to process the next batch. Monthly sales happened all around the country, every year for longer than I'd been born. In that way, they weren't much different to cattle and sheep sales for livestock that are raised for the main purpose of eating. But horses are clever enough to become faithful friends and workmates. I imagined there must have been perfectly good horses like this at every sale, despite the bad reputation of horse auctions in general. [because "rubbish" horses were still only sick, injured or spoiled by bad habits, and nearly always due to bad owners Or by kind hearted owners who lacked experience in how to solve or prevent naughty habits.] I also believed that most sick or sorry horses could be cured or retrained, if they were lucky to get the proper care and attention by responsible owners.

Within days, I'd be forced to rethink that idea, but at the time, I could only despair at how many wonderful animals like Penny and Tuppence seemed to be killed each year, and it made me feel even more powerless. I knew I'd never be able to stop it on my own, but I hated that I couldn't even stop it for this single pen. Average price they could expect for a "dogger"; $100 to $500.

Old Miss Daisy Raincoat scratched her chin, and started asking questions. I felt so relieved, I almost hugged her. I seized the opportunity to walk away, hoping she'd see that she would have no competition coming from me. If I had been brave enough, I would have kicked a few of those meatworks buyers in the shin as well and sent them up to the first aid building to ensure they missed bidding against her too.

Sadly, I didn't know that Miss Daisy Raincoat had even less cash than me.

6. Fortune Played Me Like a Fiddle.

Horace, another Roman poet from the last years BC, once said;

*Fortune makes a fool of those
she favours too much.*

Crikey, she must have loved making a fool out of me.

The auction progressed like a tightly controlled riot.

The oldest auctioneer stayed invisible, at first, inside the huddle of his three sons and five of their big burly assistants. The sons were movie-star handsome, but too old for me by about a decade. I began to see a bright side to the spectacle, finally. Or maybe they attracted my eye, because they didn't waste their time strutting about showing off, like most guys I knew. They just got on with the job, full of attractive confidence and experience as they leapt up onto the top rail - a flat plank that enabled their small band to walk along the top of the pens without getting their boots muddy.

As the youngest of them stopped at each pen to describe the horses and open the bidding, his voice swiftly accelerated faster than a speeding freight train. He had no need for a loudspeaker. The crowd heaved and murmured like a hungry beast, focused almost entirely on him, or whatever else he told them to look at in the pens. He also had his own three "spotters"; other fit young men who climbed the rails to watch different sections of the crowd and report their sightings of a bid.

I kept well behind them in the next row, and avoided all

eye contact, even though they each tried to catch my eye a few times.

I noticed most of the crowd avoiding eye contact with them too, as if most of them weren't buyers at all. That's when I realised that many were sellers, which made the numbers of potential buyers seem to shrink even smaller.

First up for sale; the foals and yearlings that had been penned away from their mothers.

Most seemed old enough to wean anyway, but at least a dozen were still young enough to need milk. All sold in the range of $10 to $200, with the mode price - most common - about $100. Thankfully, they nearly all sold to horse traders or breeders — aside from a few that "passed in" and would get to go home again. Not enough meat or bone in those pens to interest the meatworks buyers, apparently. Those harsher looking men smoked cigarettes under eaves of a nearby building to keep out of the drizzling rain a while longer, or loomed around the bigger pens for that stage of the auction to begin.

Or they volunteered to take turns as the auctioneer's "markers" — the people who used long sticks with a bulb-like sponge of paint on one end to paint the rumps of every animal with a coloured dot - more like a smudge, since the horses always moved when the stick poked through the rails at them.

Watching the process, I learned how the coloured dots enabled different bidders to win animals inside a pen, without needing to buy the whole lot. None of the animals liked it, often shying, or shrinking away from the paint stick, even on the rare occasions the marker wasn't rough with them.

Only those people who'd signed up for a bidder's card were permitted to bid, so I stayed well away from the registration table as well.

Ten minutes after the motherless foals sold out, the first row of horses and ponies sold in the range of $30 to $120, with the mode price about $60. So much lower than the usual dogger prices that I'd heard about, and I heard mutterings around the crowd that it must be because of the weather. Not enough buyers to drive up the bidding, apparently, but I wondered why nobody else seemed to notice that the meatworks buyers weren't bidding much against each other – which also made me worry again about those poor kids I'd met. As if being forced to sell their home and pets wasn't bad enough - and in weather foul enough to risk pneumonia. Selling them for such paltry amounts would mean their parents might still have a debt to repay the bank, even after they'd sold everything and lost their main income.

'Excuse me,' said old Miss Daisy Raincoat. She'd been keeping her distance too, but now she pushed past me and squeezed through the crowd to an elderly man who'd already bought two pens full of foals.

'I need cash,' she pleaded with him, and hugged him as if he'd been her best friend in another life. 'As much as you can spare please, Charlie?'

'Divorce was supposed to end the drain on my wallet,' Charlie replied, but his expression softened and he pulled out six yellow fifties from his hip pocket. 'Now I'm broke as well as broken. And you wouldn't get that much, if I hadn't scored a nice pen of fillies already.'

I caught myself smiling at them. It seemed like such a huge relief to know there were at least two other people in the crowd who cared about horses enough to set aside their disagreements.

Daisy thanked him with a peck to his grey whiskery cheek, and for his generosity, I felt like kissing him myself. He handed the cash to Daisy just as the auctioneers reached pen 13-13 with the two mares and foals.

Opening bid; one hundred.

'For the lot,' added the auctioneer. 'Minus the pig. We'll sell her separate.'

I could hardly believe my ears. Two mares and two foals for a paltry average of $25. I had cousins younger than me who wasted more than that each week on music and junk food.

From the next row, I climbed up a few rails for a better view and spotted Daisy Raincoat raise her bidder's card - which shot the price up to one-fifty. Still a shock, really, since the previous pen with six grey geldings had started at two hundred for the lot and gone up by a hundred each bid to $2100.

'One-sixty,' called the most fearsome meatworks buyer.

'Seventy!' shouted Daisy Raincoat.

'Here,' called a plump old woman beside me. Bundled up in a full length "Driza-bone" oilskin coat for stockmen, at first glance she did look like a man, until I heard her voice again. 'One–eighty, but I want the pig too. She'll make a nice pot of bacon.'

'She's pregnant!' shouted Daisy Raincoat, but a spotter turned, nodded to the plump woman and relayed her bid to the auctioneer – which put me unexpectedly in the thick of it, even though I wasn't even standing in the proper row.

'Pig's in,' shouted the auctioneer. 'What am I bid for the lot then? One pregnant pig, two lovely quiet broodmares, and two well bred foals. Just look at them. Worth every penny, people! I've got one-eighty, one-eighty, one-eighty....' he repeated – until a silent bidder near the rear of the crowd gave a nod that I only noticed from the dip of his hat.

'One-ninety, one-ninety,' called the auctioneer.

'Two hundred!' shouted Daisy Raincoat.

Bids rose from two other places in the crowd, each time out-bid within seconds by dear old Daisy Raincoat. Too fast for me to spot or identify her opposition. The plump woman beside me bid again, which took the bid past two-sixty and put me back in the thick of it.

I felt spotters' eyes on me like lasers, and had to get away. I shoved my hands in my pocket, stared at the ground and backed out until I had enough room to turn my back on the action.

'Hey, watch where you're going,' complained a cute guy, not much older than me. He wore a khaki shirt inside a knee-length Driza-bone, open down the front with shoulder caps that made him look even more broad shouldered and handsome. Then I noticed the logo on his shirt pocket.

Same meatworks logo as Mr Fearsome.

'Sorry,' I grumbled, and backed away from him too. He carried no bidder's card as far as I could see. Just a bunch of keys with a silver bulldog tag; same bulldog used by Mack trucks as their emblem.

'Four-sixty-six!' shouted the auctioneer. 'Including the pig.'

I never saw who made the final bid, but the rival bidding dried up, so I knew it had to be Daisy Raincoat. She'd been so determined.

If my head had been screwed on straight, I would have remembered seeing her ex-husband hand over only six fifties, the sum of which only came to three hundred. But the excitement of the auctioneer to declare the winning buyer was simply too much. Time seemed to slow to a crawl as everyone in the crowd turned to watch Daisy. The auctioneer watched her keenly too as he raised his hand and said; 'Going once…'

7. Bidder Number 26

Plutarch, the Greek Philosopher,
who was well known for his charming anecdotes,
once said;

*Fate leads those who follow
and drags those who resist*

... but with so much mud that day,
Fate had an easy time dragging deep ruts with me.

The auctioneer and his sons each peered at me as they scanned the crowd in all directions for any last minute bids. They'd done it every time, except now it seemed personal, as if they could see my interest so far in this pen like a neon sign blaring brightly at them.

'Going twice,' he said as his gaze settled back on Miss Daisy Raincoat. '... Last chance,' he said, stalling dramatically. 'Best bargain of the sale so far. Dig deep to help out these little kids.'

Daisy made no movement at all, as if she feared raising the bid accidentally more than she needed to.

'Sold!' declared the auctioneer. 'To bidder 26. Next, up, we've got...'

The crowd murmured, shuffling sideways in the mud to keep up with the auctioneer, while relief overwhelmed me. I knew Daisy had to be the winner, because she'd stayed behind. Yet a dark whisper warned me that something was wrong.

I needed to leave, and maybe I should have. I still had

two or three pens on my list which interested me enough that I'd planned to stay and watch the prices, but after everything I'd seen and heard, I felt too miserable to leave until I'd made sure there'd been a happy ending at Pen 13-13.

If there hadn't been so many sellers hanging close to the main auction, I could have simply peered through the rails, but I couldn't get that close. So I had to wade back around into that row and wait for the crowd to move down a few more pens.

Not that I minded, since I had to go that way to get back to my car anyhow.

'Hi, kids!' I called, and then I noticed they were crying harder than ever.

'At least they went to a good home,' I said, hopefully. I still saw no sign of their parents, which would have been enough to make me bawl my eyes out at their age.

'Canned doesn't count,' sobbed the girl. She turned the bay around, ensuring I saw the bright orange spot on her rump.

'They're going to die!' cried the boy. 'Where did you go? Why didn't you buy them?'

I glanced around, wondering what happened to Daisy Raincoat… and found her ripping up a bidder's card with the number 19 (my dad's lucky number).

'Where were *you*?' she cursed, glaring at me. She stomped her bidder's card into the mud. 'I thought you showed interest too?'

'I *wish*,' I said, and inverted my jeans pockets. My five dollars in coins spilled out into my hand and I showed them to her. 'They might as well grow a beanstalk.'

'Those horses are far too good for dog food,' Daisy said. 'And do you know what the meatworks does to foals?'

There was that question again, but I really had no idea.

Same as they did with the big horses, I guessed. Not that it made any difference to my ability to help or not.

Then Lucky caught my eye as he reared up with a snort of defiance, and whinnied, as if warning the whole world that he'd fight to live.

Something sparked inside me. I couldn't leave that auction without trying to do something to save them.

'Who bought them?' I asked. 'Point them out to me.'

Daisy stabbed her crooked old finger in the direction of Mr Fearsome, just as he won the final bid for another pen of broodmares with young foals at foot. I saw his colour on the rump of the grey mare too, and finally caught a glimpse of his bidder's card.

Number; 26.

Double thirteen. The sum of the pen's grid reference number, also equaled the date in January; the 26$^{th.}$ Australia Day; intended to celebrate and commemorate how lucky we were to be Australian.

So much for Luck; the number thirteen seemed so busy around me, it assaulted me in pairs. I was staring at a 13 day old foal, born on the 13th.

I got the feeling that Fate was laughing at me. Taunting me, since 13 had always such a bad reputation as an omen of bad luck, I couldn't help but feel that someone was trying to warn me not to have anything to do with that pen. I had no idea that I'd eventually come to think of thirteen as my luckiest number. At the time, I could only look at that mare and foal and know that I *had* to save them, just as the plump engineer had once taken a stand to save my girl Snowy.

As Mr Fearsome followed the auctioneer and crowd along to the next pen, I sucked in a huge breath for courage, and dashed after him.

Beside him stood the cute young guy with the Mack truck keys and a tall chunky man whose coat made his shape look the same as a beer can with a clipboard and hat. As I drew nearer, I heard them complaining about how their rival buyers had padded the crowd with "friends," which made it even harder to see which of them was really bidding.

'Excuse me,' I called as politely as I could manage.

Too quiet for him to hear me, apparently. I had to tug on Fearsome's sleeve to attract his attention down to me. 'Can I speak to you please?'

'Sure you can.' But before I could open my mouth again, he turned his back on me.

I scowled at him in frustration. One of my highschool English teachers used to tease our class like that too, as a way of encouraging us to use the more grammatically correct; *May* I…?"

So I knew how to play that game.

'*May* I speak with you, *please*?' I added more politely.

Arching a curious brow at me, he also seemed to notice Daisy Raincoat over my shoulder, listening intently.

'Forget it,' he said. 'She's already nagged me.' He gave me such a dirty look to go with it, as if he'd already heard every possible argument there could be on the subject. 'All complaints in triplicate, luv,' he said, and then began to turn away – until he realised I wasn't letting go so easily.

'That chestnut foal back there in 13-13,' I said, still clinging to his elbow. 'There can't be more than one tin of meat on his little bones. So do you really want him that much?'

'Nah, he's less than worthless, luv.' He shrugged me off successfully. 'Don't you know what they do to the youngest foals at a meatworks?'

I shook my head, fairly certain now that I didn't *want* to know.

'They're not worth the time it takes to kill them,' he explained. 'Their meat is too soft anyway. It turns to jelly.

So they're left out to die in the sun after their mums go.'

'You mean you let them *starve* to death?'

'No! Of course not,' he argued. 'Not me personally. Dehydration usually gets them first and that rarely takes more than a day or two in summer.'

'Not in this weather!' I complained. 'It's so cool and damp it could take up to a week for them to die slowly.'

'What else can I do, luv? I save as many as I can until I can find better homes.'

'You do?' I could hardly believe it. He looked like a total criminal.

'Then why didn't you just let the old lady win the last bid?'

'Because she didn't make the last bid before me. You see that tall skinny mongrel under the black hat?' He pointed to a cluster of black hats so I didn't pay much attention. 'That rogue dog, Stewie, would have taken them straight to the docks for export, and if you think these conditions are foul, try imagining a few hundred horses jammed into the stinking hot belly of a ship for weeks with nothing but harsh words, whips and death waiting for them.'

'And you think you're any better?'

'Honey. I love horses. Really. I save as many as I can, but our paddocks are full at home this week. Yes, the truck will be taking them straight to the works, but at least with us they'll get fresh air, feed, water and they won't be flogged all the way.'

He glanced to his companions, and I finally recognised a strong family resemblance. Brothers, I guessed. Compared to Mr Fearsome, one of them seemed young and clean cut, while the other looked older and plump.

'Can I have the foal then?' I asked hopefully. 'If the meat-workers will only leave him out to die anyway, it seems like such a waste. You could just let me...'

'Sorry, luv. I'm only an agent for the business. The foal is logged in now as their property, so his cost needs to be offset by profit, unless it can be written off with his death.'

'So how much profit would "The business" need on that foal to make it worth selling to me?'

Mr Fearsome glanced to the plump man beside him, shaped like the beer can, who checked his clip board, did a brief calculation to deduct an amount for the pig, and then divided by two, as if there'd been only two animals of equal value in that pen.

He circled the answer. 'They cost two hundred and eight.'

'Let's call it two-ten,' Fearsome said, with a friendly wink, as if I should thank him for adding only two dollars profit.

I blinked horrified. 'I can't afford *that much*!'

'Why not? It's only two bucks on top of what I just paid, and for that price, you're also getting the bay mare.'

'I can't afford *two* horses,' I pleaded.

'Why not? That mare is too good for a tin can. Haven't you seen how quiet she is with those kids in this chaos?'

'Yes, of course I have, but…' He'd just stunned me at how much he cared, and now I felt even more wretched at the state of my finances. 'It's hard enough affording the two I already have.'

'You'll find a way if you want that colt,' he said flatly. 'Bottle feeding is a risky and expensive substitute for the colostrums in his mother's milk. Unless you've got another mare on standby somewhere that not only has milk right now, she'll also foster an orphan?'

Orphan. That word slugged me with an instant chill. And another one as soon as I checked over my shoulder and saw Penny's big brown eyes over the top rail, watching me.

'Gotta go,' Fearsome said, as the auction moved on further without him. 'Yes or no?'

I hesitated – until Mr Beer Can tapped my shoulder

lightly with his big beefy hand. 'You don't need to pay at the sales office until 3pm, luv, and the gates don't close until four. So there's plenty of time to go fetch the cash from home or wherever, and make it back in time, if that's your problem?'

'Okay, yes,' I said, before I could stop myself.

The unexpected relief that swept over me came with a wave of excitement that felt like I'd won a jackpot lotto. I leapt at them with a hug for each. I knew I could borrow cash from my parents temporarily and repay them by selling the mare as soon as her milk dried up. And by selling her privately on a nice clean sunny day later on, I could even hope to make a huge profit while also finding a good home for her.

Then it hit me; I'd just hugged the most fearsome meat works buyer at the auction. I think I also stunned him more than I'd stunned myself. He blushed and grinned sheepishly as he began to turn back for the auction.

'Same deal for me?' Daisy pleaded. 'And I can offer a good home for their pig?'

Fearsome frowned at her. 'You were rude to me earlier, so if you want in, you'll have to cough up an extra hundred.' His expression softened at her. 'And you'll pay that part in cash to those kids, so the auctioneers don't get a cut from it.'

'Deal,' she said and shook his hand.

'Hey, Henry!' Fearsome shouted to the auctioneer's marker. 'You see that bay mare and chestnut colt back in 13-13?'

The marker glanced that way briefly, then nodded.

'Do me a favour, mate, and add an "A" to the bidder ID? I just on-sold them.'

Henry nodded again, and scrambled back along the rails to paint an orange A onto the rumps of my two.

My two, I thought. It seemed like Fate or good luck that he coincidentally chose to paint my first initial on them, without even knowing my name. Then it really hit me.

I had barely three hours to find as much money as I earned in a week. And it was a public holiday, which meant mum and dad had no cash at home for the business. In future there'd be magical money machines that spit cash conveniently from many walls in a city street. But those days were still many years away

8. Scraping It Up

Epictetus,
a Greek Philosopher born into Slavery,
once said;

*Wealth consists; not in having great
possessions, but in having few wants*

... which sounded so inspirational,
until the day that I really needed the cash.

It was **12:13pm**
... I needed two hundred and ten dollars, exactly
... in under four hours.
It seemed like thousands, and might as well have been. Aside from my car expenses, I'd spent my last pay on fence repairs.

Racing around the house, searching for my various small stashes of treasure, I spent half my time dodging cats and a dog who wanted to play – and the other half trying to figure out how to break the news to my parents, in a gentle way that would also inspire them into lending me a little cash, temporarily, from whatever they might have in their wallets... and hopefully without getting scolded with the old "too many pets already" speech.

I'd never borrowed money from them or anyone else before, and I'd never wanted to. For me, IOU were three letters I never wanted to write, so I wondered how much they might want as repayments until I could sell the mare when the time came...

Yeah, I know. I laugh at that idea now too; me ever selling a horse. What a joke.

My first problem; I arrived home on a rare day. An empty driveway. Gulp.

I kicked myself for not remembering they'd gone to visit my grandparents.

I tried calling their mobile phone from the house phone, but since the first mobile phones had barely turned ten years old, their "new fancy" mobile actually weighed more than a house brick and needed a full sized car battery to function, so it stayed in the car between the two front seats, hard wired into the vehicle as a trendy "new" car phone.

No reception today anyway, big surprise. The darn thing hardly worked anywhere. Even thirty years later, there'd still be black spots in that area

No response on the landline at my Nan's house either, which meant they must be out in my pop's big vegetable patch, sampling all the fresh yummies.

I realised that what the world really needed right then in the 80's was some kind of pocket sized phone, small enough they could carry it, instead of leaving it in the car for charging. But those "communicator" things only existed in Star Trek.

Stumped for the moment, I leaned against the nearest wall – until I realised it was made of brick, and I rolled my eyes at the metaphor. Me; literally backed against a brick wall.

I went upstairs to take a painkiller for my fast-growing headache, and soon found myself walking circles around the kitchen table – dodging all the lines in the tiles. The clock on the stove warned me I'd used up half an hour already, so I hurried to my room to find my old worn-out handbag. Bad luck not to keep at least one coin in my old wallet, even if I only planned on cutting it up for craft supplies - so I opened it, retrieved the five cent coin and threw the bag away, finally.

Slumping on my bed, I noticed my cherry-red piggy bank grinning at me, as usual, from my dressing table, beside my Bugs Bunny alarm clock.

'Cut that out!' I shouted at the pig. 'If you're not helping, you're part of the problem.' Then I grabbed it, knowing that smashing it would be the fastest way to end my problems with cash… I even raised it over my head in preparation to crack it open on my dressing table, but the cool ceramic somehow managed to soothe my mood.

As one of my most cherished childhood ornaments, it should have stayed safe forever. I'd dropped notes and coins into it for nearly three years while I'd been little – until my dad warned me I'd have to "kill" it when the time came for me to spend the cash. So I'd changed my childhood plans to become rich by other means, in the hope of never needing that kind of pocket change; the kind that would force me to kill a "friend".

Yet, here I paced, desperate for it. I caught sight of myself in the mirror and hesitated.

That cute little red pig had smiled at me from the corner of my dresser for as long as I could remember, so I couldn't do it. Except some idiot had designed it without a plug hole, so I had to tilt and shake it strategically and patiently to retrieve all the coins and notes the same way they went in. Through the slot, which jammed easily with the biggest coins.

It took more patience than I had, so I got cranky and fetched a crochet hook, which made it *look* like I was gutting it, without actually harming it.

Half an hour later, I'd netted an encouraging $152:05.

Helpful, but not enough, so I dashed around the house, searching down the backs of all the lounge chairs, and found $13:20 in loose coins – mostly from the three chairs where customers waited for Dad to finish fixing their cars.

That reminded me of the safe in the office. A thousand dollars had been locked away over the public holiday. I knew the combination. I even went so far as to open it, stare and even reach for it. Untouchable like acid.

My hand snapped away without committing that sin.

If ever I dared to dip my fingers into it, I knew my mum would never trust me alone with it again, and her trust had always been worth much more to me. Sappy, but true. So I slammed the safe, leaving the cash tin "safe" in the safe, while I added my precious treasures to the $5 from my pocket.

I spotted the party-loving bachelor next door at his garden shed, with his mower backed out on his overgrown lawn. Donny shook his fuel can, took off the lid to inspect it closer, and frowned.

Lucky me, my car had a full tank.

I bounded downstairs, sliding down the banister, and ran out to attract his attention.

'Why in the world would you ever want to sell some of the fuel from your car?' he asked.

'A little problem with horse power,' I joked. Aside from being a keen handy-man and party animal, Donny also happened to be a very fine mechanic for my dad, so I should have known I'd never get away with that quip.

'You realise that adding fuel to the engine usually resolves the issue of horse power?'

'Not this time. I promise.'

So he sucked on a foul tasting hose with the other end down the throat of my fuel intake, and we siphoned out a full tin of fuel, leaving me enough dregs in the tank to last until my next pay packet - provided I grounded myself by visiting no friends or relatives - and he handed me $25 in cash, which was generous. By my calculations at the current price of 50 cents a litre, I'd only sold him $22.50.

I found another $1:85 down the seat of my own car, $1:40 on the floor under the mat, where my handbag sometimes spilled around sharp corners – even though I had to pull up some of the floor to get at it. Then $4:30 loose in the handbag itself, and I really do mean *in*side it. Most of the small coins had worked down into the stitching through a small hole in the lining, and required scissors and emergency surgery to extract. Oh, and $5:15 in very small coins from the drinks-tray.

Not a cent left anywhere in the house, car or yard – which still left me two dollars short.

Two lousy dollars!

I thought about borrowing it from Donnie, but he'd vanished.

Not to be beaten for the sake of such a small amount, I bolted down the street to a house full of seven kids who often pestered me for pony rides, and I sold four quick gallops up the street and back, at fifty cents each to the four oldest, taking two aboard with me at a time - bareback on Apache, so it didn't take any extra time saddling him. Except, in my haste, I didn't bother crossing the road to avoid the preciously trimmed grass on Mr Nosey's footpath.

He chased me with a broom, shouting; 'Wait until your parents get home, young lady!'

Yeah, right, I thought. I'm already doomed.

At least now I had the cash.

9. Racing That Deadline

Sophocles,
an ancient Greek writer who tortured
his audiences with tragic plays,
once said;

*There is no success without
effort and hardship.*

Okay, sure, but a little more success from less hardship
would have made a nice change that day.

By **1:26pm** I felt so clever for scrounging the cash with so much time to spare before 3pm, but I congratulated myself too soon. Way too soon.

I still had no way to get the mare and foal home.

Not safely, anyway.

I couldn't lead or ride her across town legally without a permit from the city council office, and they'd be closed for the public holiday. That forced me to consider doing it without a permit – until I recalled seeing a Gatekeeper's sign on the exit from the sale-yards;

No Animals To Leave Without Permit.

So I wouldn't be able to sneak them out. Then I wondered how many other people hit the same problem – and realised the sale-yards themselves might be able to suggest a few solutions.

And when I rang, they did. The Department of Primary Industries had supplied them with full authorization to issue free travel permits, same as I could get from any department office during working hours.

BUTTT…with a capital B and three t's, I still couldn't ride or lead the mare home that far through traffic in the rain. Far too dangerous! Aside from needing to trust a new horse with my own life in traffic, I also had the foal to consider. To lead him meant simply leading his mother, but that couldn't stop him from startling and darting off briefly into traffic, which might in turn cause an accident to somebody else.

Putting a rope around his neck, might have been an option too, but I couldn't risk that without inviting a stack of new problems; I couldn't use a rope around his neck without frightening him or strangling him when he pulled back, and I didn't have a halter small enough to fit him anyway, so he could slip out unless I could fashion something made-to-fit using scraps of rope and rags from the trunk of my car.

I felt confident that I could train the colt to lead within a few minutes; if only the basics. But to make the lesson last for the whole three hour walk home could only risk disaster. Every horse training book I'd ever read assured me that everyone in the history of mankind who'd ever tried to force a horse to do anything for too long, always ended up regretting it. Especially with young stock. If not hurting themselves during training, then it was still possible to ruin the human-animal relationship through unintentional trauma. Patience could not be rushed, and failing to think the problem through thoroughly first from the horse's perspective equated to horse-shouting, not whispering.

I'd seen the results plenty of times, and not just from the scars that Snow still carried. I'd seen so many girls at pony club punishing their horses to force obedience, which always seemed to instill a greater measure of reluctance or rebellion in their steeds, while others like me preferred patience and a system of voice and calm repetition to help the horse figure out for itself how to do things. And coincidentally or not, our horses usually became the boldest, bravest, or most curious and willing to go almost anywhere, try almost anything. It was a method I'd learned from *Horse Control*, a series of books written by Tom Roberts, a World War Two veteran, who'd used gentle methods to teach horses to be brave and reliable, even during heavy battle.

So my personal vow had already been taken; I could not, should not, would not ever, *never* in a billion kazillion years, *ever* put my horses in a situation where they'd feel so frightened that they'd be unwilling or unable to obey me.

More famous last words.

Then it hit me. At home, my dad had a tip truck that he needed for taking old engines to the wreckers, plus a cattle crate that he'd built for a customer who'd died in an accident before collecting or paying for it. The crate seemed like a perfect solution; a simple metal frame with metal walls, and a sliding door at the back. No roof, except for bars that stopped cows from jumping out over the top. But if I could load the crate onto the truck, together the two parts would make a reasonable facsimile of a horse truck – perfectly safe, provided I could chain or bolt them together well enough - and not tip up the tray by accident.

Alas, I wasn't physically strong enough to load the crate on by myself, and I wasn't licensed to drive a truck yet (only a small manual car like Tina).

Then, as Fate and Fortune would have it, a smoking hot muscle car purred down the street - bronze, like burnished gold - and I turned in time to see the neighborhood's hottest young bachelor, Jim Bell, coming home from work at the local power station. Cutest guy in the street and six years older than me, so way out of my league, but I knew he'd borrowed the tip truck from my dad once for cleaning out his parent's garage, which meant he must have the right driver's license – which was another one of the crucial details needed for the travel permit at the sale-yards.

I bolted after him, and caught up to him just as he locked away his lovely car. Don't ask me the make or model. Daughter of a mechanic, but if it didn't have four legs and two ears, I couldn't tell one from another. If I'd been obliged to call that car anything, it would have been *The Panther*, because it rarely came out to prowl during the day. He had an old Landcruiser ute that he used as general transport to and from the power station too, and it sat under a carport beside the house. Usually covered in a thin film of coal ash, today the Landcruiser had its hood up, as if the engine had given him trouble.

Jim didn't see me coming up behind him, and my stupid tongue twisted up in knots at the thought of talking to him. Aside from being the most handsome young guy in the neighbourhood, he was also one of the smartest, so I couldn't even think the name Jim without swooning. And if that wasn't embarrassing enough, our parents were already friends and had been for years before either of us were born. So the six years age difference between us meant that he'd known about me since my first diaper.

Luckily, our paths rarely crossed. He went to primary, while I enrolled in kindy. He'd gone on to high school, while I progressed to primary. He'd always been working, going to uni or dating older girls, so from his perspective, I remained the little girl, playing with toy ponies.

In sixteen years, I'd bumped into him only three times, and all three ranked in the top five most embarrassing moments of my life. All relevant to what happened next. So freeze-frame me in the driveway for a second, with my mouth open and hand coming up to wave at him...

Embarrassing Moment #1: In primary school:

Eight years old, sent home sick on a day when my parents had been out shopping for new cars; Jim's mum offered me his bunk, and I sneezed all over it. Except sneezing isn't the worst thing I did. Carroty bits all over his pillow and mattress.

Still holding my stomach, I passed him in the hall as he'd come home from junior high with his latest girlfriend. Like all the guys I'd ever met through my dad's mechanical business, he only seemed to like blondes. Unlucky me, I was so brunette, my hair often looked black. So my tongue tangled up, so mortified that *sorry* came out as *soggy*. I barked techni-colours all over his gorgeous black shirt – while he was wearing it - and we turned matching red in embarrassment.

A decade had passed since then, during which our family had moved out and back into the neighbourhood two years later, so I figured it was about time I apologised. Starting a new life as a high school graduate by then myself seemed to warrant it. Except, that only resulted in:

Embarrassing Moment #2: Eight weeks ago; still burning fresh in my brain as my first weekend after leaving high school; in my street...

Cantering off into the sunset, literally, as I headed west on Snow (my personal white steed), I felt on top of the world at first. Last exam behind me, totally relieved from all the stress in my life. Ready to make my own rules. Be a whole new person. I had my first job, my first car and I'd completed the first stage for learner drivers, so under those old rules, I'd just gained the additional freedom of being able to drive by myself, unsupervised.

Enjoying the cool afternoon with my old mare, I rode

past Jim's car, parked on the footpath, and noticed his legs hanging out on the grass, while he worked underneath.

Snowy noticed his legs move too, and took a second look at him as we rode by. She didn't shy, baulk or even break her beat as we cantered past him. Yet that gave me an idea about how to get him to notice me first, so I wouldn't have to be first to break the ten year drought of words between us.

A little experience talking to guys might have helped. I went to a high school for girls, so the most experience I'd had with boys had been boasting sessions from all the prettiest girls in class, or from listening to my father's apprentices getting into trouble for swearing in front of his customers. Otherwise, if any local boys came anywhere near me, Apache usually put himself in the way, and threatened to bite or kick them. Just threats, really, but those boys never knew it. If anything, Apache and Snow could judge character better than me, and they had a funny way of making people reveal their true colours loud enough so that even I could see.

So I had to experiment with Jim. I tried riding "sexily" past his car a few times, hoping he'd look out at just the right moment – until I noticed Mr Nosey across the street, enjoying the show, with his face and hands glued up to his window like one of those stuffed toys with suction cups for car windows. Also, my version of sexy must have looked clumsy and comical.

Frustrated, I spun around, gave Snowy a loose rein so she could stretch her neck into a gallop, and clicked twice as the signal to bolt off at top speed. She leapt over Jim's concrete driveway with another signal from my knees, but then as she landed, and gathered herself to continue galloping, I jumped off her back, aiming to land beside Jim. I tried to make it look like a fall, rolling and landing on my back - which frightened Snowy so much, she slammed on her brakes, spun around and started sniffing me to check I was okay.

Groan.

'Hey, are you okay?' Jim asked, peering out at me from beneath his car.

'Pfft...' I spat out a clump of dirt, finding it so hard to answer huskily *and* look sexy, while trying to keep a horse tongue out of my mouth. Poor Snowy started to shake with worry, so I couldn't keep up the dumb charade. 'I'm fine,' I grumbled and rolled to get up.

Jim rolled out too, dusted off the grass from my shoulder and butt, and cupped his hands together to offer me a leg-up. 'You should try using a helmet and saddle next time.'

I took that as an insult. No compulsory helmet rules yet, so riders only wore helmets when they couldn't ride properly, or had to work with a horse that couldn't be trusted thoroughly. Ignoring his offer for a leg-up, I nudged Snowy's shoulder as the signal for her to lean down a little, and then I swung up onto her back by myself.

'Sorry for throwing up in your bed,' I said, and couldn't gallop away fast enough.

As I turned the corner at the end of the street, I caught sight of him, watching me and scratching his head.

Embarrassing Moment #3: Last Friday night

Our first date. Yes, date.

No warm up. No flirting. No conversation or preliminary warning at all really. As I rode down the street Thursday afternoon at a casual walking pace on Apache, Jim's car purred to a slow roll beside me, and he leaned out to ask if I'd be free Friday night for a drive-in movie.

'My kid brother wants to go out with your kid sister, and our parents volunteered us to be the... cough, cough... chaperones.'

'Oh, great.' I groaned. *How humiliating!*

Both too shy and polite to blink at each other, my sis and his bro came home without exchanging a single word. Not even *hello* - which only served to make the situation for Jim and me that much more awkward for the duration of the entire three-hour "date".

And now, here I was, not even a whole week later, virtually trespassing in his driveway to beg him for a favour.

10. Beg, Grovel, Beseech, Implore, Entreat…

Sigmund Freud,
the famous Austrian Psychoanalyst,
once said;

*Children are completely ego-istic;
they feel their needs intensely and
strive ruthlessly to satisfy them.*

Normally, still as a minor myself, I would have argued
about the sweet innocence of childhood,
but WOW, dude. You really nailed me that day.

At precisely **1:39pm** Jim turned around from locking up his car in his garage, and bumped into me.

'Oh, sorry!' I stammered. 'I didn't mean to… ah…'

'Forget it,' he grinned. 'You're a sucker for punishment, aren't you?'

'Excuse me?'

'Friday night? Excruciating.'

'Oh… yeah.' I blushed bright crimson. 'And that's only the start of it.'

He blinked at me, confused. 'You're not really suggesting we should try that again?'

'Ummm… not exactly.'

He folded his arms and waited, raising one brow as if he enjoyed my embarrassment as prime-time entertainment, even more than Mr Nosey and Mrs Parker.

'Whenever you're ready,' he prompted me. 'You've got maybe a whole minute before I fall asleep from exhaustion. I just finished a double shift of overtime.'

'Oh, well don't worry then. You'd better get to bed.' I spun on my heel, almost relieved to get away from him.

'Hold it.' He grabbed me by the shirt the way he used to grab me by the diaper as a toddler, whenever I used to blow raspberries at people and try to run away. 'You can't leave me wondering. I won't sleep a wink with a mystery hanging over me.'

'Now who's the sucker for punishment?'

'If it's anything to do with Friday night, forget it. Let's pretend it never happened.'

'Phew!' I said, relieved at that too. 'That's a deal, signed and sealed, but…'

'That's not the reason you came,' he said, reading my expression.

'Doesn't matter. You're exhausted, and this may take an hour. You don't need me in your hair, especially when it's for something that's borderline crazy.' I turned to leave again, but he blocked me in that suave way that guys have when they're confident enough to handle anything.

'Try me,' he said, and I struggled to stop myself from swooning and drooling all over him.

I twiddled a wild curl near my ear, wondering how I'd ever be able to explain it without sounding like an impulsive, money-wasting idiot. 'I kind of need a teensy bit of help with something,' I confessed, 'but it's okay. I might be able to ask Donny when he starts mowing his yard soon.'

'Oh, really?' He studied me with that semi-amused look again, as if he'd already guessed that I'd been up to mischief. 'And it's a secret, is it?'

'Actually, it was advertised.'

'And the headline said….?'

'Yamanto horse sales.'

'Uh-oh.' His grin fell off and he looked at me sternly. 'You bought another one?'

'Hey, I've never been to a sale before. It's not my fault.'

'So you *did* buy something?'

I screwed the toe of my shoe around on the driveway, wishing I was an ant, so I could squash myself and grind myself so small he'd never see me again.

'... and learned your lesson now, obviously.'

'I only went to look, I swear! I honestly didn't plan to buy anything. But you weren't there as chaperone, and I have all this room on the riverbank, and the vet told me that my grey mare is getting really old now, and...'

'What... did... you... buy,' he said with more patience than a Buddhist monk.

'It's not so much *what*,' I confessed. 'It's more like... how many.'

'How many?' he choked. 'If I had to count legs, how many hands would I need?'

'Only two. Horses that is. And even that's not as bad as it sounds, because one of them is really, really small. Hardly there at all, really.'

'Too big to carry home on your back seat, though, I take it?'

'Aren't they all?' I grinned.

He chuckled, rolling his eyes. 'Okay, then why are you here, instead of phoning a friend at a pony club with a trailer?'

I shrugged. 'I'm not in a club. I tried ages ago, but it was too far away. Hence no horsey friends.'

'That's rough. So what's this teensy favour you need?'

I spilled my guts and told him everything - almost. About the truck, the crate and driver's licence.

'Why didn't you just say so? It's only ten minutes away.'

I leapt onto him with a hug so tight, I stunned myself as much as him. That was my first hug with *any* young guy, and I had to leap straight off again.

Purely platonic, I reverted to all-business;
'We need to leave now, please.'

11. Thus Began The Saga of the Return Journey

Buddha,
that big cuddly founder of Buddhism,
once said;

*Chaos is inherent in all compounded things.
Strive on with diligence.*

However, that day, chaos infested even
the simplest little things too.

It was already **1:52pm** and the tailgate wouldn't come off the rear of the tip-truck. Yet we needed that off before we could slide on the crate by lifting it together, the hard way. With home grown muscles. Lucky for me, Jim had enough for both of us, but I managed to keep up my corner – until we discovered a jammed bolt sticking up from the tailgate that stopped us from sliding it on.

My Dad's trusty sledgehammer fixed the problem with the bolt. Jim offered to bash it down into place for me, surprised that I'd even try to do it myself, but I knew how to swing a sledgie well enough, because I used it all the time to drive steel pickets into the ground for my fences.

'If you want to meet a tool that's a witch to use, I'll introduce you to "it" some day.' I didn't bother pointing out the long thin scar near my eye, but I showed him all the scratches down my arms, where the wire tensioning tool had let go and caused the steel barbs to whip back and tear shreds from me. 'Using "it" is like trying to shampoo a wild cat in a toilet.'

'Are you sure you're a girl?' he chuckled.

I glanced down at the modest bulges in my blouse. 'Yep, pretty sure.'

He opened his mouth to add something, but I beat him to it.

'Don't you dare call me a tomboy, or I'll have to smack you.'

'Wouldn't dream of it,' he said with a cheeky smile. 'You looked a treat last Friday night but it's not like we could relax and talk. Most of the horsey girls I know are all snobby britches anyway. So I guess I never expected you to be so... different.'

'Different?' I pouted. 'You mean dirty.'

I gulped, realizing he might think I meant in a sexual way, so I slapped my own butt pocket. 'My jeans are always like this.' Sleek black jeans with pretty floral embroidery - currently splattered with mud. Then I realised I'd made it worse by attracting his eye to my rump, and I flushed red, embarrassed. 'Can't get any earthier than this,' I stammered, but he only smiled a little more, and turned back to my dad's truck.

Jim reversed the tip-truck up to the crate a little straighter, and together with some jiggling we managed to lift it high enough so the back came down part way to meet us. But the crate still refused to slide on. Ruts and bumps in the old metal floor made it like sandpaper – or Velcro.

'Kitchen soap!' I dashed off to mix up a soapy bucket full of dish detergent.

Splashing it over the tray of the truck solved that little problem. We hefted the crate up again, and now it agreed to slide on, but we still lacked enough strength to heft up the back end and slide it on all the way. Especially with the tray tilted uphill.

I glanced around, looking for another strong set of arms, but Donny's car had vanished with him and his lawnmower lay nuked to pieces all over his BBQ table.

'Does your Dad have any pulleys?' Jim asked.

'Beats me. But he won't mind if we look. He doesn't really care who borrows his tools around the neighbourhood, as long as they all boomerang.'

Dad had tool boxes for small tools, while most of the big stuff hung on the walls... white walls with black lines drawn around each tool so everyone knew where to find and return everything.

Also made it more obvious when something went missing.

Guess what was missing.

Ten minutes later, after searching through every drawer and bench, Jim found a pulley, finally, by looking up. Somebody had left it hanging from the last rafter used to heft out an engine.

I smacked his arm, teasing him. 'Next time, we look *up first.*'

It took a few minutes to find a ladder to get it down, but we finally shifted it out to the highest part of the truck. Jim cranked it up, while I lowered the tray, and together we finally managed to lever, pull and slide the darn thing up into place. Then I saw the weight sticker and realised we'd just lifted a whole tonne together.

I skipped and whooped and squealed with glee as I danced a jig around Jim, already knowing that he thought I was crazy, so a little more wouldn't matter.

From the tool box I grabbed some ropes, a tie-down strap and a "dog-n-chain" (which was basically just a crank and latch, shaped like a dog's tail, but with metal teeth to crank it tight) and asked him which one he'd recommend to secure the crate to the truck. Otherwise, the first corner we turned on the road could cause the whole thing to slide off – never funny in anything except TV comedies. In real life, it meant the possibility of broken legs and necks – and I'd already driven past an accident once where some guy had put a pony into an old horse trailer with a rotten timber floor, saying "she'll be right, mate"… but the pony fell through while he'd been driving along at a hundred…

I still get shivers and nightmares.

So I asked Jim if he'd mind helping me take extra care in tying it down with everything we could find.

He chose the long heavy chain first and climbed up to pass it over the top of the crate, so we could "dog it down" tight – and a good thing he knew how to use the dog. I'd never actually used it myself before, but I'd seen it done a few times by my dad and under-estimated how tricky it could be. Luckily for me, Jim had a natural knack for it. Same with the tie-down straps. Those ratchet buckles still have me beaten, but at least I knew how to tie a trucker's knot for the ropes. We couldn't carry a tipper load of hay home without them.

Jim had never seen a trucker's knot before, so at first he thought I was trying to tie up some kind of giant macramé or crochet stitch – until I showed him how the rope could be used to tighten itself using the greater power of leverage. I finished it with a bow, making him laugh.

'Better than having the long ends drag on the road,' I argued.

2:13pm Jim slid up behind the wheel like a pro, while I scrambled up into the passenger side like a drunken frog, slipping back one step for every two.

Tap, tap, tap, went his fingernail on the fuel gauge. 'Is this thing accurate?'

'Oh, crap.' I slapped my forehead, having no idea if the engine needed petrol or diesel.

Out again, it took us three laps of the old truck just to find the fuel filler cap, then another fight to get it off with a small bent key, and finally, Jim sniffed the feint fumes inside.

'Petrol,' he said, making me laugh – and not only from the new oily black circle around his nose.

'Don't tell me how you learned the difference,' I joked. 'I thought you were a good boy.' I wiped it off for him using the corner of my shirt.

Back into the garage we trudged, taking caps off all the little fuel drums for Dad's lawnmower, chainsaw, whipper snipper, quad bike, motorbike, emergency generator and firefighter pump, until we finally found a fuel reserve that smelled the same.

Refueled and back in the truck, Jim glanced sideways at me and told me to 'belt up.' I scowled at him, except he was grinning, and it dawned on me slowly that he meant my seatbelt.

'Stop, stop!' I shouted, halfway down the driveway. 'I forgot the lead rope.'

Embarrassed again, I leapt out and grabbed Snowy's halter and lead from the back seat of my car, guessing that both mares seemed roughly the same head size.

'Don't say it,' I said as I climbed back in sheepishly. 'I already know I'm an idiot.'

'Hey, at least you remembered here and not half way across the city.'

2:26pm Part way across town, an explosion lifted the back left corner of the truck. It scared the life out of me. I grabbed for my door to leap out, moving or not. My Dad watched lots of war movies, so to me it sounded like we'd run over a land mine.

Jim laughed at me. 'It's okay,' he said, braking to a halt from about sixty. 'It's just a rear tyre blowing. Luckily, not a front steer tyre, or we'd be crashing by now.'

Not just any rear tyre, however. The hardest one to get at. The tipper had dual wheels on the rear to help support heavy loads; which meant there were *two* wheels on each side at the back, running as twins, and the flat occurred on the inside tyre, on the road side of the vehicle.

Heavy sigh. We had to get off the road far enough to work without getting struck by traffic, and take off both tyres on one set in order to replace it with the spare. And then the spare tyre didn't want to unwind or crank down from its holder. The bolts on the rims didn't want to come off. The jack didn't want to retract or go back into its slot. Slimy mud made the lot slippery, after splashing up from the wet roads... Oh, and then it rained on us.

Jim looked up at me from under the truck, with his face covered in grease, mud and road grime, while lightning and thunder rumbled overhead.

The first spit of hail stung his nose.

'Do you get the feeling we're supposed to give up and go home?' he asked.

I shrugged, knowing if he chosen to give up, I'd have to as well. 'They'll die if I don't try. The winning bidder was the meatworks, so I'm actually buying from them.'

'Let me get this straight... You're buying *live* meat from a meatworks?'

'Technically, yeah... I hope so.'

'How often does that happen?'

I shrugged again, not really knowing. 'Not as often as it needs to. But there's no need for you to feel bad. You've helped me this far, and I'll always be grateful. You're also tired, wet, muddy and at risk of pneumonia, when you really should be home catching some zzz's and protecting your health. So if you say we can't make it, that's life. Just say so, and I'll hail a taxi for you to go home.' I smiled grimly. 'On the bright side, if I'm not buying horses, at least I can pay for your fare.'

'And abandon you by the road side?' He shook his head and laughed. 'Not likely. Your Dad would kill me.'

'I'll be okay.' I could hardly take a taxi home with him. I'd be mortified by complete failure. 'I'll go down the hill to one of those old houses, and pay for a call to my grandparents. Mum and Dad can pick me up on their way home later.'

'With your luck, they've left already, or you'd knock on the door to a serial killer.'

He insisted in spending the next half hour struggling to replace the slimy filthy tyre with another slimy filthy tyre that proved to be equally uncooperative, while I spent the minutes insisting on helping him, the best I could, even if only to shield him from the hail and pelting rain. As 3pm ticked closer, I felt the heavy beat of seconds increasing with every pulse of my heart.

Victorious, finally… but not for long.

We made it two more blocks when the engine coughed and cut out on us.

Jim looked at me quizzically. 'Is this a *normal* day for you?'

'Lately,' I sighed.

'Do you realise *sane* people would have given up ages ago?'

'What can I say?' I shrugged. 'I just applied for an office job at a mental health facility.' As a joke to lighten the atmosphere during my interview, I'd even asked one of the psychologists on the panel if they could write a note as evidence of my sanity for my dad as proof I wasn't crazy – and the guy in charge of the interview panel (of three psychologists and managers) had jokingly replied that he couldn't do that without testing me first, and that I might not like the results much. Then the only lady on the panel had grinned and suggested I'd fit right in with the other staff there. 'I'm expecting to hear back from them any day,' I said.

'Yeah, well, don't be surprised if they arrive at your house with a van and straitjacket.' Jim poked around under the hood. 'There has to be a candid camera in here somewhere.'

Instead, he found a leaking fuel line, which also explained why the tank had been nearly empty at home in the first place. Either that, or a thief had milked the tank, since Dad never let his vehicles get so low to empty. It risked sucking dirt into the engine, apparently.

Jim found the tool kit, so the fuel line took no time to fix. He patched it and hailed a passing motorist, who siphoned some fuel from his own tank - which Jim paid for, refusing payment from me and making me feel even deeper in debt to him.

3:13pm We rattled and rolled into the sale-yards.

'Too late!' shouted the gatekeeper. He blocked our way, shaking his fist. 'The sale's over.'

'We know,' I shouted in reply. 'We've come to pay and collect.'

'Get a move on,' he grumbled, stepping aside. 'You're late for that too.' He slapped the side of our truck as we rolled past, and closed the entrance gate behind us, leaving only the exit gate open with a sign that warned us we had to be queued to leave by 3:30 with gates closing at 4pm.

At the office, the cranky blonde secretary was already complaining about a few buyers who hadn't bothered to pay or check out with her yet. She glared at me too as I walked up to her service window of the caravan. Her mood didn't improve at all, despite my friendly smile, as I emptied my pockets onto her counter with my treasure of mixed coins and small notes.

She spanked the counter at me, like a strict school teacher. 'Is this a joke?' she scowled. 'Is there a sign out there, daring people to wreck my day?'

'If there was, it was pinned to my back,' I replied. 'You wouldn't believe the day I've had…' I apologised sincerely, and began to explain, but old Mrs Cranky Spanky waved me to silence, complaining that she'd have to start counting it all again.

Boo hoo. She'd barely made it to two dollars.

Cranky Spanky asked to see Jim's driver's licence for the permit, and as he opened the personal inner sanctum of his wallet, I noticed a thick wad of cash. And I mean t.h.i.c.k. This guy could put his back out sitting on a pile like that, and as a girl who'd just been scraping to find coins for the past three hours, I'm ashamed to say I felt jealous.

Then I shook myself off like a wet dog and got over it. I couldn't get past the embarrassment of him knowing me since birth, and knowing what I looked like in a diaper. But I must also admit to being impressed. A guy who had his head together with money and cars and didn't mind rolling around in the dirt with me through the bad times… wow, now that's the kind of guy that my girlish dreams were made of. Except I needed one who was closer in age, less inclined to date the "gorgeous blondes" and hadn't helped his mum change my diapers, each time she'd babysat me as a toddler.

At long last, Mrs Cranky Spanky handed me a receipt and a travel permit, along with stern instructions to show it to the head stockman before leaving the premises. I never bothered asking her name or how I'd recognise the head stockman. I guessed he'd be on a horse and/or at the gate, and I figured the sooner I made off from her, the better.

'Shake your tail,' she warned me. 'All gates are closing soon.'

I ran as fast as I could to Pen 13-13… where I skidded to a halt in the mud and landed flat on that tail I'd been shaking.

The pen; empty.

The mare and foal; missing.

12. To Catch a Horse Thief

Juvenal,
the famously sarcastic Roman poet,
once said;

*The traveler with empty pockets
will sing in the thief's face*

... but what do I do, when I suck at singing?

Standing amid the array of emptying pens, everywhere I looked, stockmen busied themselves loading horses onto trucks and into trailers. So while Jim guarded our own truck, I ran about, desperately peeking between side-boards and over tailgates, trying to find the two I'd bought and paid for.

Revelation; all horses look alike when they're covered in slimy foul mud.

I wish I'd been smart enough to take a photo of them before I'd left. I usually kept a little Polaroid camera in my car, since interesting things only happened away from home.

Now that I needed to look more closely at all the horses, I realised I'd only seen the mare and foal for a few minutes, and I couldn't remember if the mare had a black mane *and* tail, or not. To me at the time, she'd been all muddy brown.

Did she have a white blaze down her nose; and if so, was it broad or narrow? Crooked or straight? Did she have a white star, or merely a fleck of something white, thrown up with the mud?

I could hose off every horse and still not be sure if I'd

found them. I honestly couldn't remember any of their details, especially after everything else I'd been through, and the more I looked, the more confused I became. All the muddy brown horses looked the same to me.

I tried looking for the kids, and when that failed, I scanned for rumps with an orange dot and letter A, but most of the horses had been loaded already up into huge trucks, and I could only see legs and bellies through the side boards.

On the far side of the yards, I spotted old Miss Daisy Raincoat, hosing off her three bargains on a nice spot of concrete down near the toilet block. She tethered them on green grass under the eaves of the small building - where she also seemed to be waiting while her ex-husband reversed up to her with his very long horse trailer.

'Hey, have you seen my two?' I called out to her.

She spun around as if she'd seen a ghost in me. 'They thought you'd done a runner.'

'A what?'

'Changed your mind and run away.' She pointed to a truck on the far side of the yards which bore the logo for a meatworks - not the same logo as worn by Mr Fearsome, but a meatworks, nonetheless. A meat-works with the logo of a ship.

I ran so fast to reach it, I must have broken a land-speed record. At least for me.

'Hey, those middle two are mine!' I shouted to the stockman, just as he drove them up the ramp amid a stampede of others. 'I paid for two of those!'

Then I noticed four horses already ahead of them in the ramp, all with mixed codes of ownership on their rumps. 'Hey, are you stealing those?' I asked, in all innocence.

If looks could kill, I'd have dropped dead on the spot.

It took a second longer, but it dawned on me that my mouth had blurted the truth before my brain had engaged enough to know it for sure.

'Horse thief!' I sang out at the top of my lungs, and within seconds, I had a choir of big burly stockmen screaming and headed my way.

Mr Fearsome appeared out of nowhere, leapt up the ramp with the zeal of a guard dog, grabbed the thief by the neck and body-slammed him into the tailgate of his own truck.

'Hello, hello,' he said politely, introducing him to the tattoos on his fist. 'Been up to mischief again, have we, Stewie?' Mr Fearsome dragged the crooked meatworks buyer aside, and assisted him in his wait for police by laying him flat, face down in the mud. Terrible accidents involving his head and Mr Fearsome's knee also happened to the thief on his way to the ground. During the scuffle, the thief kissed Mr Fearsome's knuckles several times, and not in the nice way.

By the time I glanced back to the horses, my two had been forced up into the truck by the next four horses behind them on the ramp. So as soon as the police arrived – in less time than it took to deliver a pizza - Mr Fearsome and his brothers unloaded the whole truck to help sort them out again.

As I watched the horses empty out down the ramp, I saw my little foal get shoved from behind and fall down, right in the path of the other horses.

'Whoa! Whoa! Whoa!' shouted the beer-can shaped brother, waving his arms.

I shouted at the same time too, but faster than I could blink, Mr Fearsome snatched a metal paint pole from a nearby marker and shoved it through the rails of the ramp – holding the bulk of the horses back from unloading, and giving the poor little guy a few vital seconds to get up.

'Lord, is he lucky,' joked one of the older stockmen.

'Mister,' I said, catching my breath, 'you have no idea.'

'Hey, luv,' shouted Mr Fearsome as he waved to me. 'As your two reach the end of the ramp, open that gate.' He pointed to the pen nearest to me. 'We'll draft them through to you.'

I nodded, keen to help any way I could, and while the other stockmen sorted the mixed herd, I opened a second gate to invite my two through into a pen which had remained empty the whole day, so it had absolutely no mud churned up in it yet. No grass either, but solid ground seemed like blessing enough for the moment.

Six other horses burst through with them.

I felt horribly sorry for them. All lovely looking animals, all so excited and happy as they emptied out of that truck - even if they were only escaping down into that foul smelling mud. And yet, all still concemned to the meatworks.

At least I could save two of them.

Mr Fearsome's younger brother appeared by my side to thank me. 'That guy's been under suspicion for some time,' he whispered. 'He's been making off with the uncollected stragglers, by mixing them in with his, while we've been busy loading the bigger mobs. Gate keepers never count legs on the solid-walled trucks. Especially this late in the day. We've suspected him for years but never had any proof.'

They still didn't, I thought. He could argue that he'd made a mistake that should have been found at the gate.

'Will he go to jail?' I asked.

'He will if I have anything to say.' Mr Fearsome chuckled. 'He's just lucky the cops got here fast, or he might have fallen off his truck a few more times and broken his jaw and not just his nose. By the way, I heard the kids calling your mare Penny. So she has a name, if you want to keep it.'

'Penny, yes. They told me. Are they still here?' I brightened, realizing that amongst all the drama, I hadn't had a chance to talk to them or their parents yet about when the mare and foal would be due for their annual vaccinations against tetanus and strangles.

'They'd had enough,' Mr Fearsome explained. 'Poor little beggars. Ask up at the office,' he suggested. 'Their dad needed to register as a seller before he unloaded, so he must have supplied the office with contact details.'

'Thank you *so much*,' I said, clasping his hand to shake it, but that hardly seemed enough, so I hugged him one last time, expecting never to see him again.

I've never seen such a stunned look on a man, not even counting the first time I'd hugged him that day. I surprised myself again too actually, considering my very first impression of him. I thanked him and grabbed a rail to climb over the top into Penny's pen.

Mr Fearsome's older brother grabbed me by the back of my shirt and stopped me.

'Hold it, luv,' he warned. 'One of those stallions in with your mare is a rig.'

'A what?'

'He hasn't been gelded properly, and it's driven him crazy. Hey, Pete!' he called to a stockman, mounted on a big black Australian Quarterhorse. 'The two A's in this lot. Can you cut them out for us?'

'Sure, stand back.' Pete opened the gate without dismounting; his horse shouldering it closed obediently behind them and waiting until his rider had leaned across to bolt it shut properly. It looked like such a cool trick to teach a horse how to close a gate like that, I decided I'd have to try it at home myself later with Apache and Snow.

Stockman Pete latched the gate, barely, as the rig attacked him, and his horse spun to defend them both with his heels. The stockman cracked his whip across the rig's nose, sending it away briefly, and in the turmoil, the other horses nearly trampled the foal again.

Each side of the yard had a gate, and I leapt to the nearest. 'Penny!' I called, hoping she'd respond to it.

Even if I was still a virtual stranger to her, I guessed that she'd know her own name - and she did. She came bolting out from the bunch so fast, I nearly didn't get the gate open wide enough in time – and the foal stayed so close at her side he rubbed off mud from her in the shape of his silhouette.

I slammed the gate closed behind her, realizing only then that I'd let her out into an open path between the yards, where the crowd had been shuffling during the auction. Last I'd seen, there'd been a gate open around the next corner – an escape route into the carpark!

'Penny!' I called again, and she spun around and hugged her nose against my side. 'Clever girl,' I said, stroking her face.

As the mud came off in my hand, I discovered that under it, she did indeed have a lovely slim white blaze down her nose. 'What a very clever girl you are.'

I tried not to look over my shoulder at the other horses, but I couldn't help it. I glanced back and saw four long faces staring out at me, as if pleading for me to call their names too.

By then I probably would have, if only I'd known them.

Powerless, though, with a makeshift truck and already stretched way beyond my limits, the best I could do for them was pray, wipe my eyes, and be grateful that I could save two who'd get to walk away.

13. Out of the Frying Pan...

Laozi,
the legendary Chinese founder of Taoism,
(also known as Lao Tzu)
once said;

*They who do not trust enough
can not be trusted*

... which seems to be a rule with animals too.

To this day, I've never seen a horse more trusting and willing to follow a stranger – not even Snow or Apache, who'd both fallen in love with my bag of fresh bread.

Yet this wasn't love. It wasn't even trust yet. Just blind terror. To Penny and her foal, I represented the smallest danger and the only way they saw to get out of that frightening situation. I could have walked through fire, and they'd have followed me with that mare's nose still hugged firmly against my side, and her foal's nose tightly against her shoulder on the opposite side to me. As long as I kept heading away from that truck and the mud, I didn't need any halter or rope.

Seeing the gate to the carpark open ahead, I paused to harness her anyway.

I glanced up and saw Jim headed my way, in search of me with a worried expression.

'Problems?' he asked.

'Not anymore.'

'I saw a police car race in through the wrong gate, and leave with a guy in handcuffs.'

'Yeah, horse thief, apparently. I'll explain on the way home.' I glanced over to the back of our tip truck, and saw the whole rear wall had fallen down into the shape of a ramp. 'Is that supposed to do that?'

'Design feature... I hope.' Jim grinned like a kid who'd just found the button to turn his toy truck into Megatron.

'Can you get it up?' I bit my tongue, realising what I'd just asked him. 'Again, I mean. The ramp.'

'We're about to find out.' He winked at me with a grin. 'So how do you want to do this? Keep it as a ramp? Or shall I fold up the wall again and slide open the smaller rear door to let them jump in?' He glanced around at a slope which could serve as a more natural kind of ramp, and to the row of timber ramps on the yards that had been purpose-built.

I hesitated, weighing the risks of each choice. Seemingly simple, and yet a step wrong with either one could mean injury or worse. I didn't know the mare well enough yet to know which would worry her the least, but I did know that she'd already been through one trauma with a truck, so getting her into another truck so soon could easily become a tug-of-war with an animal much stronger than me. And as a mare with a foal to protect, she'd already warned her baby to keep to the far side of her from me, which suggested if I tried to force the foal anywhere, she'd be compelled to defend it, in which case she could become deadly with a capital D.

'Give me a second,' I said, and led the mare to a bright patch of clean green grass near a fence to give us both a little more time to get better acquainted.

Penny plunged her muzzle into the fresh grass as if she hadn't been fed in a whole day – and she probably hadn't.

Not a good thing for a skinny mare producing milk. Under stress, if those conditions were prolonged, she could develop all kinds of nasty stomach or systemic problems. Sour milk for a start.

The moment she began grazing, she calmed down straight away. Her sides stopped heaving in fear, and although her pulse must have dropped too, I still felt mine throbbing with a beat like a clock ticking off the seconds to our 4pm deadline at the gate.

The foal spun around against her side, and nosed up between her back legs for a serve from the milk bar. Penny took comfort from that too, obviously, because her expression softened and she shifted her back leg to give the foal easier access.

'Good girl,' I crooned, stroking her neck. 'What a good, clever mama mare you are.'

I let the rope hang loosely between us and crouched on my haunches, making myself appear small and unthreatening to them, while needing to check the foal was suckling okay. Most importantly of all, I also needed to spend this quiet moment with them, so they could associate me with something pleasant and familiar, instead of just the frantic chaos that I'd been appearing in and out of, unreliably, all day so far.

Penny kept a wary eye on me as I tried to lean closer to her foal. My fault. My eyes have a weird focal problem that can't be corrected properly yet by either lenses or surgery, and I thought I saw something on the foal's side that looked like blood.

Waiting until he was busy suckling, I edged closer, even though the foal kept switching to the far side of his mother suspiciously.

Watching him from the other side of her tummy, I noticed a few scratches on Penny's legs. And worse. A drop of blood fell from the colt's umbilical cord, right where it joined onto his stomach. I also saw a shallow gash down his side, a deep scratch on his near-side hind leg and a nick on his chest. All seemed filthy with mud, which meant they also had to be stinging him.

No wonder he didn't want me to touch him.

I tried to walk around for a better look and check his other side, as well as hers, but he scampered around her rump, or ducked under her tummy, always keeping as far from me as possible without leaving his mother.

To earn his trust, I knew I'd need to earn his mother's thoroughly first. So I started talking to her again, even though I had no idea what to say and could feel our deadline tick-tocking nearer with every second. So I just kept telling her how clever and brave she'd been so far, and what a handsome colt she had, and that they'd both be safe finally, just as soon as I took them home to a nice juicy paddock.

Yeah, I know there are people who'd be rolling their eyes at me for expecting an animal to understand details like that, but I didn't really expect it... *yet*. I only knew from experience that it was more about body language and tone of voice at first – and I'd much rather make sense than talk nonsense. It's also a bonus when months of repetition make it possible for pets to understand more and more of our language. How can we expect them to learn, if we don't speak to them often, right?

'Gate closing!' shouted a stockman. 'Ten-minute warning!'

'Oh, great,' I muttered.

'Ready or not,' Jim said. 'Here we go.'

I nodded, knowing I still had to convince the mare that she *wanted* to be on my truck, even after she'd fled so desperately from the last one, and I had to do it quickly, in direct contravention of the first rule in forming a long-lasting trusting relationship with a horse.

My only chance was to look at the situation and appreciate it from the mare's perspective.

If her previous owners had been there, I would have asked for one of *them* to load her for me, so that if she baulked, the mare could blame them, not me, for loading her back onto a truck.

But that wasn't an option for me either.

So I reached through the nearest fence and snatched a sweet handful of the greenest grass I could get from the other side - because that's where most horses seem to think it grows — and I offered it to her as a final token of friendship. She took it from me keenly, so I repeated it a few times until she stopped eating on her own and waited for more juicy handfuls from me. All the while, I kept talking softly, and explaining the situation to her, and thanked her for accepting food from me.

Sane or not, logical or not, it worked. I no sooner finished explaining the situation about the truck, while walking her around it in a decreasingly small spiral so she could smell that no danger lurked within it – she promptly turned her nose for the ramp and walked straight in with the colt still glued to her side.

I had to jog to keep up with her.

'Close it now please,' I called to him. 'Before she changes her mind.'

'How will you get out?'

I glanced up at the bars, deciding I could jump, swing up and climb out... *if* I morphed into a real athlete for the first time ever. 'I'll be the girl falling from the roof.'

He started cranking the winch, while I got busy tethering Penny into a corner. The foal ducked under her neck, trying to get away from me again, but he effectively wedged himself into the corner, which allowed me to get a much better look at him – and to touch him finally. First time I'd ever touched a foal in my life. Much softer than an adult horse, not counting the mud and slime.

I checked out the mare more thoroughly too, and to my horror, I found she had a long gash, high up inside her hind leg, which also stretched over her udder and bled near the tip of one teat. Over half a ruler's length in all, but thankfully, the cut seemed only shallow.

'Steady, mare,' I whispered to her, and I leaned up under her back legs for a better look. Not too smart of me, sticking my head up inside the hind legs of a horse I'd just met, but I made sure my hair didn't tickle her stomach, which could make her kick in reflex and - my trust in her paid off.

'Hey, Jim!' I called, as I chose to stay in the back with them a while longer. 'Before I get out, can you please drive us down to the toilet block? I saw a hose down there earlier, which could help clean up these wounds a lot - provided it stretches enough for you to hand it up to me.'

No complaints or hesitation from him. No nagging reminders about the time limit either. Or telling me "she'll be right, mate, until we get home". I really appreciated that, and wanted to tell him so, but I had no idea if guys liked to hear such things in public or if he'd find it embarrassing.

He drove down far more cautiously than I'd expected, and helped me hose off the worst of the mud from them. Penny seemed both relieved and grateful, actually, but the foal hated it, even though I tried to make it seem like normal rainfall on him.

After the last river of slime fell away from them, it took another few minutes to hose it all out of the back door as well, because the slime turned the metal floor of the truck into a deadly slippery slide. Broken legs would have been guaranteed at the first rough bump or corner… until Mr Fearsome appeared unexpectedly, with two long wide strips of rubber carpets.

'Bump strips,' he said, passing them up to me. 'I heard your mare slipping about in there, and these were marked for demolition anyway.' He pointed downhill to the older sections of the yards, that were roped off from the public, and I saw where he'd taken them down from the rails, where they'd been hung to prevent animals from trying to escape.

'Lay them down on the floor,' Fearsome said, 'and their hooves won't slip on the way home.'

'Wow, thanks,' I said, wishing I had something to give him in return. I reached down to shake his hand one last time, and remembered one of the inspirational quotes from our Little White Throne Room's Great Wall of Wisdom.

'Thank you,' I repeated more sincerely. 'May fortune favour you for all the kindness you shine into the world.'

The right thing to say, apparently, and the complete opposite to the way I'd felt about him when I'd first met him. He choked up a little, in a manly fashion, and simply nodded in reply as he turned away. I watched him climb up into his huge Mack truck with his brothers, and drive away with a full payload of condemned horses. It still seemed so tragic, but if those poor animals really did have to die – if he wouldn't be able to find homes for them all, then at least I knew they wouldn't be flogged all the way.

'Five minutes,' Jim called. 'There's a stockman out here giving us the evil eye.'

'Coming.' I wiped my eyes, trying to pull myself back together while I still had a little privacy. 'Can you please check if there's a first aid kit behind the driver's seat?'

I knew my dad liked to keep one in every vehicle, and

that antiseptic cream for humans seemed to hurt horses a lot less than anything I'd ever bought from the vet.

Jim also handed me a few bandages that turned into perfect wraps for the foal's leg and chest - which also gave him something to suck on, aside from his mum's wounded udder.

I couldn't put antiseptic cream anywhere that Lucky might get it in his mouth, obviously, but I knew enough about being female to know that mother's milk always carried its own antibodies, no matter what the species. Same as "mother's spit," mum often told me. So I spat on my fingers, and used saliva as an antiseptic lubricant to milk out a small dose of her own medicine, catching it with my other hand, and soothing the whole area by applying it to the clean cut on her udder.

Penny flinched when I touched her udder, and she laid back her ears unhappily, but I realised my hands were still cold from the hose water. The cream seemed to soothe her almost instantly. Not only by soothing the sore area, but also by guarding against any painful air from getting into the scratches. A good thing too, because we'd soon need that level of trust between us for something far more deadly serious.

Out of the frying pan, as the old saying goes…

We had a long road ahead together.

14. The More the Merrier, I Hoped

Bugs Bunny,
my hilarious hero,
once taunted Yosemite Sam by saying;

*I dares ya ta step
across this line*

... and yes, for horses separated by a low fence that they
could easily step over, it could look just as funny,
but also much scarier.

As Jim and I drove home with the mare and foal, it finally dawned on me that I hadn't prepared the paddocks for new tenants.

It's not like I could simply dump two new horses in with the others. From that one disastrous weekend at pony club camp, I knew that horses had a pecking order based on age, sex and aggressiveness. So it wasn't possible to simply let them run loose together, without risking a few more injuries from their horsey shenanigans. The mare and foal had been through enough already. They also needed the last two hours of daylight to learn about the natural dangers of their paddock; the barbed wire fences and steepest sections of the bank, which dropped straight to the river.

I'd never planned on having a foal, so I needed time to fence off the most dangerous areas first – areas that Apache and Snow were both big and smart enough to handle. Yet, I could already expect nightmares of the little guy rolling over in his sleep and falling into deep water. My mind had a way of dreaming up all the worst case scenarios, and then I'd never get a wink's sleep unless I'd done everything I could to prevent such horrors from actually happening.

'Can you wait here?' I asked as Jim braked to a halt at the river paddock. 'Give me five seconds to shift the other two into the steeper paddock.'

Too late, though. They'd already caught wind of the newcomers.

Apache and Snow stood at the gate and called *hello*, like a formal chorus from a welcoming committee.

I almost changed my mind about moving them to free up the safest allotment for the mare and foal. For a fleeting moment, I thought everything would be perfect from the first moment.

Wishful thinking.

Apache started up with his alpha-male hormones; rearing and galloping up and down the fence like a playboy on steroids. He'd only been gelded a month before he'd been put up for sale to me, while most colts are gelded well before they turn two. So even though he couldn't make babies any more, he'd still had four years to develop all the muscles, instincts and attitude of a fully grown stallion. Perhaps that's also why he took such great care with my personal safety, protecting me as if I was one of his herd and family. But in any case, I couldn't put a foal in with him in case he trampled it by accident, or spooked the youngster through a fence, or into the river – which dropped to a depth of five metres almost instantly. So unless the foal could learn to swim in seconds, he'd drown before he could find anywhere to scramble up the bank. Ordinarily, I would have fenced it off already, except the other two loved to swim in the river on hot days.

Penny stamped and pawed inside the truck, growing

worried and restless. I doubted she could be ready for mating again so soon after giving birth, but she began to behave as if she was. She lifted her tail and squirted a milky urine inside the truck that even I could smell outside, and it made Apache go crazy wild with excitement.

'Are they going to fight?' Jim asked.

'Worse,' I said. 'They want to *like* each other too much.'

He looked embarrassed, and I tried not to giggle, because it embarrassed me too. 'I didn't know you had a stallion down here.'

'I don't, but try telling *him* that.'

It really didn't look safe to put a tiny foal in a paddock with three over-excited adults. But before I could lock my first two away in my newest river paddock behind a neighbouring house, I'd need to lead them down there. So, leaving the mare and foal in the truck for a few minutes longer, I ran home for more halters and lead ropes. I tethered Apache and Snow to a tree next door, well away from the dividing fence, and set about unloading the mare and foal in relative peace. They all still whinnied a lot and stamped their feet impatiently, especially when I swung up onto Penny's bare back and committed the traitorous crime of riding another horse within sight of them.

Jealousy flared up in Apache so fast, it was like I'd thrown petrol on a wildfire. He reared up, threatening to break his reins, until I called out to him, and gave him all the commands to calm down.

Putting only one dividing fence between the two pairs no longer seemed like far enough. Yet that's all I had. They'd still be able to bite and kick at each other over the fence at any time, day or night.

I couldn't dismount the new mare just yet either. For safety's sake, I needed to make sure Penny and the foal visited every corner and knew every kink around trees inside the boundary of their own yard to minimise the risk of accidents through their first night. If we'd arrived much earlier in the day, I wouldn't have bothered, since a horse can find its own boundaries fast enough, especially in a yard the size of a small house allotment. But I wasn't taking any chances in case she got spooked and bolted through one of the wire fences. Her injuries suggested it wouldn't be the first time that week.

As I turned the farthest corner, I realised Apache had fallen silent, and when I checked over my shoulder, I saw Jim at his side, stroking his neck and shoulder. Impressive for a city boy. Snowy seemed to take an instant liking to him too, which was strange, because she never liked any men to touch her, aside from my dad on the rare occasions that he could spare time to help me trim her hooves.

Penny walked obediently around the obstacles and boundary, and felt really nice and relaxed under me, so I hugged her and set her free to graze, leaving the halter on her, just in case I needed to grab her again in a hurry.

Instead of grazing, she trotted to the dividing fence and called to Apache and Snow as if to challenge them.

They strained at their tethers, but when they failed to meet her, she strode to the corner where Apache and Snow usually did most of their business, sniffed around for the cleanest spot, and deposited her own contribution for the local gardeners. Then at last, her hunger won over and she lost interest in all but the juiciest grass as she began to graze. The foal mimicked his mother in all things too - until his first nibble of grass. He wasn't old enough yet to take as much interest in it as his mother. For him, milk was the main meal that went down easy, while grass was a treat he was still learning to chew and swallow upwards, while keeping his head down.

'How long do you leave your first two tied up?' Jim

asked.

'We can let them go now,' I replied. 'You can go too, if you like.' He had to be exhausted by now, surely, after working a double shift of overtime and then everything else we'd done.

'I told you, I'm not leaving you by the roadside, no matter how close to home you are.'

'It's okay, honestly. Take the truck to save yourself the walk, or it'll be fine parked where it is. Either way, I need to stay until dusk to make sure they settle down properly.'

'What makes you think they won't fight over the fence as soon as you leave?'

'That's always a risk, I guess, but they need to sort out their pecking order, and hopefully they'll do it while I'm here.'

Lucky spotted me releasing Apache and trotted back to the dividing fence to watch us. He looked cuter than anything I'd ever seen as he reared up and whinnied like a real little rival stallion.

Apache whinnied too, but it sounded more like a chuckle. I led my big boy to the fence and warned him to play gently before setting him free. He'd always been kind and cautious with my dog and cats, so I wasn't really worried about him hurting the foal deliberately over the fence. And he certainly didn't. If anything, the two males bonded almost instantly as mentor and apprentice. Lucky copied every prance, stamp and arch of Apache's neck.

Penny trotted over defensively, and the two mares met a little further downhill. Apache joined them, and the posturing finally grew serious. Penny pawed the air, striking out at Snow with her front leg, and tangled herself in the wires.

'Whoa! Steady mare!' I called and pushed into the midst of them.

'I'll hold her,' Jim offered, but I had Penny's leg untangled before he could reach us. Then she spun around, offering her tail to Apache, who hung out his garden hose, sniffing, licking and nickering keenly.

'Flirts,' Jim said with a grin. 'Is it normal for them to fall in love that quick?'

'Apparently. I just hope his hormones don't drive him crazy enough to try riding her over the fence. He's only a gelding who can't satisfy a mare no matter how hard he tries.'

'Yeouch. I can imagine. Poor fella.'

I grinned and turned away, trying to settle my little herd with my voice and hands. I probably should have left them sort it out themselves, but the sun had sunk perilously close to the horizon. So I kept stroking their shoulders and necks, reminding them constantly to behave and play nice. I also took care to give most attention to Apache, Snow and Penny, in that order, since that seemed to be the most likely order of dominance, and I suspected it wouldn't hurt to support it from the very beginning.

Then Snow surprised me by barring her teeth for the first time ever, biting hold of Apache's ear and wrenching his head away from Penny's tail.

And that settled that.

Snow established herself as the matriarch.

They settled down fairly promptly after that.

'To be doubly safe,' I decided aloud, 'I'll keep them in separate paddocks for a few weeks or months, until I'm absolutely certain that they're all getting along well.'

As it happened, it only took until Monday, and the trouble headed their way on that night would not be their fault. I didn't know it yet, but all my care in building relationships was about to pay off *big time* – with the scariest night that any horse could ever have in a city.

15. Night of the Raving Lunatics

There's an old Proverb
that advises us;

If you love something, set it free.
If it comes back, it's yours.
If it doesn't, it never was.

Nice... but what do you do,
when those things that you love most are
FORCED to run away from you?

All things considered, my neighbourhood seemed relatively safe. Quiet usually too, despite being a suburb jammed between the city and the river.

Aside from the grey gossips and local hoons, our small pocket-shaped suburb centred around a few semi-organised bullies with peach fuzz on their chins. Plus a few brainless idiots who dwelt at the shallow end of the gene pool and would occasionally gather after dark to beat their chests and mix alcohol with street racing.

Luckily for me, a power pole with a corner light stood at the bend in the road where I paddocked my horses, providing one corner of their paddock with a city-funded security light. Apache and Snow had always chosen to sleep under that bright circle every night, and Penny and Lucky followed their lead on their first night together in the same paddock.

Ordinarily, the bright light kept the mischief-makers

away, pushing them back, like rats into the shadows. But that first night, the novelty of seeing an extra horse-and-a-half down there must have been too much for two of the dirtiest rats.

I woke at 5.13am to the sound of frantic knocking on the glass doors downstairs; the entrance to our main living room which also doubled as our customer waiting area.

I threw back my bedcovers and cracked open my side window, which overlooked our driveway.

'Who's down there?' I called, nervously.

A middle-aged man wearing dirty grey overalls emerged from beneath our front verandah. I recognised him as Mr Robinson, a tenant from one of the houses near my horses, who worked night shifts at the railway maintenance yards across the river.

This night he'd come home early, feeling ill. Thank goodness.

'Your horses are loose on the main road!' he called up to me. 'I nearly crashed into them. There's two raving lunatics chasing after them on motorbikes.'

'Are you sure they're *my* horses?' In my haze, I couldn't imagine them being frightened of bikes, motorised or not.

'Who else has horses around here? Two brown, one white and your big coloured gelding jumped over the nose of my car.'

I shook myself awake properly. 'Right. Stupid question.' Two other horses had moved in recently along the river a few streets away, but Snowy remained the only grey, and Apache had such strikingly coloured patterns that there could be no mistaking him. Not even after dark, because his white patches seemed to glow under moonlight.

'Which way were they headed?'

He pointed east.

I shuddered in fear. That was the way to Brisbane, our state capital, barely half an hour's drive away. The main road had only two lanes in each direction, but the first 100km/h speed limit was only two blocks away, on the far side of a railway crossing, and every step on that highway was deadly dangerous for pedestrians.

'Need help getting them back?' asked Mr Robinson. 'I'll show you where, but you'd better fetch your family down too, because you'll need two teams. One to herd your horses home, and one to repair your fence to keep them in. Those lunatics cut the wires, right under the street light.'

'Just a second.' I rubbed my face, still trying to wake up and still finding it hard to believe my horses would run away from home, even Penny and Lucky. As herd animals, they should have followed the lead of the strongest. That was Apache, hands down, and he wasn't scared of anything. If he'd been running away, there could be only one reason. He must be having trouble keeping his little herd together and safe. He may have been a gelding, and his mum may have been the matriarch but herd protection is the stallion's job, and he was the closest they had.

I knew I had to get to him first, before those idiots cornered him and forced him to take care of them, as he would with any dogs or snakes that threatened him. My luck, a court case would side with the Neanderthals against the horse, even if Apache only attacked in self-defence.

I also knew he'd never fail to answer when I called him.

So I threw open my window wider, and heard the distant rev of motorbikes waaaay over in the neighbouring suburb of Booval, and I heard whooping and shouting echoing to me. Apparently, Mr Robinson's description of the riders as "lunatics" didn't seem like hyperbole.

Faintly, and for the briefest moment, I heard the clatter of hooves on bitumen.

The sound made me shiver again, and not just from worry about the risk of a vehicle accident. My secret fear: broken bones, since a horse with a broken leg is usually an animal with an instant death sentence, and the cumulative damage that can be done to hooves and leg bones from jogging on bitumen rarely shows up until years later. Or months if they wear metal shoes. Thankfully, mine were all barefoot that week, so at least I didn't have the extra worry about law suits from motorists getting struck by damaged horseshoes flying off. There's absolutely nothing lucky about a horseshoe if it hits you.

Biggest worry; they were being forced to gallop on bitumen – after I'd been so careful to teach them how to stop at the curb, look both ways, just like little kids, before walking calmly over it. Knowing Apache as well as I did, I knew that forcing my normally placid, sweet boy to run away from his home against his training and my wishes would have been making him extremely cranky. So I brought my hands up to my mouth in the shape of a loudspeaker, and called his name at the very top of my lungs – long and slow - to help the sound travel as far as possible over the crisp dewy rooftops.

'Apaaaaa-Cheeeeeeeeeeeeeeee.'

Dogs and cats barked and screeched and howled in chorus up to three suburbs away. As much as I loved animals, I wished them all silent, momentarily, until I heard my faithful friend reply in his very loudest whinny.

With ten times my lung capacity, his cry seemed to echo over the whole city, also silencing the other animals. Such a strange sound for the suburbs.

'Paaatch-cheee,' I called again, using the nickname that better suited his patches of colour. 'Snowwweee, Pennee, Luckeee.' I emphasized the eee's on the end of each name, using the old bushman's trick of using vowels that seemed to travel much further over distances – like the generic Aussie catch-cry *Coo-eee*. It worked and all four horses responded within seconds.

I heard a distant crash, and more hooves pattering on bitumen; as if Apache had heard his name, then spun back on his hunters and taught them some manners, finally, now that he had the vital information about which direction promised his small herd the greatest safety.

In the still morning air, I heard the clattering of hooves growing louder.

'Hey, they're coming,' said Mr Robinson a moment later. 'That was lucky.'

'At least one quarter Lucky, I hope.'

At the pace they were coming, I couldn't dawdle. 'Stay there, please, Mr Robinson. Don't be scared when they come. They'll be scared of you, probably, but if you flatten yourself against the wall and don't move, you'll be perfectly safe. Even if one of them rears up at you. Simply say 'Hello, big fella', calmly.

I grabbed the first jeans and shirt I could throw on over my nightdress, knowing I had to get downstairs and out onto the footpath before Apache turned into the street and spotted a strange man between him and me. After being stirred up so badly and hunted so far from home I doubted he'd tolerate a man in shadowy overalls. Especially if those overalls bore smudges of train-grease that smelled a little too much like motorbikes.

Bursting out onto the street, my bare feet discovered the icy grass, where frost crystals seemed as harsh as glass shards. I saw Snowy turn into the street first, closely followed by Penny, the foal, and finally Apache. Herding them up onto the grassy footpath, he slowed their pace from a gallop to a long-strided trot – the best pace for a horse to travel over distances without tiring, and to ensure the youngest of his herd could keep up with him.

He herded them straight for me. Penny veered for the nearest open driveway gate with her foal, seeking any peaceful "paddock", but Apache cut her off and kept her moving towards me. Then she spotted me too, and as I opened my arms wide and called for them to steady down, all four of them skidded to a halt and surrounded me.

Noses in, nuzzling me. I didn't need ropes to lead them. I simply turned and walked in down our driveway, past Mr Robinson, who stayed as still as a painting. Their only reaction to him was a few warning snorts and a little shying as they veered wider around him, while keeping me safe from him.

Upon reaching the backyard, they trotted happily through the brick arch to our BBQ patio, and stayed close at my side, while I strung up a rope at hip height as a temporary boundary. There was nothing else in the back yard, aside from the clothes line, a few towels left out overnight, three citrus trees and a mulberry tree; nothing for them to hurt, or get hurt by. They could eat leaves and fruit from the huge mulberry tree all week and only manage to trim it and maybe scare a few silk worms.

'That was amazing,' whispered Mr Robinson. 'I've never seen anything like it.'

'You can move and speak normally now,' I assured him. I tightened the rope so it hung about a metre off the ground, stretching it about fifteen metres from the garage to the side fence, to show them the boundary I wished them to stay behind. No need to do anything between the other side of the garage and Donny's fence. It was a narrow corridor blocked by a huge, heavy oil drum and the smell always kept them away from there.

'Will that rope hold them?' he asked. 'They were pretty stirred up, and that foal looks small enough to walk right under without even noticing.'

I glanced to them, peaceful at last in the moon-shadows under the mulberry tree.

'I doubt I need the rope at all, actually. As long as you don't try to hurt me, all they want to do now is sleep. They're basically just big puppy dogs. Vegetarian puppy dogs.'

'Vegetarian lap dogs, nearly. For a second, it didn't look like they were going to stop until after they'd trampled you. Do you need help with their fence now?' He glanced up at the other windows, as if surprised that we hadn't been joined yet by anyone else. 'They could sleep through a nuclear war,' I chuckled. 'Thanks for the offer, but I built the fence, so repairing it should be easy enough.'

I thanked him again with a promise to send around a carton of his favourite beer - then gave him a smile and a wave as I overtook him a few minutes later on my pushbike loaded with fencing wire and pliers.

Fortunately, the fools on the motorbikes hadn't cut the fence. They'd only opened my bendable wire gate and dropped it in a way that made it look cut and tangled from a distance. I closed up the fence and decided to add a lock as soon as I could, although I doubted those particular hooligans would be back.

When the gate was done I followed the horses' tracks in the dew, over the hill, across the railway and the highway (I gave thanks at every step that they hadn't been hit) before veering off into the carpark at Booval shopping centre - where there was a long bike-tyre skid and the debris from a smashed headlight and helmet—which also sported a hoof print. Foot size: Apache.

I'd learned my lesson too. I couldn't follow the training books and leave the foal untouched by ropes for his first year. I owned a young animal in a city and he needed to learn how to lead safely in any direction. To do that, he needed to know he could trust me, no matter what.

I didn't realise it yet, but that decision would soon save his life.

*My first photo of Lucky
in the paddock behind
homes along the Bremer River,
in the small suburb of East Ipswich.*

*Yes, he looks cranky.
A rude magpie had just swooped past his nose.*

16. Option C; by Bitter Experience

Confucius,
China's most famous teacher,
once said;

Wisdom is learned by three methods;
By noble reflection,
easy imitation,
or bitter experience.

He made it sound like I had a choice.

The foal had been traumatised so much during the night of the raving lunatics, it took three days before he'd let me close enough again to touch him.

Until then, it was impossible to tend all his scratches from the sale-yards properly, because I could only crawl under their big hay feeder during meal times and sneakily spray a little salty water, antiseptic or honey onto him before he realised it wasn't flies pestering him.

The honey had been recommended in a health magazine as a cheap and painless way to kill germs, microbes, fungus and promote healing, thanks to its natural antibiotic properties, but it also seemed to attract dirt, ants and cause stains on his short hair. So I switched to using the leaf from an aloe vera plant – offered to me by Mrs Parker, of all people. She grew it in her garden; a cactus plant that looked more like a fat lily with blunt prickles down each side of the leaves.

'Oldest leaves near the bottom are the most medicinal,'

she said as she dug out an adult plant from a huge clump with her skeletal hands. She'd called out to me on the footpath on my way home from taking a donation box of empty toilet rolls to the kindergarten craft group for Mum. The skinny old woman had a way of extracting information from passers-by that always bugged me, but I didn't want to be rude to her, in case she complained to the council about me keeping my horses inside the city limits.

'Here's the trick with it...'

Avoiding the blunt thorns along the side of the widest leaf, she snapped it off. Then using her thick yellow fingernail, she split the leaf down the centre, peeled it open and revealed a pale green gooey gel.

'Wipe it straight onto the wound like this,' she said, smearing it along her own arm where a patch of excised skin cancers had healed. 'At least twice a day.'

'Ew! That's repulsive!' I cried, screwing up my nose. It smelled even worse than it looked, and it looked as if she'd swiped the nose of a snotty kid down her arm. 'Thanks, but I'll stick to salt and antiseptic cream.'

'I didn't know you were so cruel,' she said. 'Antiseptics can sting and slow down healing.' She pushed the pot at me, insistently. 'This kills germs and promotes healing.'

'Nah, I'm fine.' I turned to leave, but she grabbed my arm and poked at a scab where "It" had scratched me during my last few fencing sessions.

'Ow, hey!' I complained as she slimed half of the injury. I could hardly believe that she'd force her will on me like that.

'Listen here, young lady.' She shook her crooked nobly finger at me. 'Treat the other half of that scratch your own way, and if you don't see a difference by tomorrow, I'll embroider a fancy new rug for your saddle.'

That shocked me. I'd planned on running straight home and washing it off, but I had to admit I was already noticing a difference. The plant gel felt cool like antiseptic cream but much faster drying, and it formed a clear skin like plastic that kept off the air and soothed the sting.

'Fold the rest of the leaf into plastic lunch wrap so it can't heal itself, and keep it in the fridge until you've used it all up.'

'You're on,' I said. 'I need a new saddle rug.'

'Wait, there's more,' she said. 'Instead of salt-water for washing wounds, try silver water. It's more expensive — about twice the price of diet cola, but painless and longer lasting.'

'Silver, as in the metal element?' It sounded too bizarre.

'It tastes metallic, but it's better than harmless. There's no visible particles. Germs can't live in it.'

I blinked at her, unable to believe it, but she only rolled her eyes at me.

'Didn't you study history?'

'Chemistry,' I replied

'Then you should have learned it there too. Switch to eating from silver plates and cups and you'll self medicate against most germs and bacteria. That's why the black death affected mainly the lower classes in the 14th century. Fleas lived in rich homes too, you know, but the poor didn't have silver cutlery.'

'The 14th century..?' I tried not to giggle. 'Wow, Mrs Parker. I had no idea you were *that* old.'

She frowned at me, making it clear that she didn't appreciate my little joke. Escaping her deadly glare, I left swiftly, looking forward to returning the next day with measurements for my new blanket. But it wasn't to be. By the next morning, the slimed part of my small wound had nearly healed, when a scratch like that normally took three days for me.

So now I was using aloe vera on the animals too, and

tending to their wounds twice a day seemed to be working well enough.

There were no signs of redness anywhere, for either of them. Not even on the foal's tummy, where his umbilical cord had dried and fallen off naturally.

I thought we were home and dry.

By February 7th, Lucky would follow me anywhere – with or without a lead rope. I remember the date precisely, because the crew of the Space Shuttle *Challenger* celebrated the world's first untethered space-walk together. They'd be doomed soon too, but for the time being, everything seemed to be going so well in my life. I felt totally elated, like I was up there celebrating with that history-making crew, simply because my little friend no longer needed a tether either. He'd not only come to trust me, we'd become best buddies and playmates.

Fate, however, had other ideas.

Extreme weather changes ruined those next few days of autumn, ping-ponging from the heat of summer to winter chills. Bizarrely the cold rainy nights, icy winds and morning frosts evaporated abruptly, giving way to harsh suns and muggy hot days, making it hard for young and old, human and animal alike – especially with flies and infections - which reminded me to book the vet for the first annual vaccinations for my two new dependents.

Having never owned a foal or a lactating mare before, I relied on his advice that I needed to seek out the mare's inoculation history. Otherwise, there could be a risk of killing her and the foal with the same diseases that I sought to prevent IF they'd already received their shots within the last three months. Or so the vet-o-matic told me. A World Book Encyclopaedia on vaccinations told a different story; that vaccinating an animal couldn't cause the disease, and neither could re-vaccinating too soon, but my library's copy of the book had missing pages and a publication date older than me. And I'd expected the vet-o-matic to be more up-to-date than a dusty old book.

So first thing Monday morning I contacted the sale-yards and asked for records of the previous owners. I explained why I needed their phone number, so I had no trouble getting it – just in using it.

Thirteen days had passed since the sales and the phone for Penny's previous owners had been disconnected by the phone company. I drove out to the address, and found nobody home, just the old farmhouse with mortgagee sale signs plastered all over it. I rang the real estate office using the phone number on the for-sale signs, seeking the forwarding address details but the agent told me she didn't keep those details on record. I found that hard to believe, so I asked the agent about which bank held all of the mortgagee contact information. Then I called them too, but they refused to give it out to me. Rightly so, of course, for security reasons, but they refused to even pass on my urgent message or my phone number.

So I rang the vet-o-matic again, who told me not to panic. Provided I made sure their injuries stayed clean and showed no sign of redness or swellings, and as long as they cleared up within another week, he recommended that it would be better to defer their tetanus and strangles needles for three months from the date of purchase. The foal was 13 days old when I bought him so if we followed this plan he'd be 14 weeks instead of the usual 12 weeks when we started his inoculations.

'Three months old is just an approximate age,' he reassured me. 'As long as they get their needles at some time within that third or fourth month it should be fine, pet,' he said.

More famous last words.

Just my luck, the only date that this expensive old vet would be available in my area was a wee bit over three months anyway and wasn't only a Sunday, but Easter Sunday, when I'd have to pay him double-double time.

'Until then,' he advised me, 'Lucky should receive an adequate level of protection through his mother's milk.'

I'd found the same vague advice in books about horse care.

What neither of us knew at that stage, was that in addition to the cuts and scratches I was treating, Lucky had a tiny but deep puncture wound up under his hairy jaw. No bigger than a pin-prick, and concealed by mud at the sale-yards. Or maybe it happened the night of the raving lunatics. Either way, the puncture itself remained so small and the surface sealed too fast for me to notice it. But inside the puncture had gone deep enough to touch bone. It had created a tiny abscess that slowly festered undetectably, still hidden deep between two bones, up under the foal's jaw, near an artery with a rich and crucial blood supply.

Being such a sweet-natured little fellow, he never complained or gave any sign that it ever hurt, even though it must have ached more than a wisdom tooth rotting inside his jaw.

After the third day of me pretending I didn't want to touch him after that night of the raving lunatics, he grew so curious about me, we became great playmates. Especially when it came time to fill the water trough with a hose – a daily routine that all three adult horses loved. They much preferred their drinking water sucked directly from the clean hose, or sprayed over them on hot days. So the foal quickly learned to play like them. Three big ducks and one duckling.

By the third week, he trotted up at first sight of me, and

by the next, he'd come galloping at the first shake of a bridle or halter - bizarre, since most books warned me that young horses would often run the other way at first sight of a lead rope, much preferring a game of catch-me-if-you-can.

Learning from the daily routine with the other horses, Lucky also quickly understood how to let me handle all of his feet without a single game of "try to catch my hoof with your mouth." He also expressed curiosity about saddles and rugs, often licking or tugging the other horses', so I made him his very own set, in miniature, using my hobby craft skills. I sewed about as well as I cooked, so they didn't look too great, but he loved them. He also idolized Apache so much, following his moves like a little apprentice, that he took to lunging around me in circles on a long rope obediently with every command at barely six weeks of age - including voice commands for halt and back up. That's like teaching a human three-year-old how to sing the alphabet backwards.

All I'd had to do was make it a game that he wanted to play.

Then came the news I'd been hoping to hear for weeks; a letter that congratulated me on landing the office job at the century-old asylum for the criminally insane on the far side of the city, near Yamanto.

Ordinarily, a workplace like that with so many confined, dangerous people, would have terrified me, except that renovations and government policy changes had remodeled the whole medical facility into a comfortable "health sanctuary" set amidst sculpted sub-tropical gardens, surrounded by a golf course. All the most dangerous patients had been moved to higher security facilities, leaving only beds and apartments for a much safer clientele of adults who suffered severe handicaps. Mostly, the clients were innocent, gentle people who suffered from torturous health problems.

A career helping other people also appealed to me, even if I could only play my part in the office where my talent for handling money could be put to better use than at a cash register at my local supermarket.

I didn't know it yet, but the drop in pay I'd need to suffer as a first-year office clerk would hurt my pocket so much, I'd be glad that I'd already done so much overtime and budgeted for a worst-case scenario.

My Aloe Vera, still going strong.
Ugly as ever too, but I keep it proudly on my patio, where I nearly never need to water it.

17. Legalities of Life

Stick with me. I thought such things would be
torturous at first too, but;

Albert Einstein,
that witty, wild haired scientist,
once said;

*Strive not to be a success
but rather to be of value.*

He made me wonder how much value I could ever be
when I was already so small and insignificant
in a world reeling from so many historic upheavals,
and, I'd soon learn, with two nasty lawyers
hunting to find me.

After two sleeps of freezing rain, the sun came out with a vengeance, drying up the mud and coaxing up a thin sheen of green from thousands of tiny fresh sprouts of grass. Life settled into a comfortable routine - almost paradise in my small corner of the universe - while the rest of the world seemed to go crazier.

I tried my best to tune out to it; all those daily threats of World War Three becoming not only imminent, but seemingly inevitable. This was 1984, the year that George Orwell had set his famous dystopian novel, forecasting a world gone mad with Russian-style repressive regimes. He had published it way back in 1949, four years after the end of World War Two, when the whole planet was supposed to be settling into a new era of Peace.

Instead of Peace, fear electrified the air, every time we turned on a TV or radio. If it wasn't news of terrorist bombings in UK, Chile, Lebanon, Turkey or Kuwait, often including French or Americans, it was chemical weapons in the Iran-Iraq war, or Russia's cold war getting icier after they shot down Korean passenger Flight 007 on Sept 1st, 1983. It had mysteriously strayed into Soviet airspace after leaving New York with over 260 civilians aboard, including a US Senator. Apparently Russians believed that former President Nixon should have been sitting beside him. Crazy times.

Yet my new job at the old asylum was fun and filled with delightful characters amongst the staff and patients – even though they all wore normal clothes, so it was often hard to tell them apart whenever I ventured out of my second floor office for a walk downhill to the canteen.

From the dawn of February and deep into March, all the pressures of the world kept building around me, while throughout our neighbourhood, the gossips fell silent. Shock perhaps. Many were veterans of World War Two. Yet a Russian officer called Stanislav Petrov had recently averted a nuclear start to WW3 in September, only 26 days after the attack on Flight KAL007, by questioning an early warning system alert. So the whole world remained on high alert over Christmas. A nuclear war became the grim future that everyone seemed to silently accept, and we would simply have to deal with it.

'Did you know photons have mass?' joked my dad, in his own way of coping by cheering us all up. 'I'll bet you didn't even know they were Catholic.'

I couldn't help but smile. His nuclear "dad joke" was bad, but his grin was always infectious.

Posters appeared in every newspaper and mailbox with

instructions on how to survive a nuclear winter. I planted daisies the same day I helped mum to stash tinned foods and bottled water into every wardrobe and closet. We stacked towels in a corner of our dining room, ready for shredding into bandages, and we all learned how to escape a burning building; everyone behaving as if these were normal survival skills that we should have been learning anyhow. Every morning and afternoon I'd spend hours with my horses, planning where and how to hide four full sized horses from a nuclear blast wave, or from starving hordes of mutant survivors.

It all sounds crazy now, obviously... or maybe not, with the world on the brink of nuclear war again, this time with Russia over Ukraine... Or China over Taiwan... or North Korea, Iran, Palestine, Israel, Yemen... Crikey, take your pick. But back then, I'd overheard two journalists discussing which pets could be eaten raw, if it ever came down to it.

That just made me angry. Not only the idea of eating beloved pets, but also that people would spend so much time and energy planning to give in to such a terrible situation, instead of pouring *all* of their efforts fighting or solving the core problems and disputes between countries - especially when the repercussions of failure would be so horribly severe.

That's too simplistic on a world political scale, I tried to remind myself. I knew nothing about politics, but I knew from primary school that caving in to a bully only made things worse, so I was grateful that America's president Ronald Reagan and England's first female Prime Minister, Margaret Thatcher, were not caving in to scary threats.

Either way, their situation would soon impact my decisions in my own upcoming war between life and death. The parallels of my fate and fortune seemed to run parallel with society on a grander scale. As if we were all stuck in the same rut, and headed over the same cliff ahead.

It had taken the foal barely a month to learn how to trust me enough to run my hand down his hind leg - the same time it took the United Nations to condemn the use of chemical weapons in the Iran-Iraq Gulf war, which made those "world leaders" seem like dunces compared to the foal. I mean really. I was only sixteen, but even I knew that nuking your neighbor with chemicals was a *bad* thing.

Strangely, that was only the beginning of odd coincidences in Fate. Large scale and small; my little life's rut may have begun fresh after graduation from highschool, like footsteps in newly fallen dew. For example, the foal tried his first set of reins in the same weeks the reins of power shifted communist hands in Russia from Andropov to Chernenko. Nobody cared about my political opinions one way or another, since I was too young to hold any more than minor influence in my own small paddock, and that was borrowed territory anyway. My world seemed to be so small scale and inconsequential that I felt practically invisible.

I ached to find my own way in life, not noticing how much the world had already changed me, nor how much these outside influences would colour the decisions I'd have to make soon.

Still only sixteen years old, I realised I needed my own block of land the day a lawyer wrote me a nasty letter demanding that I remove my horses immediately from their client's property, after the owner had died, leaving it to warring children. They didn't know my age, just my name, and they gave me barely 24 hours to somehow comply with their demand by finding somewhere else for my horses. City or country.

Overseas the same day, Palestinian gunmen seized the passengers of Israeli Bus #300 as hostages in protest of their own ongoing land dispute, and Israeli special forces responded by storming the bus: far more serious than my own situation, with tensions and tragedies on both sides dating back generations but from the perspective of my horses, a forced sale would be a life or death crisis too.

My dad rolled his eyes at the TV news and said, 'They'll never resolve anything through terrorism…', which inspired me to have a go at solving my much milder situation of legal intimidation through negotiation. I bypassed the legal system, and contacted the owners directly to ask nicely in my own way, and achieved the reprieve that I needed. They even seemed *keen* to discuss it with me.

It turned out the nasty letter had only been sent by a legal secretary who'd been following a checklist of standard procedures to ensure the owners could list the property for sale, free and clear of any chattels or obligations.

'What's a chattel?' I asked in all innocence.

'Anything that can be moved from one property to another, like furniture, car bodies, livestock or temporary fencing.'

'Oh, is that all? Then why phrase your letter so nastily? Why not just call me and discuss it peacefully and maturely?'

'Business law is war,' replied the legal secretary, snarkily. 'The winners are always the biggest bullies.'

'Not in my experience. Customers are like family; and strangers are only customers or friends we haven't met yet.' I hung up, feeling sorry for her and the ugly, cruel way that she chose to conduct business. In highschool, I'd learned that society developed, setting us apart from animals, by caring for each other, and taking care of the weakest among us, so if it was becoming a dog-eat-dog world, then it seemed to me that people like her were to blame. Naïve of me perhaps, but if I kept any baggage from my childhood, I wanted to keep believing that helping each other through our darkest times was the best way to help ourselves too.

A similar letter came soon after from a different legal firm, on the other side of the country. This time from the buyers, a faceless conglomerate of investors; and the wording by their legal team was even nastier.

So I called their secretary too, finding bravery again in the need to defend my horses. Me, a mere minor negotiating with trained lawyers, and yet they never knew it. I hid behind the phone and the four thousand kilometres of Simpson's red stony Desert that stretched between us. I achieved my goal of a free extension for the paddock, simply by asking for it nicely in a way that would also appeal to them.

'The fences are mine,' I explained. 'I'll be taking them with me, but I can keep the land clean and fully supervised, saving you the expense of any mowing contractors or inspections from hired property managers until the time comes for your building plans. Is that okay with you?'

'Deal,' they agreed, and we didn't even bother with paperwork. They just warned me that bulldozers would be headed my way at some time between six and ten months away, and that the best they could promise me was a week's notice, even though they'd try to give me as much notice as possible.

Now I had a rough deadline for getting my own place: five months to be on the safe side.

I sacrificed one of my lunch breaks to window-shop for land instead of the usual quick trip home from work to share a sandwich with my four legged friends. I found a clean paddock out past Yamanto, on the far side of our modest city, with nice shady forest and a little creek. It was supposed to be a house block, so the creek had been the drawback that made it cheap. But with so many lovely homes and more expensive blocks around it, I suspected it might be a fair investment. I didn't realise a developer had plans to buy next door and remake the whole district, trebling the value. At the time, I could only lay down a hundred bucks deposit, with a long contract of three months before it could become mine, because I figured it would take me that long to save the rest of the deposit by settlement day. The owners didn't mind. They signed and faxed the contract back to me before I'd finished my first cup of coffee at the real estate office.

On the way back to work, I dropped into a bank to organise a loan to borrow the rest. Ads on TV made it seem so simple, but the loan officer laughed at me. She told me I was a minor.

'I'm not a miner,' I replied, joking about the half of town who owed their livelihoods to coal. 'I worked across the street at that supermarket for a while, and now I've got a permanent government job, managing payrolls and pocket money for intellectually handicapped patients.'

She looked down her long nose at me with a scowl. 'You're too young to know this,' she said coldly, 'but making deductions from other people's pay for other people's loans and pocket expenses doesn't mean you can afford a place of your own. Unless you plan on doing something very naughty with their pays?'

'Listen, lady,' I said, offended, but attempting to stay polite. 'I'm part of a team who handles over two million in cash every fortnight. I really need this paddock, but I don't think I deserve this kind of crap, just because I may look too young and naïve to you. How much cash do you handle every week at this little loans counter?'

'Only a fraction, obviously. It's all done electronically. The way of the future. But that's not the point. I'm paid at senior office rates, and it'll take me 25 years to repay my loan, same size roughly, and that's counting the second income from my husband.'

I waved my copy of the contract as evidence that I'd already begun, but she opened the dictionary to the word 'minor' and pointed to the bit that said I wasn't yet a responsible adult.

'Why should my age make any difference?' I complained. 'That's discrimination. I've got a job, a deposit and every intention in the world to repay it, same as anybody else who applies for a loan.'

'You can't make repayments on good intentions,' she argued, and then she sent me home disappointed, and with a brochure on loan products, which she'd curled in to the shape of a dunce hat for me. I doubt she did it deliberately, but I certainly noticed it.

I refused to be beaten. She'd made me furious with the suggestion I wasn't responsible enough to provide a home for my four "dependents" when I'd already been the primary carer for so long; four years for Apache and Snow.

Determined to prove that woman wrong, or at least double check her facts, I hunted through my old maths books from primary and high school, until I found one with the formulae for calculating interest on loans and savings.

I plugged in all the variables, including savings I'd be making in the meantime + the compounding benefits of reducing the loan before it became mine officially + extra repayments, timed to maximise some of the freaky quirks of the formula for daily interest when it compounds only once a month, blah blah and so on…

Then I deducted all my regular expenses from my pay, along with a little "sanity allowance" to spend each pay on myself, and then I circled the bottom line — which proved how I could pay it off in *three* years instead of twenty five.

As it turned out, I made the property start earning money by growing flowers and I built a shed to rent storage space, so I paid it off much sooner... but at the time, my battles with banks were only beginning.

I queued up at her counter again the next day - at a sign that should have said "stand here to be ignored". She eventually waved me over with another stern frown, this time with her own big calculator.

'Well, there's your first mistake,' she said, and pointed to my predictions of a dollar per litre as part of my car fuel expenses in the third year of my loan. 'Petrol only shot up to fifty cents because of all the fuel ships that sank in the Tanker War this month. The price will go down again as soon as Iran and Iraq are done bombing each other. Assuming we're not all killed in a nuclear war, everything will calm down, and fuel prices will take another hundred years before breaking a dollar.'

More famous last words.

'Great,' I said. 'I'll have extra cash in my budget. That's only one more reason to approve my loan. More power for extra repayments.'

'Listen here, young lady,' she said, using that common insult disguised thinly behind faux respect. 'It doesn't matter how clever you think you are. You... are... a... minor. That's m.i.n.O.r.' She opened her dictionary, this time to "guarantor", and told me that's what my parents would need to be before the bank would risk a single dollar on me.

So I went home, explained the situation to my parents while watching world news after dinner. Dad called it the sour hour, when a sweet dessert helped to end the day better.

'Let me get this straight,' Mum said, as she turned down the volume on the TV. 'You needed a block of land, so you saved up a deposit and bought one - without discussing it with us first?'

'You were busy.'

'Listen here, young lady. You… are… grounded.'

'I'm *what?* I'd never been grounded in my life. 'You told me the horses were my responsibility, entirely!'

'And yet you just committed us to making all the repayments for their paddock?'

'No I didn't.' I showed them my budget and loan calculations, worked out by long-hand in five pages of tables that included weekly reducing loan balances, while my repayments increased once each year in time with my annual wage increases. No harder than any maths assignment, or the pay packets I calculated under supervision at work every fortnight.

'What about inflation?' Mum asked. 'Prices for everything go up every year. And it's not like you can count on keeping your job, let alone these annual basic wage increases.' Mum pointed to the TV, which was covering Margaret Thatcher's latest war with mining unions in her role as the UK Prime Minister.

'The Brits have lost over 20,000 jobs in one stroke,' Mum reminded me.

'So what's that got to do with us down here? Just because the rest of the world has gone crazy, doesn't mean I can't try to scrape up my own little island of sanity. Look,' I said, pointing to a column in my budget called "sanity allowance". I'm already saving for it. That's my little safety-net to help spoil myself or tide me over.'

'Twenty mines just closed with the stroke of a pen,' Mum argued, 'and not because the coal ran out. This is a coal-mining town too, love. Exactly the same political problem starting here in Ipswich, and when it all happens, saving your little loose coins every pay won't make a scrap of difference. If twenty thousand of your neighbours lose their jobs, the whole city suffers. The value of your land will drop, you'll owe more than it's worth, and then the bank will foreclose and end up owning everything, including all the repayments you've already made.'

'Plus, they'll add on an administration fee that can be as high as the price of the property,' Dad warned me. 'And if selling the place doesn't recoup the whole lot – and it never does in a depressed or shonky market – they'll send debt collectors after you until you can cough up that too.'

'I'll have loan insurance,' I argued.

Mum rolled her eyes at me. 'Who do you think pays the men in black suits? And don't think you can simply buy back the property with a different bank. The whole system is rigged to screw the little guy and kick him while he's down… or in your case, *her.*'

'I could already tell most of that from reading the contract. Listen, I know I'm barely out of high school, but can you please just look at this clause down here, in the fine print?' I pointed to the group of paragraphs about extra repayments. 'Doesn't that make it impossible for the bank to renege on my loan, if I'm ahead in repayments? Even if I'm only ahead by ten dollars?'

My parents leaned forward to study the clause briefly, then shared a glance with each other - and finally, a grin.

'Leave it with us,' Mum said. 'We'll need to double and triple check all of your calculations. And we'll have to run it by the best solicitor in the city.'

They did, and the next day - while international headlines screamed of the biggest global economic crisis since the Great Depression with over 50 banks going under so far, including one in the US that was supposed to be "too big to fail," I strolled into my local branch again, this time with my parents riding shotgun.

I'd just beaten the bank to engaging the best solicitor, who also happened to be on their board of directors - so I asked his advice on bolstering my deposit with another hundred bucks, and on moving back the settlement date to help me shortcut a few hitches in the fine print that didn't quite suit my special circumstances.

He warned me that I'd need to get the sellers to agree and counter-sign the changes, but by that stage, I'd researched enough to have answers for everything. And I still had two weeks to spare until my seventeenth birthday.

On Sunday, 26th February, I celebrated the big day on the riverbank at dawn. My birthday also marked my first-month anniversary with Penny and Luck, so I had a lot to celebrate, including my victories in purchasing my own block of land and securing my first permanent office job.

Sitting on the foggy riverbank, I shared a whole carrot cake with my four-legged friends, hardly able to believe my tidal wave of good luck.

Three big horses, twelve long legs, all crowded politely around me. Plus one cheeky foal, ducking and weaving and playing with icing that stuck up inside his lip.

'Back up,' I said, as he tried to steal an extra share.

The other three obeyed instead. One command, one team. I felt so proud of them for being so well behaved, but it also revealed a command that I hadn't taught the foal yet. I decided that would be the very next trick he'd need to learn … one more skill that would soon become critical to his survival.

With every day down on the riverbank, the foal grew friskier and smarter.

By the time he was ten weeks of age, I could walk him all the way down the street, away from his mother, without the slightest twitch of his ear in search of her. He now trusted me so much, he preferred to spend time with me, investigating and meeting all the other pets in the street.

Then came April Fool's Day.

18. Fright of the April Fools

Albert Einstein,
yes, that legendary genius again,
also said;

Two things are infinite:
the universe and stupidity.
Not necessarily in that order.

How right he was this time too,
unfortunately.

Mid-morning, Sunday April 1st, I put Lucky on a long lead rope in a vacant allotment beside the river paddock while I rode Apache, teaching the little guy to trot and canter calmly along beside us without trying to switch sides or cut us off unexpectedly. Voice commands helped enormously. He knew 'whoa', 'steady', 'stand', 'walk', 'trot' and 'here, boy', which he'd learned from the other games we'd played so far, mostly running circles around me. So it wasn't much of a stretch to apply them to the new game of a straight line, up and down the footpaths that had become as familiar to him as his own paddock.

Testing him first, with a few lines zigzagging across his paddock, he behaved so well he'd earned the reward of an adventure up the street.

At the far end, near busy Jacaranda St, he continued to behave well and enjoy the outing so much, I decided to risk stretching the lesson to an adventure around the block –

and not just any block. Our suburb of East Ipswich sat in that little pocket of land surrounded on three sides by the Bremer River, with housing and streets shaped around two creeks and our primary school. It produced a bizarre boot-shaped block, meaning that riding around one block was the equivalent of riding three. Four corners later we picked up a tail of five male BMX riders, all old enough to be driving. I recognised the two oldest; Poker and Donkey, the hoons who'd jumped the curb in their car and killed one of my cats a few years earlier. Appearing even nastier than usual, they deliberately wavered all over the road behind us, making screech noises and trying to spook my horse and foal. Apache laid his ears back, angrily, listening to them.

The smallest of them raced ahead, jumped the kerb and halted abruptly in front of us, forcing us to stop, or run over him.

'Go Spike!' cheered his squad.

Apache champed at his bit, sidestepping to keep himself between them and the foal.

'Ha, look!' Spike jeered. 'She's got a spare for when the big one breaks down.'

'Yeah, she's like a boat with a life raft,' teased Donkey.

'I want to ride the mumma horse,' said Poker. He skidded to a halt in front of us too.

'Yeah me too. Me too.' chimed the other two. 'Can we have a go, huh? Can we?'

'Back off!' I shouted. I didn't bother trying to explain that both horses were male. 'I'm licensed to ride here.'

'Oh, yeah?' Spike laughed. 'Where's your L-Plates?'

'Unlike you, I don't need them anymore.' Despite being older than me, he'd lost his licence several times for drink-driving. 'Get out of my way, please. We've got every right to be here.' But those April fools only blinked dumbly at me briefly... Which gave me an idea. If they believed I was riding the foal's mum, then who was I to argue?

I gave Apache subtle leg commands to make him prance on the spot. 'Watch out!' I shouted. 'She thinks you're threatening her baby.' I signalled Apache to rush forward a step and back again to make him look even wilder.

'Hey, keep that nag under control or we'll rip its head off!'

'Yeah, rip its head off!' chorused the others.

'She'll kill you first. She can kick your heads right off your shoulders.'

They swore at me, closing in for a tighter circle – which made me realise I had to do something serious to make them think twice. Not only then, but for all time, since cowardly idiots like them might try to visit my horses at night, and then the fools would be in real danger of getting themselves killed or injured, with my horses copping all of the blame.

'I want to ride the baby horse,' Donkey said, braying like a real ass. 'We didn't get a chance last time to see how many riders it takes to break its back.'

Last time? I guessed they must be the lunatics who'd opened the gate and chased my horses out to the highway.

Spike leapt off his bike and made a grab for the lead rope. Lucky tugged backwards, shying to dodge him, and between them, the rope wrenched out of my hand.

That's it, I thought, and spun Apache around until his rump had forced them to widen their circle. Spike dropped Lucky's lead, and I made sure he got an extra close look at Apache's heels. The scariest part of a horse to most people is the back legs, so I kept my big boy turning around wildly to ensure they kept widening their circle away from us.

'Run!' I shouted. 'She's out of control!' I made a wild show of prancing and spinning around on one heel, and then threw Apache into reverse, backing towards the thickest cluster of them just as fast as he could go. 'She's attacking! Watch out!' All the while I used my legs and hands in small movements to keep signalling a string of swings from left to right which made it look like Apache had gone feral.

'Not again!' shouted Spike, and they took off, swearing at me and the crazy wild horse. I spun him around one last time to give them a head start, and then I gave Apache the cue to take off after them. 'Watch out! I can't stop her! She's trying to kill you like she does with wild dogs and snakes!'

My lie was so big, it's a wonder my nose didn't shoot out like a beak. I zigged and zagged behind them and bolted up amidst their pack, needing to hold him back so he couldn't overtake them too easily.

Apache loved the game too, laying his ears back and putting on his fiercest game face, which he'd only used twice before, while learning to hunt cattle at the pony club camp. Throwing out his front legs more than he needed to also made him look like he was trying to strike down their bikes; same trick he played on the bull that tried to attack me a few years back.

Behind us, the foal cantered along with an utterly grumpy expression – directed at me I think. He snorted and whinnied, as if we weren't supposed to be running away from him. I steadied Apache down to a halt, and the colt bolted up to me, lifted his head into my hand and made it clear he wasn't impressed with me. All this time, I thought I'd been teaching him to lead, but the look on his face that morning made it clearer. Cheeky little man thought he was teaching me how to hang onto a lead rope, and I just failed.

As I turned him for home, with only two corners to go, I caught a glimpse between houses and trees to Mr Nosey's yard, where I saw him watering his vegetable garden -

watching me.

He shook his head, as if he'd seen the whole show. 'Better not try that on *my* footpath,' he called out to me. 'I'll have your permit to keep horses in town cancelled so fast, it'll make you squirt fertiliser.'

'Lovely,' I muttered to myself. 'And it's my generation that's supposed to be the trouble-makers.'

Soon after, on April 20th, a bomb went off at Terminal 2, Heathrow airport, injuring more than 20 innocent people. In my small corner of the world, it was a painful reminder that terrorism was a festering infection which so many good people, in so many countries were struggling to battle. Little did I know that my own small community also had a deadly problem festering...

Just as Lucky turned twelve weeks old, on the eve of Good Friday, April 22nd, the skies opened up with a deluge. Rain fell so hard and fast the gutters couldn't cope. I had to get all four friends away from the rising river, which meant I'd need to find somewhere safe outside the city and load them up into the back of the tip-truck. But I had room for only two at a time. I was acutely aware that mud and cuts from any jostling about in cramped quarters could make for dangerous bedfellows, and that horses had a knack for bumping and scratching themselves in transit - and that I still had four days to go, before the mare and colt could get their inoculations on Easter Sunday.

So I called the sellers of the block I'd arranged to buy, to ask if I could move my horses out there, even though the property wouldn't become mine officially until settlement day – another two months away.

'Sure, no problem,' came the reply. 'We moved most of our stuff out already. But you'd better hurry. The bridge over our little creek will be under water in half an hour.'

'Perfect,' I muttered. I didn't have time to shift all four horses by then because I'd need two trips - and my instincts warned me to keep them together anyway.

So I had to find a new paddock in 24 hours, inside the city, high and safe from flooding, away from neighbours who might complain, and preferably with shelter, fresh water and healthy grass. And me; working full time and not allowed to make any calls from the office. I also had to do it all in the days before mobile phones were common and when the phones at home were being repaired, which meant I couldn't make calls until morning.

Then it rained hogs and logs all night.

19. Change of Scenery

Aesop,
a mysterious Greek pen-name, circa 500BCE
allegedly once said;

It is in vain to expect our prayers to be heard,
if we do not strive as well as pray

... as hard, fast, and desperate as possible,
I was about to learn.

Rain turned the river paddock into a bog.

The steep slope became treacherous and far too slippery for goats, let alone a playful foal. The river level also began to rise dangerously faster, and I worried that any one of the four might slip and fall into the raging torrent - which now had a large constant whirlpool downstream, within sight, where the nearby creek and drains emptied into it.

Our local weather bureau warned us; more coming.

I figured I had less than 12 hours before the Bremer River broke its banks. The fact that it was the last working day before the Easter long weekend and school holidays also heightened the challenge, since most people seemed keen to party somewhere sunnier. On my lunch break, I raced home to make calls; and noticed the water rising even faster than expected.

First call; to my new boss to request the rest of the afternoon off for a flood-related emergency. Then I ran down to the paddock with four halters and lead ropes and moved the horses to our backyard temporarily, leading all four at once. Two either side of me; a new trick all by itself. They all walked at different speeds, normally. Plus the rain bucketed down, and my mum wouldn't let me go out without a plastic raincoat...

'You'll catch your death!' Mum shouted. 'Don't you dare take it off.'

... and the foal discovered that raindrops on plastic tasted deliciously clean and sweet. Not just wildly attractive and curiously noisy, but also delightfully lick-able. Even so, they all behaved like beautifully trained Spanish Dancing Stallions marching a parade, and in no time, we made it to the mulberry tree in the back corner of our yard, where they could shelter to some degree under its thick, wide canopy.

Dashing inside to the phone again, and shaking off like a wet dog, I tried calling all the stables around the local racecourse in case they had any vacancies. About a dozen calls - and they all had plenty of stalls available, but only because the nearby creek boiled angrily on the rise, so all the most valuable horses had been trucked over the border or up to the mountains overnight. Taking no chances, the rest would be leaving soon.

Next I rang the local showgrounds; high on a hill and right beside the century-old asylum where I worked.

Just my luck, many of the racehorses had already moved in.

'No crossbred hacks allowed,' they warned me. Angry, but with no time to spare for venting it, I started calling real-estate agents all over town, hoping they'd have a vacant lot somewhere - preferably fenced, but I felt so desperate, I'd take anything I could get.

The only two suitable allotments had already been filled with new and used cars from the low-lying sales yards.

Sale yards! *Ding!* The idea hit me like lightning.

I called the Yamanto sale-yards where I'd bought Penny,

and asked about renting a few yards.

'I also need permission to camp there in my car to make sure nobody sells or takes them by accident, please?'

'Sorry, but we've just taken delivery of several truckloads of valuable breeding cattle from the lowlands that needing saving until the waters recede.'

'But…' said Mrs Cranky Spanky who'd been so ill tempered with me on Australia Day, 'I happen to know the meatworks own fifty acres next door to us which can't be used for cattle anymore, because they have to muster them across the road to be killed, and since the new housing estates began squeezing tighter around us, some of the new neighbours have complained how cow manure on the road splashes up under their pretty cars, making their tyres smell.'

'Ridiculous,' I said. 'To think anyone can be so rude as to move out into a semi-rural or business area, and expect the current community to change to suit their city ideals.'

So old Mrs Cranky Spanky earned a new nickname, Goddess of the Week, while she gave me the phone numbers for the meatworks. They seemed keen to rent the paddock to me — and very cheaply at only $50 per week.

I'd come full circle; right back to where I'd started with Lucky and Penny. Right next door to Pen 13-13, with a direct view of it.

I needed to hike over the paddock first to re-assure myself there'd be no hidden dangers such as rabbit holes or tangles of old fencing wire anywhere to break or snag any beautiful legs. I soon learned that the meatworks had even higher standards for animal safety than me. Their fencing contractors had not only used more wire than usual to contain their stock — and used higher quality materials - they'd also performed a clever twist of wire at every join along the fence, which prevented any sharp snags from scratching hides. I looked closely and learned their trick, which I've used on every fence I've ever built since then.

I raced across the road to the meatworks' office and paid for two months in advance.

A paddock that size in such a lush area could also feed up to 20 horses quite comfortably without overstocking – not that I'd ever be that greedy to risk ruining the soil or grass coverage. And at less than five minutes' drive from work, it would be more convenient for five days out of every seven than having them closer to home. The only proviso which made it cheap was that three stockmen had horses that needed to come and go occasionally, without any warning or notice. No big deal.

I'd also spoken to nine other people at work, so far, who'd expressed an interest in keeping their horses closer to the city too. So I decided to offer agistment to them at $5 per horse per week - provided their horses didn't pick fights with the others, more than the usual initial pecking order squabbles. That meant it would cost me less than $5 per week to house and feed all four of my horses. A real bargain. My picturesque paddock was not only safe, but also clean, lush and shady, with a creek, two dams and excellent fencing. And my four-legged friends were safe from rising flood waters.

Another bonus; the paddock had a lovely healthy mix of grasses and good drainage that would help to avoid hoof rot, which often developed with thick or swampy mud, which there would be on the riverbank after the flood waters receded.

I raced home to tell Dad the great news. I spotted him down in the garage with his legs hanging out from under a car, but as I opened my mouth, I saw the jack slip, the car fall and land on him, crushing his ribs!

I screamed out for Mum and anyone else who could hear, and Donny leapt the fence in one bound to help me lift it straight off him.

Ambulance medics arrived in no time. Police too, for some reason. Something about suspicion of tampering, and a prowler; seen lurking the neighbourhood.

As luck would have it, it was the same two cops who had turned up to the sale-yard to arrest the horse thief. I wondered if that made them the fastest in town at responding, or just the only two with a working cop car, in the current economic climate.

This time, I caught the older cop's name; Sergeant Cook (sounded like Crook the first time I heard it). He asked us all a stack of questions, separately. That was the first I'd heard of a prowler. I told them all about the April fools and the night of the raving lunatics way back in January, so they took Mr Robinson's name for questioning, but they doubted the three incidents were related.

'Hey, aren't you that girl from the sale-yards?' asked Cook before he'd done with me.

'She is,' replied his partner. 'She's the one who spotted that horse thief.'

'What horse thief?' Mum asked.

'Nothing to worry about now,' Cook said. 'The stock squad took charge and returned all the horses to their rightful owners – even the ones he'd hidden at home and stolen from kids and other private properties.'

'Did he go to jail?' I asked, keenly.

'Court case is still pending,' Cook said without looking at me, as if I was still just an inconsequential kid. 'Horses weren't the only thing he'd been stealing.'

They never told me anything more than that, and I never saw anything more in the newspapers. I heard the adults whispering and looking my way occasionally, as if talking about me a little more, but the focus shifted back to the medics, still stabilizing Dad and preparing to transfer him up to the hospital for suspicion of cracked ribs.

'Don't bother,' Dad complained. 'I've had cracked ribs before and they heal.'

'Not if you've got a bone fragment working its way for your lungs,' argued the biggest, meanest looking medic. Scary enough to rival Mr Fearsome from the meatworks. 'You just lay back and behave or we'll have to strap you down for the ride.'

In the meantime, I simply had to wait and accept there were some things that would always be out of my reach. Like the mystery of why some people chose to do evil things that could hurt innocent people like my dad, or my horses. I had two other things on which to focus;

I needed a new driver for the tip truck, and fast.

And many other horses had found happier endings because of something I did that day when I'd bought Lucky and Penny.

20. The Desperate Search for a Driver

Novalis,
a wise German poet,
once said;

*Character and Fate are two
words for the same thing.*

I know he meant that the choices we make, and
the actions we take, determine whatever happens to us
in our own life's stories...

Yet today it seemed like Fate had its own character with
a wicked sense of humor, and
enjoyed using me as its favorite toy.

Still *Thursday, April 19th*
... and 19 was supposed to be my dad's lucky number.

By 2pm the rain stopped only long enough to transfer him from the garage to the ambulance. Checking my watch, I knew it was too early for Jim to be home yet from the power station, so that left only one person I knew with a suitable truck licence – and she had to follow Dad up to the hospital. I'd have to wait until Mum returned, before I'd get a chance to ask her.

Fate kicked me in the shins again. About ten minutes after I'd seen Jim's parents go out, he rolled by in his bronze panther – with a pretty blonde in the passenger seat. They went inside his house, presumably to have some time alone. An hour later, I saw them heading out again. I heard slow romantic rock from his stereo - loud enough to make the whole street throb, let alone my heart.

Another fifteen minutes passed, and then he rolled quietly home again. I guessed that he'd returned her to wherever she'd been in the first place.

I turned away from my bedroom window, realising I'd been watching the street as fervently as Mr Nosey. Still, with Jim home and unoccupied, my options opened up a little.

I raced down to the phone in my mum's office.

Jim picked up my call almost immediately.

'Are you home?' I asked, then slapped my own forehead. 'Stupid question. I mean, are you heading back to work today?'

'Nah, I took a day's leave to make it a longer weekend.'

I scowled, twisting my hair into a knot, imagining him out with that other girl, dining, wining, or whatever it is that older guys do with girls who are old enough.

'What's the problem?'

I frowned, hating that he equated me to problems. 'Not a problem exactly, just wondering if you'd appreciate a chance for a little more time behind the wheel of a truck. It's fun, right?'

'Oh, yeah. With you it's a real hoot. Has it got fuel, tyres, spares and a working jack this time?'

'It should. But if you're after a challenge, I'm sure I can break something.'

'I'm sure you could.'

'Now who's the sucker for punishment?' I asked, grinning when he strode in a few minutes later.

Loading the horses turned into an unexpected challenge.

Penny saw the tip-truck with the crate backing down the driveway and turned tail to bolt off down to the mulberry tree. She probably feared going back to the sale-yards.

'Don't open the back yet,' I said as I headed down to fetch them. 'I'd better take Apache and Snow first.' So I called them and they came straight over to hang near the truck, but for my next trick, I needed both Penny and the foal to watch, so they'd know there'd be nothing to fear.

Jim scratched his head. 'If you're taking this pair, why fetch the others so soon? The truck is only big enough for two.'

'It's a herd thing.' As I turned around, I saw Apache and Snow sniffing at Jim, checking him out, and letting him pat them. Jim seemed to be the only human male they both agreed to let get close to me, without laying their ears back or putting themselves in the way as they'd always done with the apprentices and young male customers.

'Forget it you two,' I said, wagging my finger at them. 'Not going to happen.'

'What are they doing?' Jim asked.

'Making a choice for me. Don't ask. You don't want to know.'

Jim stood by the latch to the ramp, ready to lower it down, while I tethered the mare and foal along the fence, using fast-release knots so if they wrenched back, frightened, I'd be able to get to them promptly to calm them down again.

Instead of the ramp, I opened the sliding gate, clicked my fingers and Apache took it as the cue to jump up, all by himself. Impressive to watch. He reared up right beside me and leapt up using mainly the power of his hind legs.

'Move over, boy.' I patted his heel to remind him – dangerous with most horses, who flinch or kick at flies, but he already knew my head was at his heel, the only part of him I could reach.

I clicked and repeated the process with Snow, and as she climbed in, I found the little colt on the other side of her, with his lead rope dragging, waiting for his turn to jump in.

The only way to get free from a quick release knot is to tug on the trailing end of the rope. Clever little fella. Either that, or coincidence. Maybe I hadn't tied it up tightly enough, but he certainly behaved as if he was guilty.

'That's too high for you, little man.' I closed the door in his face.

He stamped his foot and reared, prancing about wanting to follow the truck, so I had to lock him and his mother in the back half of the yard again until we returned.

Apache and Snow had never been let loose in such a big field as the new paddock. They'd never been in anything bigger than three acres, so their first instinct would be to run and find the boundary. Normally, I would have let them explore at their own pace, but being fifty treed acres, with lots of amazing little nooks and glens to distract them, I needed to show them around it personally, to ensure they didn't miss any of the unusually shaped corners or tricky bits before nightfall.

Riding Snowy bareback and leading Apache, we cantered around the boundary together, which also ensured they would settle down promptly to graze with much lower chances of running through any fences. I offered to take Jim with me for his first horse ride on Apache, but I'd neglected to pack a saddle, and the instant I gave him a leg up onto my Apache's spine, we discovered the reason why men had invented saddles in the first place.

'Yeouch!' he squeaked, and doubled over with his eyes watering. 'I think I'll sit this one out.'

My own eyes watered as I tried not to laugh.

When I arrived home, I could hardly believe my eyes. My Dad was back already from the hospital. I'd ducked inside for cold water for Jim, and found Dad in the kitchen, cutting off the bandages from his ribs, while Mum watched, rolling her eyes and shaking her head.

'Swallow a magic pill?' I asked him. 'Should you be doing that so soon?'

'Hurts worse with them on,' he complained. 'I can't work if I can't breathe.'

'You're not supposed to work at *all*,' mum complained. 'You're supposed to rest for eight weeks.'

'Yeah, right. Sick leave is for employees.'

I shared a pained expression with Mum and bounced down the stairs with a cold drink for Jim, knowing there was no arguing with Dad when it came to his work ethic. With money tight and getting tighter, they needed to work seven days a week already, so he wouldn't be taking time off.

Downstairs, Jim had already laid down the ramp for Penny. I took my time, leading the mare around in a spiral so she could reassure herself that the truck didn't smell like the sale-yards. Or antiseptic. The colt snorted at it once, then bolted up, beating us inside, and once Penny saw her foal up there, she wanted up too. She hadn't read all the books that said; first load the mare, then the foal.

Unloading at the other end, we did it back to front again, because Lucky spotted the others in the paddock, and bolted down the ramp for the happy reunion. I played the boundary game again with all of them, and after a third trip to fetch their long hay feeder which kept their meals of hay off the ground at a comfortable height, Jim and I sat on the gate with a bucket of takeaway chips and watched them settle in before dusk.

'Nice,' he said, thoughtfully, watching them graze in the mottled shade of the trees 'Like a postcard.'

'Thanks for your help,' I said, toasting him with my diet cola. I didn't have the nerve to ask him about his hot date earlier. As a mere neighbour, it wasn't any of my business if he got lucky anyway. I'd seen the light switch on in his living room, so more than likely they'd only been watching TV.

For the time being, I couldn't believe my luck. The new paddock in the new suburb would cut the vet-o-matic's bills in half, because he serviced that area on normal weekdays - which meant I could meet him during my lunch breaks. I called his nurse to cancel my booking for Easter Sunday at double-double rates, and tried to bring it forward to later that afternoon - which also happened to be my latest payday and would have reduced the wait for the foal's inoculations from four days to four hours.

Just my luck, the vet-o-matic had a full diary already, so he had to put me back by an extra fortnight instead – unless I trucked the horses back to East Ipswich to keep my Easter Sunday appointment.

I tried to argue that Lucky would be older than three months, but the vet-o-matic countered that three calendar months was closer to thirteen or fourteen weeks anyway. He also assured me that an extra fortnight wouldn't make any difference.

For any normal horse and owner, under any normal weather conditions, I have no doubt he would have been right. As a vet, he could be expensive and cranky, but he also had a reputation as one of the best in the business. So aside from this one little hitch, it all seemed like such a great sweeping stroke of good luck for me to score such a beautiful paddock where the health risks for the little guy were indeed comparatively slight.

I gave in, and agreed to rebook for a fortnight, with only the slightest twinge that I might live to regret it. The Easter long weekend combined with a computer glitch at head office where my own paypacket was calculated, which meant my pay hadn't gone into the bank yet, so I wouldn't have enough cash to pay him anyway. I didn't even notice that it was thirteen weeks today since the Black Friday storm in which Lucky was born. And there was already that other minor injury still going un-noticed.

The sun set one last time on those blissful days of innocence.

The secret abscess inside my little colt's jaw had already burst internally, and begun to leach poison into his bloodstream, sending out a neurotoxin that would soon affect all of his major organs and body functions. The nerves for controlling his muscles and movements would begin to paralyze, including those in his brain, heart and lungs, also creating painful spasms that would shudder throughout his entire body.

Yet I still had no idea. He seemed perfectly healthy and happy, galloping around with the others playfully. But the countdown on his life was already ticking down with every heartbeat.

I took this image during a break in the rain, that day Thursday, April 19ᵗʰ

Age 12 weeks. This was taken near the top of the vacant allotment at the river, waiting for me to lead them around the street corner to my house, where our truck would take them all out to the new big paddock that I rented from the meatworks.

Yes, that's Penny behind him, yawning. You can also see the street light they liked to sleep near every night.

It's still painful to look at this image now, knowing the little guy was so close to dying and I had no idea. He seemed curious and playful with me, as ever.

21. Dawn of the Ordeal

Bugs Bunny,
my cartoon hero,
should have warned me weeks earlier;

What's up, doc?

I wish I'd known, Bugs.
I really do.

Good Friday began with the same innocent ritual as any other day.

7:13am... *Splat!*
That stupid blue-ish bird struck my window again. Seriously, what was it with that bird? Virtually every day for more than a year, and he still hadn't knocked any sense into himself.

'Hi Bruiser,' I said as he shook himself off.

Throwing back my covers, I didn't want to waste a single moment of my four day-long weekend. I leapt for my bedroom door, trying not to land on my little "monster" kitten Muffy, as she raced out from under my bed.

'Grr-ow-ow-ow!' Doggo complained, as he crossed paths with us in the dining room as usual. Muffy tripped me with her typical flurry of playful fur and claws, but I laughed as we tumbled together into the hall against my parent's bedroom door.

'Anita's up,' Dad said, as I heard him roll over.

My mum listed feed-time for pets as a chore, but for me it was like club time with friends. I filled all their bowls with "squishy" food, a spare with only kibble and a tub for water while they all lined up in order. I didn't bother feeding myself yet, as usual. I just tugged on a pair of jeans over my pyjamas, grabbed my car keys and drove across town to see how my four biggest friends had spent their first night in a strange suburb.

I pulled up at the gate to their new paddock and leapt out to greet them. The foal cantered up with his mother, beaten only by Apache, who whinnied and bolted for me the moment he spotted my car in the street. I tossed a few tasty biscuits of hay into their big feeder to share, and groomed them all, leaving the foal until last, as usual.

Everything seemed fine – except for a strange look in Lucky's eye that resembled fear. I could see the whites of his eyes in full circles, instead of the usual small triangles at each corner. Yet I could see no reason for him to fear anything. He didn't really behave fearfully, either. He seemed keen and friendly for attention, as ever. So much so, I took a pic of him being cheeky to his mum. [P162]

At first I wondered if dogs might have bothered them through the night, so I double-checked all their legs thoroughly for bites or scratches.

Satisfied, but still cautious, I fitted Lucky with his little home-made halter to give him another leading lesson. My goal; a familiar activity that he enjoyed, to see if anything else seemed a little off in his responses or behaviour, but just as I buckled up his chin strap, I discovered a small amount of pus under his jaw. An abscess. It seemed like such a tiny hole. Barely a pin-prick, but I took the time to clean it thoroughly with salt and clean water.

I always kept a bottle of clean drinking water in my car

anyway, along with a few sachets of salt. Together, they made the all-purpose wound cleaner. Or, separately, they came in handy with hot takeaway chips. However, the yellowish pus seemed a little too much for such a small wound, which made me suspicious. Especially since I had no way of telling how long ago it started to weep. So I decided to dash up to the nearest shop for some proper antiseptic — something good enough for humans so there'd be less chance of it stinging, while still keeping away any blowflies.

By the time I returned fifteen minutes later, I found Lucky holding his nose out straighter more often. I'd already noticed him do it several times in the last few weeks as a tactic whenever he cheekily tried to tease the older horses into playing with him. So it didn't seem strange by itself. But now he also shouldered against me quite often, and that was definitely odd. He'd never tried to push me around before, and it wasn't really bullying either. Most books about horse training had already warned me that young colts would try to bully me at some stage during training, so I'd already learned a few strategies, but to me, it seemed more like he was trying to tell me something, and his body language wasn't quite co-operating. He tried to lick my hand, which he often did anyway, but his tongue felt slightly stiff to me, and he worked it against his teeth as if it annoyed him — same as I often did with a numb tongue after a trip to the dentist.

To anyone else, he might have seemed like a normal naughty or cheeky colt. One who'd grown a little too bold from being handled so much. So I began to wonder if cheekiness might really be the case. Or maybe he was only pining for his old paddock. But everything I asked him to do, he obeyed immediately. All of his tricks. Every... single... one... as if the routine helped to comfort him.

Every animal went through stages of maturity after all, so this might easily have been his next stage. Except he kept cuddling up to me and obeying everything I asked of him, as if pleading for more.

I knew he wasn't trying to be naughty.

Something was wrong.

Either way, I needed to get that wound clean.

I raced home and back again to fetch my full kit of medical supplies. Traffic was hell both ways. An ambulance blocked three lanes of an old intersection where new traffic lights had been installed recently to prevent accidents. Police too, and fire brigade gearing up to hose down the road as soon as the medics and wreckers drove clear of a fatal accident.

'She didn't stop,' I heard one woman say as I rolled slowly past the fallen pedestrian. An old lady dressed in pink. She'd failed to stop at the new don't-walk signal. She'd stepped out in front of a car on her way home and met her maker amid a scattering of spilled groceries and milk.

The whole scene seemed too surreal, with all those people milling about, busy or watching. All that spilt milk, and not a single tear in sight for the old lady - until I checked my rear vision mirror and saw my own face. I still had all my grandparents, and couldn't bear the thought of losing them, but just at that moment, the inevitability of facing Death hit me.

I wasn't ready, I decided, and wiping my face, I accelerated back up to the speed limit.

Turning off the main road through Yamanto into Berry Street, I tried not to speed downhill to the first of two dangerously blind curves. More cautious than ever, I only wanted to get back in one piece. I needed everything to go right for me, but as I turned the corner, the paddock came into view and I couldn't see the foal or horses anywhere. Certainly not near the gate, where I'd left them.

Slewing to a halt in the short rocky driveway, I leapt out and called for Apache and Snow at the top of my lungs. My voice echoed over the creek and back at me off the concrete walls of the meatworks.

They both answered from the far side of a fallen tree. Dead for years, with the spiral scars of lightning down its main trunk, I'd hardly noticed it on previous visits – aside from a passing fancy that it might be fun for Apache and me to jump over occasionally. I hadn't realised it had been large enough to hide all of them from view at once. Penny answered me too, when I called her specifically, then the three adults came galloping around to me.

Without the foal.

That wasn't just strange. It was downright peculiar.

I couldn't see Lucky anywhere out in the paddock. All three horses galloped ahead of me to that fallen tree, where they stopped and encircled it.

I gulped, knowing this couldn't be good.

Wading over through a sea of waist-high lush grass, and whistling while stomping to ensure any sleepy snakes had time to clear out of my way, I soon found my colt standing inside the fallen tree branches, with his head buried into the darkest shadows.

His eye turned to greet me, still seemingly frightened. His whole neck seemed stiffer, along with his jaws, which clenched tight, while his nose remained stuck out for no apparent reason. Overall, he seemed terrified, yet also defiant of whatever had a grip on him.

He stood unusually still while I cleaned the tiny wound under his jaw again. Taking care to remove all the scabs of dried pus first, I open it as wide as I dared. He flinched, like it stung him, and I realised he must have had a pretty bad headache to go with it.

Stiffness made me think he might have picked up a "paralysis tick" at the new paddock — the main reason we needed strict rules for travel permits in the first place.

Grey, like a small soft squishy beetle that could grow fatter from ant-size to that of a marble within a day as they sucked out more blood, these little cattle ticks could hang on and continue to pump disease or neurotoxins into an animal - even after death if I pulled off their body without getting their much tinier head. Actually, it's a blood parasite that's carried by the ticks that is the real culprit of the paralysis, but the tick itself often gets the blame and the bad nickname since it's the only creepy crawly that's obvious without a microscope.

However, I'd seen symptoms of paralysis in cows, who either urinated red from the tick-born parasite disease called redwater, or went limp and weak from the tick's neurotoxin — and the colt showed none of those symptoms. A thorough search of Lucky's body and legs revealed no ticks on him, but that didn't mean they hadn't fallen off already. Most diseases took two days to a fortnight to develop, and I suspected that ticks could also carry other diseases, so I double checked the other horses.

Still no sign of the little grey gremlins.

The thought that my colt might be exhibiting the first symptoms of tetanus never occurred to me. I didn't know much about that disease or how it looked. All I'd taken in was the warning; Tetanus is deadly. Vaccinate Yearly.

Readjusting the little red macramé halter I'd made for him, I tried to lead Lucky back to the car for a rub-down - his favourite game - but he didn't want to back out from the dark shade of the fallen tree.

That was odd too, because I could lead him anywhere by now; backwards or forwards, even well away from and out of sight of his mother. Yet now he wouldn't even follow his mum when she called to him.

I had to go right back to basic training, which consisted mainly of voice and patience plus a few serves of nudging, tapping or clicking. To begin with, I also laid my hand flat against his chest and pressed back slowly on cue, while also repeating the command with small nudging movements until he complied. Then I ceased immediately as a reward for obedience and promptly repeated for another step. And the next. Ask, step, reward. Ask, step, reward.

He finally got the idea to take more than one step at a time - enough for me to see a full sized step - and I noticed that his front legs seemed stiff at the knees, while his whole body seemed top-heavy and wobbly. I didn't have a mobile phone like my parents – brick-sized or not. So I ran back to the car and drove home as fast as I could to ring the vet-o-matic. Then reality struck me.

As a public holiday – at the start of a four-day Easter long weekend – I couldn't contact him at his clinic. I'd already cancelled our appointment for Easter Sunday. So when I finally made contact on his after-hours phone, and explained Lucky's symptoms, he chastised me for messing him around and refused to come out at all, ever again, to any of my animals.

He dumped me, saying; 'Listen hear, young lady. You are too much trouble. Never call me again.'

He hung up, leaving me on the end of a dead line.

Now I had a very sick foal and no vet at all.

22. The Epic Quest for a New Vet

Buddha,
that wise founder of Buddhism,
has been paraphrased, sadly too often, in stables, barns,
and vet clinics all over the planet;

Without health, life is not life;
it is only a state of suffering;
an image of death

... but I had my own camera, and my images reminded me of how close to 'healthy' my foal had been.

I didn't understand the full severity of the situation yet.

I didn't have time to get angry at my old vet either. Only frustrated. Most of the other clinics around town specialised in smaller city-style pets. Dogs, cats, guinea pigs... so their vets seemed to lack either the knowledge, experience or equipment for handling the bigger animals. Even so, I called them all again, looking for one who cared enough about animals to pick up their phones on a public holiday to service clients, and in particular, new ones.

There were plenty of animal-loving vets in South East Queensland, I soon discovered. I spoke to fourteen clinics between Brisbane and Toowoomba - a full circle of 150 kilometres around me, and not counting the vets who had already closed up for the weekend, but each time, after describing the symptoms, they all said virtually the same thing;

'How soon can we put him down?'

I tried to describe his symptoms different ways, in case the words *stiffness* or *locked jaw* might be making them overlook something less dangerous, but they all asked about stiffness with his neck and jaws anyway.

I couldn't believe my ears. I'd grown used to my vet-o-matic who'd always seemed to care enough to try anything, albeit at a steep price. In comparison, the cold maths of the situation seemed so cruel.

'The time and expense in attempting to deal with such a lethal disease is a cruel exercise in futility,' one vet told me. 'There have been no successful cases in either humans or animals. Or none that recovered well enough to be worth the effort. A smaller animal, may be less expensive as a test case…' Yet nobody could even guess at how long it would take. Or could provide an approximate quote for expenses.

'The disease,' I was told more than once, 'is 98% fatal across all species. And of the 2% that survive, less than 1% recover fully with no lasting effects.'

I kept asking about the 1%, but nobody could tell me anything more than that. All accounts from survivors were anecdotal and lacked any details to replicate.

My shortlist of potential vets contracted to two after-hours clinics. One at Pine Mountain, twenty minutes away, which had an answering machine that encouraged me to leave a message because he was out, attending to other emergencies. And an older-sounding man from the opposite side of town, who prioritised Lucky ahead of a dog who needed his hind leg removed after a car accident. He agreed to meet me at the paddock in twenty minutes, which equated to dropping everything and racing up the highway from his outer suburb at the edge of Brisbane. I felt so grateful, and told him so.

Yet, it took only one glance from a distance for his face to shadow over with worry. He checked Lucky's heartbeat and temperature, and then sighed heavily, keeping one hand on my foal's neck, patting him.

He looked at me without needing to say anything, but I still had to hear him confirm what the others had already warned me over the phone.

'It's tetanus, I'm afraid, and it's gone chronic.'

My heart stopped, I'm sure of it. He patted my shoulder and told me he needed to explain a few things so I could come to the most responsible decision on my own.

'The tiny, but deep puncture wound under your colt's jaw has been contaminated by the common bacteria, Clostridium tetani - most likely penetrating his skin on a nail, timber splinter or maybe a piece of wire.'

My own suspicions were that it had happened on a wire fence at his home farm while being yarded to leave for the sales. All my fences were shiny new, while bankrupt farms often suffered derelict yard facilities and rusty fences, especially after bushfires. I also recalled the two kids at the sale-yards explaining how Penny had broken into an old coal mine during a storm to give birth – which explained the initial wound up on her udder. I showed the vet Penny's scar and explained my suspicions.

'The incubation period is only supposed to range from two days to two months,' he argued. 'Considering the events at the sale-yards and the weather that day - and the fact that the deepest of Penny's other scratches seem to be healing cleanly on her leg - it seems most likely that the little guy has been fighting off the bacteria for two and a half months, and only survived this long on antibodies from his mother's milk... And,' he added, patting my shoulder, 'because of the excellent level of care they've been getting from you. As a belly wound, your mare's gash should have been one of the hardest to heal. You've also done an impressive job because having to tend their wounds so regularly as a virtual stranger for so long should have made them resent the sight of you, rather than trust you.'

'Oh, that's only because of the daily treats,' I confessed. 'Kitchen scraps mostly. Bread and Weetbix. Most of the time, they see me and lick their lips.'

'At least you had those memorable times together.' He paused and stroked Lucky's wispy mane. 'Tetanus is usually fatal in horses.'

'Usually?' I clung on to that word like a drowning girl onto floating debris – and trying to hold it together for Lucky's sake, since my horses had always been so sensitive to my moods and attitudes. 'The survivors,' I asked. 'How did they... do it?'

'You misunderstand me, I'm afraid. If the tetanus doesn't get them ... There can be terrible complications. That's why responsible owners put them down before it gets that bad.'

'Oh, but my colt only presented his first symptoms this morning. If he's had it so long already, then maybe...'

'By this stage, I'm sorry, there's no known successful course of action. If he'd been inoculated sooner, maybe he'd have a slim chance to survive as a cripple, but that's no life for a horse. Which reminds me, you'll need to get two shots yourself as soon as we're done here. One to work immediately and one slowly.'

'Can't we do the same thing for him?'

'Too late. The bacteria is already causing a creeping paralysis, and the inoculations only work by exposing patients to a small dose to trigger their bodies into responding in order to guard itself. And since his little body is already responding, inoculating him now may only tip the balance further against him.'

'What about in humans? How do doctors treat the

disease? They can't just put people to sleep when they show up with a little oozy boo-boo on their face?'

'Mostly, humans can feel the onset of stiffness and pain before it becomes obvious to others. So they usually receive treatment before it gets to this stage. Ever heard of the American civil war general Robert E Lee? His favourite horse, Traveler, succumbed to tetanus after standing on a nail, and he had the very best veterinary care possible in the day. But it's just as lethal in *every* species by this stage... I'm very sorry to advise you, but this little colt is not going to live up to his name today. He's already in a lot of pain, and it's going to get worse. Much worse. So you need to ask yourself, how much are you going to make him suffer first?'

I blinked back tears and patted my colt's neck - on the opposite side to where the vet was still stroking him. I'd read books that warned me of sick colts tending to sulk more than sick fillies, but my little man remained standing up defiantly. I couldn't help but feel proud of him.

I hugged his head against my tummy, shielding his eyes from the harsh daylight, and wishing I didn't have to make such a decision for him at all. How could I do such a thing after all we'd been through in such a short time together?

'He's such a good little fellow.' I kept patting him, needing him to know how terribly sorry I was for him. How much I... loved him. 'He doesn't deserve this.'

'They never do.' He placed a reassuring hand on my shoulder, but Lucky needed it more. I returned the vet's hand to the colt's neck. This wasn't part of my deal at the sale-yards. I'd tried to save him. It wasn't meant to be this way. We'd won... *Won*, damn it. And yet the professional in front of me was insisting otherwise.

'You don't understand,' I pleaded. 'This little guy has escaped dogs, a meatworks and a night on a highway with raving lunatics, and now you're telling me it's *me* he needs to fear most?'

The vet shrugged. 'I wouldn't put it that way.'

Seconds ticked by, and still the bacteria multiplied.

I felt rushed to make the decision, but not rushed by the vet himself. To his credit, he stood back, waiting patiently. Yet every second I delayed, the bacteria multiplied. And that poor dog at his surgery still needed to lose its leg.

'Every passing minute is making pain worse for your colt, and his chances slimmer. You need to face facts, young lady. It's the only responsible thing to do. Much better to put him down now and save him from the worst of it.'

I blinked back tears again, knowing I'd have to agree. I'd have to open my own locked jaws and say it myself.

Lucky hugged his head tighter against my tummy, and my heart shattered into a billion tiny pieces. He trusted me to make the right decision.

He trusted me to death

Mum was right. I couldn't do this for a living. I couldn't even utter the words for this little friend who couldn't speak for himself. I could only nod, and I felt like I'd betrayed him for doing it.

'Are you sure?' asked the vet.

What a question. My heart pounded high in my throat, wanting to scream NO, and my whole body trembled, struggling to hold back my tears. Don't be childish, I scolded myself. I had to agree. Too cruel otherwise. My body shook again and again with sobs that I tried to hold in. I needed to be brave for his sake, or else his fear at the very end would be worse.

The other three closed in around us, watching. Trusting me too. Not just his mother, Penny, as I'd expected. Apache looked so worried about his little apprentice. Even Snowy seemed intently concerned, despite tolerating Lucky's cheeky pestering most other days with annoyed swishes of her tail.

I hung my head, feeling the full weight of my decision, and accepting it - along with all the guilt. Our little family would be one less tonight, and it was all my fault. I'd played with him every day, and all the while, his life had been ticking away in time with his heartbeat.

'I can't let him suffer any more,' I conceded. 'Not because of something I missed, or failed to see. I'd never be able to sleep again.'

'It's the best thing,' he assured me. 'But I'll need you to sign a consent form first.'

'Get it,' I said, hugging the colt one last time. 'The sooner the better, I guess.'

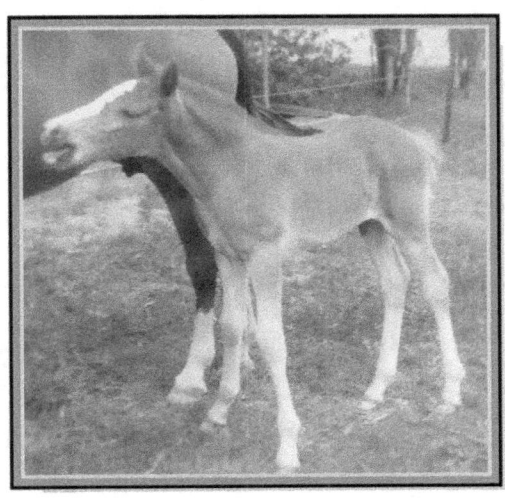

This photo shows Lucky's first symptoms: Stiff neck, splayed feet and his tongue is annoying him. His muscles also strain occasionally, but this is also how he looked every time he was cheeky to the bigger horses, making his symptoms so much harder to notice.

23. Consent for Two Lethal Injections

Stick with me, it gets better, I promise.

Although, Leonardo da Vinci,
the famous Italian artist and scientist, once said;

While I thought that I was learning how to live,
I have been learning how to die.

For years, I never understood what he meant,
but I trusted that his wise words should make sense
to me eventually, perhaps when I was old and grey.
So I kept the quote on a note in the back of my diary...

In my wildest nightmares, I never imaged that it would
make sense only after I was forced to make the choice
for somebody else. How long to live, or... not.

The vet fetched the consent papers and handed me a pen.

I, {.......insert name.......} hereby acknowledge and consent...

'Wretched pen.' No ink. 'I scratched the nib of the ballpoint a few times, trying to get it to work.

'Sorry, I meant to grab the other one.' He headed back to his car. 'I had one ready on the seat, with the needles.'

Part of me hated that he'd come so prepared to kill. He handed me the new pen, and stepped away to fill two huge fat syringes with a dark green fluid. Each one as long as my hand, and as thick as my thumb.

'Why *two*?' I asked, breaking out in a sweat. I didn't know if I should be worried about another horse, or that he planned on puncturing my poor foal to death.

'It's the dose.'

'So that's it?' A stupid question, since he'd practically answered it already, but I couldn't believe it had come to this, and so soon. I could hardly bring myself to say the words, but I needed to, partly to reassure myself that this new vet knew what he was doing, without upsetting him, since I'd need him from now on for the others. 'Is that really what a lethal injection looks like?'

He nodded and instructed me on how to hold Lucky's neck and head still.

'Aren't you going to give him a painkiller first?'

'He's in too much pain already to notice these little pricks. This works faster anyway.'

'Okay, but why *two* needles?'

'His body weight determines the dose.'

'I meant, can't you use a bigger syringe, so at least he doesn't have to feel the needle twice?'

'He'll be past feeling anything by then. The second syringe is just to be sure.'

I didn't like the sound of that.

'When I push in the needle,' he said, 'stand back, because he'll go down fast.'

I didn't like the sound of that either - abandoning him, right when he'd be falling and be the most frightened. 'What if I lay him down first? He knows the command.'

'His legs are stiffening up, so trying to bend them to lay down will be more painful.'

'But he'll be going down anyway, and you said he's already in pain?'

'It's easier on my back to get at his jugular this way.'

Oh, well just so long as *you're* comfortable, I thought bitterly.

I stared at the needles - the volume of fluid – and knew they'd have to be painful, no matter how gentle we tried to be. I'd had vaccine needles smaller than my little finger and they'd stung like wasps.

I held my breath... stroked his bushy little brown mane... I decided I'd keep a small tuft of it, afterwards, so I could remember him forever.

Using two fingers, the vet poked down along Lucky's neck - his jugular groove - in search of the main vein, the direct line to his heart - and that's when it happened. Lucky wrenched back from him with all his strength. He jerked the halter out of my hand, and tried to run away on stiff legs.

The vet swore and leapt to block him from getting away, and then many things seemed to happen at once. Penny rushed up to one side and slightly in front of Lucky, to guard him, Apache went to the other side and I found myself in a line of three. Us against the vet, and Lucky behind us, jerking his head defiantly and trying to rear up on his hind legs.

'Stop!' I shouted. 'Let me calm him down first.'

I didn't need to catch him, though. He'd staggered around behind me. For protection. Poor little guy didn't know I'd already betrayed him with my signature.

'Grab him!' shouted the vet. 'Get these other horses out of the way! Shoo! Shooo!' He flapped his arms about, trying to scare them off, but they didn't budge. They only raised their heads up out of his reach.

'Don't!' I snapped, lunging and grabbing his hand just short of striking Apache's chest. I spread my arms wide so he couldn't get past me. 'Nobody hits my horses. Not for anything.'

'Then you do it! They shouldn't be here anyway. Get rid

of them.'

'The foal is part of their family. They have every right to be here and comfort him to the very end.'

'Then tie them up over there.' He pointed to a circle of trees around the big feeder.

'Can't do that either, sorry.' All three horses closed ranks behind me as if they understood every word now, body language or not. 'Look, they're issuing a formal protest.'

'But you signed the consent form already.'

'I know… but they didn't counter-sign.'

'Don't be ridiculous! We must do it before he takes his first fit, or he'll die in agony.'

I could read the horses well enough. The three adults would guard his body and mourn him for the instinctive three days after death, but I needed a closer look at the little guy. I needed to see if he'd spooked out of mindless fear, or something greater… So I sidled down the narrow space between Apache and Penny.

'Steady, mare,' I said, keeping one hand on each all the way down. 'Steady boy.'

They held their guard against the vet, while I crouched behind their back legs, opening my hand to invite the foal closer.

He staggered nearer. Two steps only at first, both rigid and painful, so I met him halfway.

'Steady little man.' I hugged him, then crouched again and looked him straight in the eye. 'We only want to make the pain go away.' I clicked my tongue as the command for him to walk forward alongside me – a command he'd never disobeyed.

Until then.

I tugged on his halter, clicked my tongue – I even tapped his shoulder constantly, taking him all the way back to his first basic lesson. I tapped lightly on his shoulder until he figured out what I wanted of him. But he knew what I wanted, and flatly refused.

'I'll come to him,' the vet said. 'He's in too much pain to move already.'

'No, it's not that. You don't know him.'

The vet took one step, and Lucky reared up in defiance – something else he'd never done on a lead. He snorted at the vet, and tried to whinny. Sounded more like a gurgle, but also like the cry he'd made on that first day we'd met.

I noticed the broadening whites in his beautiful brown eyes, and finally I saw it – behind his obvious pain, I saw fierce determination to survive.

I WANT TO LIVE.

He couldn't write it, or say it, or even tap it out in Morse code, but I recognised that message loud and clear. I felt stupid for not recognizing it sooner. Finally, I could see it, even through my own bleary eyes and the haze of advice from all the vets and books I'd consulted.

'Look at him!' I pleaded. 'He wants to live.'

'Listen here, young lady. He's only a horse, and a baby at that. He's got no idea about long term wants or will be-s. Or about vets and needles. There's no such thing as tomorrow for him. It's only now and how empty his tummy feels. But right now, there's only pain or no pain, and your decision as to which it will be.'

'How can you say that, after such a reaction? He's choosing pain over death.'

'He wasn't choosing anything. He wasn't even reacting to me, specifically, or to the needles. I simply prodded him a little too hard, and he reacted by moving away. That's why you were able to catch him again so fast. He doesn't perceive you as pain. Only me.'

I shook my head, refusing to believe it. 'He's smarter than that.'

'Perhaps he might have been, one day, but a foal can barely recognise their own names at this age. Right now, in this moment, and the next and the next, there's only pain for him. Or milk. And the starvation that comes when his muscles begin to lock up so painfully, that he'll be unable to feed himself.'

'Then I'll help him. I'll find a way.'

'Sure, if his heart doesn't stop first. Or his lungs. Or brain. Or kidneys. Any one of which will be a cruel agony. So you need to be responsible again right now, and put an end to it for him.'

'But if he's trying so hard to stay alive, how can I justify giving up on him?'

'You need to be brave... How old are you, by the way?'

'I just turned seventeen. What's that got to do with anything?'

'A lot, actually. It explains your difficulty in coping with the situation.'

I wanted to scream and pound him with my fists. I didn't understand how anyone who chose to be a vet could be so blind to an animal's body language.

'Minor or not,' I said as maturely as I could manage, 'how can either of us deny him a chance at living? Just one chance. Maybe that's all he's asking? The symptoms only started showing this morning. If we can treat each one and keep up with them, maybe...'

'You don't understand, Anita. I need to speak to your parents.'

'Why? These horses are *my* responsibility. I bought them. I care for them. If you ask my parents anything, they'll only turn you around to face *me* for *my* decision.'

'Enough!' he shouted, and flapped the signed consent form at me. 'This cannot be tolerated. I won't stand by and watch you torture this animal! You're still a minor for another year, so unless your parents show up in the next ten minutes, I'm well within my rights as a veterinary professional to override you.'

'Try it,' I snarled at him.

He took one more step towards me with his arm still raised, holding the consent form, and Apache lunged forward and put himself between us.

'Whoa, boy!' I called, and calmed my biggest horse by simply raising my hand softly against his shoulder.

'I think you'd better leave,' I said, keeping my hand in place. 'For your own safety.' I doubted the guy was in any real danger, since Apache never actually hurt anyone in his whole life, aside from the one hoofprint on the helmet of a raving lunatic. But he was so big, he could look pretty scary if you didn't know what a big cuddly bear he really was, and if the vet reacted aggressively towards me, then maybe it was possible...

'That horse is dangerous!' he shouted. 'Get him under control, or I may be forced to put him put down as well.'

'He's *not* dangerous! He was just raised at a kennel for Rottweilers so he thinks he's a guard dog.'

'This is insane. I'll be back with police and the council stock controllers.'

'On a long weekend?' I laughed. 'Yeah, good luck with that. In the meantime, we'll get a second opinion. Everyone has that right, don't they? Age and species shouldn't make any difference.'

'Listen very carefully, young lady. You're being both foolish and selfish. You're projecting your own desires onto the foal. You want him to live, so you think he wants it too.'

'I'm the one who signed the form,' I argued. 'He's the one protesting. Seems fairly clear cut to me.'

No matter what the vet said to me now, I knew I couldn't be his kind of responsible. I couldn't be his kind of brave. Not with Lucky. Quite the opposite. I felt like a coward taking this long to defend him, but it wasn't entirely my decision any more, and as I looked into Lucky's eyes again, I doubted it ever had been. *He* wanted to live. *He* wanted to try. All I had to be was strong enough and diligent enough to be worthy of him this time.

'I've got your back, little mate.' I patted and cuddled him. 'You'll get your chance for a happy ending. Even if it is only one chance.'

'The odds are against you,' said the vet as he headed back to his car.

'Always have been. But thanks for your time, because I really do appreciate it.'

'You can always get another chestnut foal, you know. There can always be another Lucky.'

I laughed and shook my head. 'Mister, you have no idea.'

My pay was still held up by public holidays, so using my first credit card - which came with the loan for my property - I paid him for his time and the two lethal injections, since the drug couldn't be returned to its bottle... which seemed odd, by the way. Was he worried about his next victim getting infected for all of ten seconds? Maybe it lost potency, or something. I didn't ask. I didn't care. I only wanted him to dispose of the doses well away from my paddock. Sparing a thought for the poor dog whose surgery had been delayed because of me, I gave the vet my genuine thanks again for rushing to see me.

'I'll be back with police before the day is out,' he warned me. 'I've still got this,' he said, flapping the authority to euthanize in my face one more time. 'I didn't become a vet to sit back and watch people torturing animals.'

I snatched the paper off him, ripped it to shreds and shoved all of the pieces into my pockets.

'I'm getting a second opinion,' I reminded him. 'And if

you really want to come back here, you'd better call my solicitor first, as well as the meatworks for permission to enter, so you're not trespassing.'

One glance across the road revealed what I'd already guessed. Closed for Easter.

'You don't have a solicitor.' He screwed up his nose, snidely. 'You're just a minor.'

'Wait right there.' I bounded off to grab the legal firm's business card from my purse, where it had been since I bought my property. 'Ask for Leon. He's the senior partner.'

The vet scowled at me as he drove away.

Now all I needed was a second opinion, and hopefully one prepared to give him a chance. Just one chance. If I had to send my little mate to eternal sleep after that, so be it. I could sign the form again. I knew I could, provided we gave it our best shot first.

Only problem; I couldn't keep calling vets until I found one with a prognosis that suited me. This was tetanus. No known survivors. If the disease didn't get him, the complications would.

I only had one vet left within 200kms—Norbert Gaulton's clinic at Pine Mountain, which hadn't returned any of my calls yet. He was still too busy with other emergencies.

But I could still hope, and keep trying.

24. Meeting Norbert

a Catholic nun,
known as Mother Teresa,
whom I'd seen on TV rescuing those of the poorest
who had no other chance of surviving,
once said;

*If you love until it hurts, there can
be no more hurt, only more love.*

She must have suffered agony in her love for so many. I only had this one sick little horse, yet being powerless to find any help for him was killing me.

I hated leaving the foal alone, especially after the vet's threat to return with police, but Lucky wasn't entirely undefended with the other three horses watching out for him. And I had no choice. I had to return home to make more phone calls, and I couldn't stop at 150-clicks, or even at a 200 kilometre radius. I'd pay almost any travel allowance to give my little friend a chance at life.

I left another message for Norbert to return my call, and then I kept dialing up and down the east coast of Australia from Cairns to Sydney and Melbourne, and even Tasmania, then west across to Perth and out to all the major regional centres in every state and the Northern Territory. (Geographically for distance calls, that's roughly the span of the United States, not counting Alaska and New Mexico.) Basically anywhere that listed an after-hours clinic I called, trying to find a vet who had actual experience - or even knowledge of case studies - on how to treat this mysterious yet ferocious condition called Tetanus. No details anywhere to be found, although I did begin to glean more about the symptoms and various stages that had been reached before.

The bacteria affected humans the same as animals, and existed in almost every environment, so I also called human doctors and nurses at hospitals – and hit my first major moral snag.

The first three hospitals refused to speak to me because I'd called them about a horse. They couldn't understand – or didn't care – about how much they might have been able to help me, and to me, this was still life or death.

So the next three calls started out like this, each keeping it simple with the most basic truths:

Ring, ring…

'Hi, I have a twelve week old baby, who's been really healthy up until today, but he's had a little puncture wound on his jaw that burst with pus and he started having trouble with his tongue. His neck and jaw are going a bit stiff, and he seems to be in an increasing amount of pain or discomfort…'

At which point, the nursing staff would stop me, if they hadn't already, and they'd either demand or strongly recommend me to bring him in for emergency treatment.

'What treatment?' I begged to know. 'Please tell me.'

None of them could. They all said it would depend on the symptoms, but they couldn't or wouldn't give me any suggestions for those either.

Scarily, they all leapt to the same diagnosis over the phone – mentioning either tetanus itself, or its common name, lockjaw. All reacted as if I was dealing with the black death, and they all responded with dire concern for the "baby…" which would have been wonderfully comforting if he really had been a human baby needing their help. Yet it only managed to worry me more, hearing their relief to hear it was "only" a horse – as if the difference between human and animal also made the difference between the right to know how to save him, or not.

I grew so sick of it, I decided the next time, I wouldn't tell them it was a horse at all. Except it took only seconds before I heard the nurse beginning to panic - trying to remain calm while attempting to convince me of the extreme urgency required.

'It's okay,' I tried to reassure her. 'I just need information. I know I must sound young, but I've had four years' experience treating minor wounds to prevent infections. Except I can't find anything about this one. So if you could please just tell me how to treat it, we'll be fine. Honestly.'

'You need to tell me your address immediately,' she insisted. 'If it's tetanus, then it's extremely serious. I'll send out an ambulance right away, and they can begin treatment on his way in.'

'Can't you please, *please,* just give me a hint?' I burst into tears, and so did she.

'It's okay... it's okay,' we tried to reassure each other - for different reasons.

'He's a foal,' I confessed, but I had to say it a few times before she heard it. Or maybe she didn't believe me. At first she misheard me and thought I'd called him Noel. I had to tell her the whole story before she stopped pleading for my address, and even then I think she remained suspicious. She asked me if I was calling from East Ipswich, which struck me as odd, because as far as I knew, it was only police who could trace a call like they did on TV.

'Honestly, I'm really sorry I worried you. I'm just so desperate. I can't find any vets with experience at treating any of the symptoms.'

I explained the whole human-animal similarity thing, how the disease didn't care who it killed, and I begged to be put through to a human doctor who might be willing to suggest a few things. What I really needed right then was a phone that I could use to send photos to prove my situation. But that was years away. Instead, all I could do was explain the same thing over and over with each call – explaining that whatever worked for human babies was likely to work for baby horses.

Every vet recommended lethal injection immediately, but I drew comfort and reassurance from the human hospitals, which all had a completely different mindset;

'We'll send out an ambulance urgently and get him on the road to recovery.'

Sure, I knew why humans needed preferential treatment over animals, and I never would have questioned it. What I couldn't understand, was why so many veterinary surgeries didn't have the same can-do attitude for any client who prioritised life and responsibility ahead of expense and difficulty. It sickened me to think they might only be reflecting the general needs or preferences of society in regards to "mere animals". Especially livestock, where the value of an animal is measured not by its ability or potential, but by the average price of the breed at the slaughterhouse.

Forget a treatment plan, they couldn't even seem to come up with a rough price. I didn't care if their guess-timates were two or three hundred dollars out, but the nature and reputation of this wretched disease meant they couldn't or wouldn't give me even that much. I had to rely on their own perceptions of value when I didn't know or trust any of them.

'Not worth it,' one female vet told me bluntly. 'The medicines alone would cost $100 to $200.'

'That's cheap for this foal,' I said, taking it as a good sign.

'How soon can you see him?'

'I'm off today for a week's holiday,' she replied. 'And he won't last that long. Then even if he did, I'd have to ensure that police charge you with cruelty for making him suffer.'

As with many of the previous calls, I assured her that I'd never put him through anything I wasn't prepared to go through myself.

'Yeah, right,' she said, and hung up.

I found plenty of nurses and doctors who were far more willing to speak to me than veterinarians had been. From a medical perspective, most *wished* they could help, and tried to hunt up more information, if only for their own database. And many wanted me to let them know how I got on, eventually.

Unfortunately, most had very limited information or experience to offer, no matter how hard they tried. Yet it was a human doctor, not a vet, who confirmed my first instinct – to treat each symptom individually, and each new problem as it arose, and to try to keep up with them all, while also inoculating against tetanus *every day* – yes every day – using toxoids and anti-toxins, and pumping Lucky full of antibiotics.

I also sent my mum to the town library for all the books she could find on veterinary or medical science – virtually any book that mentioned the word tetanus, even if it was only a sentence. As Fate would have it, the Ipswich library was open nearly all weekend, hosting special Easter events for children and disadvantaged sectors of the community. Two of the staff stepped aside to help, and even granted Mum permission to bring home everything we needed, far above the normal lending limit. (Until this story was published, there was still no full accounts published anywhere that I could find.)

Of the dozens of books she brought home that day, the

only helpful text came from an old reprint of Pottie's Horse Dictionary, first published in 1882. All other books described the disease and how to prevent it with inoculations, but not how to treat it. Not a single word. They all described it as fatal.

But the first edition of the pocket-sized Pottie's Horse Dictionary had been published over a hundred years ago, when horses were valuable enough for their owner's livelihoods to be worth saving, if at all possible. The reprints had been updated with new terminology, so the tattered edition I read was a mish-mash of old and new. Packed with all kinds of old remedies for many different diseases and ailments, it suggested a few tactics for other ailments which seem barbaric, by modern standards - and in some cases, bizarre. Eg; For a "curb sprain" in the rear hock, considered hereditary, the recommended treatment was "fire and then blister". I suppose that explains why the book is out of print now, even though the advice for tetanus is as valuable as ever. (For the extract from *Pottie's Horse Dictionary*, see Appendix II.)

3.50pm Norbert returned my call, finally.

Such an unusual name, now synonymous with *hero*. First thing he did; apologise profusely. He'd been a long way out of town with his hands up the messy end of a pregnant cow, who'd gone down while attempting to birth a tangled up set of twins. Usually that meant sacrificing one to save the other, but he'd been successful at seeing two new lives enter the world, both valuable to their owner. At last, I'd found a vet with the right mindset for me. But I couldn't afford to lay all my trust in him yet. His clinic advertised his services for Pine Mountain, while the address in the phone book said Blacksoil – out on the edge of the city limits between city and country.

Pine Mountain certainly sounded more hygienic, I had to admit. But he sounded so young compared to all the others, and his clinic seemed virtually brand new. He also seemed a little too keen to know how many other horses I owned. On the other hand, his phone listing advertised that he cared for both large and small animals. He had no stable yet for sick horses, but he agreed to examine the foal to provide a second opinion. Specifically, I needed to know if it really was the deadly disease tetanus, and if he had the same prognosis.

Within the hour, Norbert met me at the Yamanto paddock.

He came wearing a black t-shirt, which he pulled off and wrapped around Lucky's head, effectively blindfolding him. I'd never liked that blind-folding tactic for handling wild horses, and especially not now since my colt wasn't wild and wrapping it around his head seemed to upset him more at first. So I wasn't impressed. I reached to sweep it straight off - but then I noticed him settle. Norbert explained that tetanus made victims hypersensitive to light, so the darker we could make it for him, the milder his headache. Then my perspective flipped, and I truly admired Norbert, a vet who'd rip off his own shirt to make an animal more comfortable.

Returning to his Landcruiser, he donned a spare set of coveralls.

'So it's definitely tetanus?' I asked, still trying to stay hopeful that it wasn't.

He gave me the bad word with only a nod, except this time, I'd come prepared with Pottie's Horse Dictionary.

I opened it to show him what I'd found.

'This suggests it was possible a hundred years ago,' I said and pointed to the heading *Treatment and nursing*. 'So with modern medicine and modern practices, it should be even easier to defeat, shouldn't it?'

'That depends a lot on the patient and how much he wants to live.'

'Mr Gaulton,' I said and led him out to sit on the trunk of my car. 'You have no idea… But I think you need to. If any animal can beat it, I suspect it's this little guy.'

'That's a lot to say about a twelve-week-old baby. We're talking about one of the deadliest diseases in the world. It literally knocks down elephants.'

'Then let me tell you a little bit about him, please, and afterwards, if you can look him in the eye and still say it's the end, then I'll sign your consent for lethal injection and I'll do it with relief, knowing we crossed off all our options first and didn't just say that it's terminal, just because everyone else says it will be.'

He made himself comfortable, crossing his arms. 'Hit me,' he said, and I did — with our whole story, and how Lucky's slip from the grip of the meatworks buyers had been only the smallest part of it. Compared to the rest, that was pure luck. He'd also survived that dog attack, two tramplings and a night on the town with raving lunatics.

I became acutely aware that every beat of Lucky's heart meant more bacteria and more neurotoxins to fight, so I spoke quickly while sparing no critical detail. I'd armed myself with a photo album too, so I could also prove how special he'd been so far during training.

'He can do more than most two-year-old horses,' I explained, trying to sound rational, not emotional. 'If he wasn't so stiff, he could demonstrate.'

Instead, I could only show images of the colt learning how to lunge, lead, and back up, all by voice command, plus a few other tricks outside the norm for his species, let alone his age, like fetch, jump and sit… Okay, so he never really mastered that last one, but at least he tried.

I had the evidence with me.

'That's impressive,' Norbert conceded as he flicked through the pages. 'Unfortunately, co-operating when they're healthy is completely different to when they're sick, in pain or frightened, and he's going to be all three. His primary instinct will drive him to escape pain, and tetanus is entirely painful. You'll find it surprising how strong he can be, fighting you, even at this tender age. All he'll want to do is run away with his mother.'

'Is it the same if he trusts me as much as her?'

'Possibly. I've never heard of such a case. Every patient is different.'

'Okay then. How would you rate a terminally ill patient who is racked by pain and still does this..?'

I waited until he looked back to Lucky, then from the rear of my car, outside the fence and a full bus-length away - and with Lucky's head still resting inside the black t-shirt, looking worse than he had all day - I called his name. We saw his ears twitch under the material, and when I gave the command to back up, he did, even though he'd been effectively blindfolded.

Only one step, taken very slowly and in obvious agony; but he still chose to comply. He tried again, breaking my heart as he tried to turn his stiff neck and body to come towards the sound of my voice.

'Whoa, boy,' I called before he hurt himself any more. 'Steady, little mate.' I glanced back to the vet, hopefully. 'I'd rather not put him through anything more than I have to, so can you come over with me now and look him in the eye please?'

'No need. Leave him be.' Norbert folded his arms again, his expression darkening, and my heart plummeted. I could virtually hear the consent form rustling – except he stared at the colt for a longer moment, and only moved his hand enough to scratch his chin.

'He can't stay here,' he said, finally. 'We're going to need a stable, a sling, and 24-hour monitoring.'

'What's a sling?'

'I've got one in my car. Where's the nearest stable you can get to?'

'At home in Blackwood Street. Over in East Ipswich. Dad's got a spare shed I can clean out, and I can do all of the monitoring… wait. Do you service East Ipswich?'

'I drove further to get here, but travel costs won't be your main expense. You'll need a bucket of medications.'

'I'll pay cash every day if I have to. I don't know how yet. My credit card only has a $500 limit, but I'll find it. I'm not giving up now until after he does.'

'Is that your determination speaking, or his?'

'All his. Truth is, he's been my teacher every day, and all I've ever had to do is hang on.'

'Better tighten your grip then. This will be a steep learning curve for all of us.'

25. Back to Blackwood

Bugs Bunny,
my cheery hero,
once said;

I'll be scared later.
Right now I'm too mad.

In my case, it was mad at myself.
Downright furious.

Norbert offered to stay with the foal, instructing me to drive home to fetch our truck.

Instead, I ran to the nearest house and rapped on the door, pleading to use their phone for an emergency.

An old lady answered the door – knitting a Christmas sock, with a ball of red wool tucked down her cleavage. A little bizarre for April, but she accepted a dollar in payment for a ten cent phone call.

'The engine wouldn't start this morning,' Dad replied a minute later. 'I dropped out the guts to fix it, but if you give me half an hour I'll find something.'

By the time I returned to Norbert, he'd noticed three other horses at the top end of my paddock. 'Didn't you say you had only three adult horses here?' he asked, pointing to them.

'Oh, they're not mine. They belong to stockmen at the works, so they're not here all the time.'

'I only brought enough needles for yours.'

I felt stupid. I thought he'd been quizzing me about my other horses as a means of making extra money out of me if the colt died. I'd grown so accustomed to coping with the vet-o-matic's methodology, it never occurred to me that Norbert might have such a kind, considerate reason. 'Sorry. I'll contact them as soon as I get home.'

'Cattle dogs too, if there's been any in here.'

'Apache and Snow had their annuals on Australia Day,' I said. 'I don't know about Penny. I tried to contact the previous owners but no luck there yet.'

'Your first two should be safe, but my goal is to guarantee it.'

'Hang on, if we vaccinate within three months of their last shots, won't that risk infecting them with it instead?'

Norbert shook his head and reaffirmed what I'd read from the tattered old World Book Encyclopaedia. The vaccine couldn't cause the disease. So he administered all four of mine with a Tetanus antitoxin AND Tetanus Toxoid needles. One for immediate coverage, and one long-lasting. He also shot Lucky full of painkillers and muscle relaxants to help him cope with the trip to Blackwood Street in the back of a truck, and rinsed the wound as they took effect. Then he administered intravenous shots of Tetanus antitoxin and penicillin close to the wound itself to help fight the infection at the source. And amazingly, Lucky didn't resist any of those needles like he had with the other vet.

'He may need more today,' Norbert warned me. 'These just get him started until we can clean him up properly after the truck ride.'

Except Dad didn't arrive in the tipper.

He didn't arrive as soon as I'd expected either. I kept glancing at my watch as the minutes ticked by, unsure if I should be worried or angry. I could have driven home and back again myself by now, and it wouldn't be the first time that a customer had delayed him. As the only 24-hour emergency breakdown service in town, he often had to drop family matters to attend to other people. I'd never felt bitter about it before, because we needed it to keep food on the table, but this time....

I had to blink twice when he finally rounded the corner. I could hardly believe my eyes when he drove in behind the wheel of his mobile mechanical van – towing a double horse trailer. It looked so bizarre, as if he could fix any horsepower problems with real horse power.

Opening the gate to let him drive through into the paddock, I tried not to sound angry. 'Where did you get *that*?' I called as he drove in and around me. In all the time I'd owned horses, the only trailers we'd ever used had been rented.

'My cousin, May.'

'Your cousin may what?' Dad had such a big family, I had trouble keeping count of my own cousins, let alone any of his, so we always used their titles of uncle, aunt, cousin or whatever, as well as their first name to help keep them sorted – except my head was so messed up, I wasn't thinking straight when he mentioned a cousin I'd never heard of before.

'Not may what, May *who*.' He parked and climbed out beside me. 'I grew up with May. She breeds and trains trotters over the hill.'

'Why didn't you just bring the truck? It would have been faster.'

'The truck is too tall for loading a stiff foal. Is it really tetanus?'

'Not for long, I hope.' I hugged him, appreciating how thoughtful he'd been, when I'd been imagining the opposite.

'You'll need to scrub out that float with antiseptic after

we're done with it,' Norbert warned us. 'Plus an extra two rinses to flush it thoroughly.'

'Is tetanus contagious?' asked Dad.

'Not as such,' Norbert said, 'but we're dealing with an active concentration of the live bacteria, so you need to make sure you remove all traces of the bacteria from the float.'

'To be safe,' I suggested, 'I want to handle everything as if it's contagious in the worst way.'

'But the risk is the same as every other day,' Dad argued. 'It lives in the soil anyway, and my cousin's horses are ritually inoculated, so they should be safe regardless, shouldn't they?'

'Probably,' Norbert replied. 'The bacteria needs a wound to enter the body. If you're vaccinated, you're safe, normally. But any skin rupture or abrasion will do, from paper cuts and hangnails to punctures and burns. It can be small, like a scratch inside your ear that can get infected from dust in the air. Or internally, from eating peanut brittle that scratches your throat after it's been sitting on a dirty bench. Risks are negligible most of the time, obviously, but we'll be maintaining a high vigilance for a month after the last symptom, just to be sure.'

I liked the sound of that; thinking that far ahead, like a human doctor and already aiming for an end to successful rehabilitation.

'Let's not set our hopes too high,' he warned in the next breath. 'We still have to take each problem as it comes. So first, you'll need to get some milk powder to feed him. I gave the last of mine to the calves, but a store for farm supplies should open first thing tomorrow and until then you can get by on bottled milk with egg, honey and sugar.'

'What about *her* milk?' I asked, pointing to Penny. 'Or is it no good anymore, after the needles?'

'It's the best there is, but getting it into him is the problem. It'll be too painful for him trying to twist his head up under her to serve himself.'

'What if I do this?' I strode over to Penny, nudged her side like a foal, then leaned in and squirted some milk into my hand. 'Can he drink from a bucket?'

Norbert grinned; a quiet man of few words. 'If you can keep that up, you'll also solve the complication of her milk drying up and having nothing to offer him if he survives.'

I noted the word *if* without argument now. The situation was still way above my coping skills, but at least I was trying. I kept focusing on what seemed to be a fifty-fifty chance either way. Which sure beat that lousy one percent. Or worse; zero.

We heard clumping, and turned around to find Apache loading himself into the float, and I had to grab Snow before she loaded herself too.

'Patch!' I called. 'Back-back, buddy. Get your big butt out of there.'

He complied without hesitation, but stayed close, watching while we loaded Penny and the colt. As keen as Lucky had been for the last trip, loading him this time became a slow, difficult task for my poor, stiff little foal, whose body had begun to set like concrete. At twelve weeks, he was already too heavy to lift in bodily. But the two men managed it, aided by the low slope up into the trailer.

I bid my farewells to Apache and Snow with a quick cuddle for each, and as we drove out in our little convoy, Apache bolted along the fence, following us and calling as if he wanted to come home too.

'Whoa, boy,' I called to him out my window. He and I had jumped higher fences than that boundary while competing at the showgrounds during our first year together, so he could clear those six strands of wire with heaps to spare if he chose. 'We'll take good care of your little apprentice.'

Lucky answered with a shrill, gurgly whinny – and that was the last sound we heard from him, although Penny nickered softly to him all the way back home to Blackwood Street. And I tried not to notice, the river still raging, brim full and threatening to flood us out.

A police car tailed us the last two streets, and pulled into the driveway behind us. Good thing I hadn't travelled in the float with the foal, or I could have been in real trouble for breaking that law. I recognised the same cops as always, which made me worry they'd be curious to see our travel permit - which we didn't have. Since the sales, Mum had organised a new annual permit to travel stock anywhere inside our red zone for cattle ticks in south east Queensland, but in his rush to get to me, Dad had left it in the glove compartment of the truck by accident.

No big deal.

The situation didn't faze Dad at all. As a respected businessman, he'd never had any trouble with the law, so he climbed out first and greeted Sergeant Cook, while I grabbed the chance to slip back into the float to check on Lucky, unnoticed. As far as the police cared, I was still only a kid and not worth much attention.

'Emergency quarantine,' Dad said, exaggerating to ensure he had their attention. 'Unless you're both inoculated for tetanus, I'll have to ask you to step back outside the gate for your own safety. We need to unload these animals urgently.'

Norbert drove up onto our footpath; a no-no that our council usually rewarded with a hefty fine for everyone except emergency vehicles. As a vet, that seemed to qualify, since the cops didn't question him. Instead, Norbert filled them in quietly and calmly about the whole situation.

'Tetanus?' asked Sergeant Cook. 'The hospital reported a call from this number by a young woman with a sick baby.'

'Baby *horse...*' Dad said, and explained the whole human-animal thing along with my difficulty in finding anyone with experience. He apologised. They wished us luck, and watched from a distance, also keeping back a small crowd of the usual gossips until we'd finished unloading. It took me a while longer to notice my sister and five of her friends above me, glued to windows upstairs inside the house. Friends who'd never expected their weekend pyjama party to include a few days in quarantine – even if it was only voluntary isolation.

At least they enjoyed the show.

Unloading what felt like a concrete foal proved to be a lot more challenging than loading one. We had to reverse Penny out first, then turn Luck around and walk him out forwards – still wearing Norbert's black t-shirt over his head, but only looped over this time, instead of sleeved up over his ears, because he seemed much happier if he could see his front feet.

'He may not be able to feel his legs much by now,' Norbert explained. 'Aside from the pain, the toxin interferes with nerve communication between the muscles, spine and brain.'

'And we treat them separately, or together?'

'A little of both in a daily routine of therapy, four to six times a day. His legs are locked at the knees from the muscle contractions, so he can't bend them by himself any more. At least not easily. So you'll need to keep his muscles strong or they won't be able to support him. You'll need to lay him down to do it properly, on both sides. And you'll need at least two people to flip him. Too fast, you'll risk injuring him or triggering a fit. Too slowly and it will kill your backs. He'll also need constant stimulation to keep his blood flow, and nerves communicating with his muscles. But first we have to make sure we haven't missed any injuries, no matter how small. That means we need to clean him up until he's sparkling, and go over him again thoroughly.'

That meant washing off a thick layer of mud down his legs and sides.

'Has he ever been washed down by a hose?'

'Has he?' I grinned, remembering our good times filling the trough. 'He's a duckling. But since he's sick, I'd rather fill warm buckets, if that's okay?'

'Better than okay. Do you have any puppy shampoo or mild dish detergent?'

'Sure do.'

I handed Lucky over to him, and left him speaking with Mum about tetanus shots, while I dashed up to the kitchen and set about cleaning the foal gently but thoroughly all over - until he sparkled like the elegant old Mercedes that awaited Dad's repairs in the garage. Next came a warm rinse of clean salty water, then a rub-down and blow-dry, followed by the most thorough inspection I'd ever witnessed.

Norbert went over him with a fine tooth comb – literally, since his comb resembled a human nit comb. Despite everything, I'd managed to keep all his other wounds healing cleanly – so well that Norbert commended me.

With scarring that looked the same age as the cuts I'd witnessed him getting during his near-tramplings at the sale-yards, the puncture up under his jaw went right to the jawbone, as suspected.

Hidden between the under cleft of his jaw, once muddy it had been able to fester un-noticed. So Norbert opened it up properly, and cleaned it out thoroughly. He showed me how to do it too, because I'd need to clean it four to six times a day with salt water and a dark green gooey gel called prednoderm, containing chlorophyll, cod liver oil, neomycin sulphate, nitrofurazone and prednisolone, amongst other things – all of which combined to look, feel and behave like dark green petroleum jelly. It even came in a similar tub. It didn't seem to sting him, and even seemed to dull the pain of the wound itself quite effectively.

'I'll stay until we get him fully dosed and settled, and then I'll need daily updates,' Norbert said, patting the foal's neck. 'I hope to see him every second day, with phone calls night and morning, starting tonight.'

I grinned – more grateful than he could ever imagine.

He was the first vet who hoped to see Lucky another day.

Next, Norbert expanded his explanation of how and why the foal needed constant 24-hour care in a dark environment. 'His eyes are especially sensitive right now.'

Best solution; a stable with a soft floor and bedding hay. But I only had an old boat shed beside Dad's main garage, so we had to make do.

We'd had no boat for years. Mum kept getting seasick, so we'd sold it and a pile of junk had grown up in its place. Dad packed up most of it, by shifting it into a tighter pile in the back half, and covering it under an old oily tarp. Not an easy task, nor a quick one. It took almost an hour, but left the front half clear as a makeshift stable.

But the big old shed remained too bright inside - even with the windows blacked out using newspapers, duct tape and spray cans of tyre black. Cars and customers coming and going from the neighbouring bay of the shed also made it too noisy.

So we'd cleaned out that shed for nothing. Every clank of a spanner or hammer caused the colt to tense up more painfully.

'I don't understand,' I confessed to Norbert. 'He shouldn't be afraid of those noises. He's used to all kinds of weird rackets around here.'

'It's not fear,' Norbert explained. 'It's an involuntary reflex from the muscles. Normally, his brain has time to say; "Hey, it's okay. We're not scared of that. No need to flinch," but remember, the toxins are interfering with communication along his nerves and spine to his brain. The pain is also screaming through his body, while his muscles are trying to talk to each other in tiny bioelectric whispers.'

We persevered with the stable an hour longer, lacking any better option. But the hard concrete also risked more bruising and scrapes to the horses' legs and, as a broodmare used to paddocks, Penny hated being cooped up inside with her baby. We couldn't let her come and go without rolling up the whole door – which let in too much light, and caused him pain. And we couldn't lock her out either, or she'd run about whinnying, trying to get inside to him… which meant the next thing I had to do after returning Lucky to the shade of the mulberry tree, was visit all our neighbours who shared a boundary fence, explain what was going on – ask if they were okay with it, which I probably should have done first before bringing him home - and apologise for any inconvenience or noise in advance.

'Don't forget to explain the needles to everyone who comes down here. Especially if they come in contact with him,' Norbert reminded me. 'Your mum has been able to arrange bulk-billing with a local after-hours doctor, and she'll pick up the tab for any difference.'

I'd seen her chatting aside with Norbert a few times while I'd been washing Lucky, but I wasn't quite sure what he meant. 'Do you mean booster shots for their pets?'

'Humans too. Anyone who hasn't been shot in the last 3 to 6 months, or can't remember, should be advised of the situation here. Same goes for your nearest neighbours. If their pets are wanderers, they can speak to me about them.'

'Oh, great,' I winced. 'My sister will hate me. She's having a sleepover.'

'And I run a business,' Dad reminded him. 'So does that include visitors and employees?'

'To be safe, yes. You'll also need to warn any customers who come this far into the yard. The word *thorough* has to be our catch cry. The odds are stacked against us already. Obviously, you can't make them get vaccinations. Some people have strong opinions against them, which you need to respect. They can't catch tetanus from just being here, or looking at him over the fence, but you still need to recommend the vaccinations, or at least raise their awareness to take extreme care.'

'Taking medical advice from a vet. Yep, that's going to go down brilliantly in this neighbourhood.'

'If you're having second thoughts...?'

'Oh, no.' I gulped. 'I'll take my medicine.'

So I volunteered to be the bringer of such festive Easter tidings to our five nearest neighbours, only one of whom I'd ever met before and that was Donny. The others seemed to work such strange hours – if at all – that I barely even knew what they looked like and ironically, those closest to us remained the biggest mystery. Amongst all the doom and gloom in the media came regular warnings for kids and young women to avoid speaking to strangers, so the only ones I knew were those who were customers already and who'd paid me for chores elsewhere in the neighbourhood. But how bad could they be if they lived so quietly?

I bit the proverbial bullet and approached the scariest

house first; a dark little two-bedroom rental shack next door, where a family of Vietnamese refugees kept entirely to themselves. They rarely came outside, except for three little kids who walked to school alone each day, so I wasn't even sure how many lived there. I only knew it was a lot more than at any other house in the street, because they needed three vans whenever they did go anywhere.

Drab, run down, overgrown by weedy gardens, and growing spookier with every step...

I knocked, then heard a soft babble of arguing amongst two elderly women and a man inside, soon followed by the door opening with a teenaged boy pushed to the front of a small crowd of eight, as their representative. Same age as me, at a rough guess, but much smaller in height and frame.

'Hello,' I said, weirded out by all the faces peering back at me. I didn't know if their culture or religion frowned on girls being independent, but they'd chosen to come to Australia, so I figured they'd also chosen to accept our free way of life. 'Welcome to the neighbourhood. I probably should have said that weeks ago when you moved in, sorry. I just wanted to explain - about my horses...' I pointed over my shoulder. 'So you know there's no need to worry...' Their looks grew weirder, so I spoke slower and clearer. 'Does anyone speak English?'

'No English,' the boy said, and closed the door with the most polite string of bows and nods I'd ever seen before, or since.

I scratched my head, feeling sorry for them, and wondered if baking a tray of Aussie lamingtons or scones might help them to feel more welcome – but decided against it, in case they mistook it for interest in their son.

Next house over belonged to Mr Nosey. He'd seen us unload the horses in the first place, and probably knew as much as I did by then, but he may not have seen that I'd seen him seeing... and if I failed to keep him informed, he'd say I'd failed to treat him with the respect he deserved, and then he'd find a way to make me regret it later. On the other hand, he could talk the ears off a field of corn, so I didn't want to get trapped in a conversation with him. Instead, I let my fingers do the walking – from my mum's office phone.

Ring, ring...

'Oh, hello. You may have heard a horse whinnying? ... Yeah, no, that wasn't a western. I wanted to let you know what's going on - out of neighbourly courtesy - and make sure you're okay with it.... Yeah, sure, of course we'll be doing our best to keep the racket down... yes, and the smell... yes, yes, yes, and I swear absolutely zero hoof prints on your lawn ever again... oh, and you'll need to speak to the after-hours doctor in Jacaranda Street, because even if you're fully vaccinated, you now also need two tetanus needles in your butt and arm. Tell him my vet sent you. Bye.'

The sound of his silence made me splutter, trying not to burst out laughing. Now I wish I'd told him face-to-face, because that stunned silence must have been accompanied by a hilarious facial expression.

Outside again, I hopped the fence to try the next neighbour, but by then, Nosey had warned the next two, who'd warned the next two, and so on up and down the street - until the whole neighbourhood came around visiting in the hope of getting in on the subsidized tetanus shots. Luckily, most were pensioners who'd get them free anyway.

Dad stopped them in the driveway and closed the gates. Too late to stop a pair of young guys in white shirts who'd been doing the rounds to sell their religion, but hey. Serve them right for coming in and heading straight down the driveway to Dad's shed, instead of knocking on the front door, like they should have. Welcome to Christianity, Pilgrims. Now turn around and drop your pants... literally.

I couldn't help but smile as I spared an extra thought for the after-hours doctor, a polite young Muslim, who'd be getting the last laugh on all of us that day by shoving needles into our arms and butts.

It reminded me of wise words that Dad had contributed to the *Great White Wall of Wisdom* when we'd first established it in our little white "throne" room so long ago;

Community is family.

I had an inkling that I was only just beginning to understand what that meant.

26. For as Long as it Takes

Laozi again,
(Lao Tzu)
this time for his wisdom;

Being loved gives you strength,
while loving gives you courage.

Yet I never felt courageous.
It was more like a sliding scale from fear to terror,
but I had 16 years of love from my parents bottled up,
which powered me with enough strength to last all night,
alone in the darkness.

As dusk drew down around us, Norbert's prediction for Lucky's feeding problem came true, preventing him from suckling on his own.

Without Penny's milk, the colt would die, and without his suckling she'd dry up - with the added risk of milk fever into the bargain.

So now, I had two patients to watch over.

I commenced the new program - milking Penny at least eight times a day on my own. A cupful at a time. Then mixing her milk with bran, oats or pollard flakes, I sucked it up into a clean, fat syringe and pushed it gently between Lucky's rigid lips onto the back of his tongue so he could swallow. Twenty mLs at a time- the same size as the lethal injections he would have received earlier that day.

He seemed to love it. He could barely move his head by now, so it should have been impossible for him to express much emotion at all, but each time I filled the syringe, he'd turn his neck the little he could and lean into the syringe to help get it over his thick, swollen tongue.

Feeding him seemed easiest for us both if I lifted the side of his lip first, at the corner of his mouth, and slid in the syringe through the natural gap between his front and rear teeth – where the bit of a bridle would eventually sit.

After I'd ejected the porridge onto the back of his tongue he'd need a minute or so to swallow it down his long throat, which seemed sore. So Norbert helped enormously, by feeding a long plastic tube down into the foal's stomach – double checking that it hadn't gone down into his lungs – and then pouring down a full meal, ensuring that Lucky started his program of recovery with a full belly.

Our next immediate problem; his hypersensitivity to light. Not only sunlight. House lights, street lights, car lights. So I strung up my horse blankets around the mulberry tree to provide a corner where he could get away from most light, day or night. I made him a rug to keep him warm, using hessian potato sacks with black plastic garbage bags sewed to the outside, which also helped to keep him dry during the regular rain showers.

I sat on our old metal swing-set for hours, rocking back and forth watching him, and trying to think of other things I could do to help him... and realised there'd come a time soon when I'd need to learn how to inject needles. Big ones. Painful ones. And little ones that would sting.

He needed a whopping 20ml Penicillin needle daily for five days into muscle, plus smaller, daily Tetanus antitoxin needles and Tetanus Toxoid needles – yes, *daily* - and they all needed to be injected into a different place each time. Poor little guy would feel like a pin cushion if he survived.

6.45pm I needed to get my two booster shots. We all did. So by 7pm, as soon as the colt and his mother seemed to be settled, finally, in the backyard and sleeping on their feet, we all set out for the after-hours doctor. I didn't want to leave Lucky alone, but I couldn't miss the convoy. It would take at least four cars to fit all of our staff and my sister's sleepover friends–after discussing it with their parents first, naturally.

The loading up began and so did the traditional bickering over who'd get to ride "shot gun" in the front passenger seat. While they sorted themselves out I retreated to the semi-privacy of my mum's office to make a call. I needed to check if Jim's vaccinations had been up to date when he'd first helped me with the colt at the sale-yards. Being too much of a chicken to face him with this kind of news so soon after the other debacles, I tried calling him first…

Ring, Ring…

Gulp. I swallowed my pride as his stepfather answered. 'Hello, Mr Bell, is Jim there..? No we don't expect you'll smell them that far down the street. Is Jim there..? No, I agree a backyard is no place for two horses. Is Jim there, please?'

Waiting, waiting…

'Ahh, yes, hello, Jim..?' Gulp, wince, gulp… 'Yeah, it's definitely me again, sorry…. Yes, I suppose I really am a sucker for punishment. Sorry to bug you, but… actually, speaking of butts… I mean, on a scale of one to ten, how much do you hate needles?'

He chuckled, and hung up.

I hung up too, deciding I'd have to try again in person to make sure he didn't think I'd been joking. But as I stood up to leave, I glimpsed his bronze panther through the window, squealing backwards as he reversed out of his driveway.

Turning my way.

'Wow, nice Monaro,' whistled one of my sister's friends just as he pulled in through our gate.

Monaro, I thought. So that's what that is.

I headed out to meet him at the front door. 'Clouds coming over heavy,' I said, wondering why he'd come such a short distance in his best car. 'If you're going out, you should take your ute. Unless you didn't get it going yet? Maybe dad could-'

'That's only a flat battery, but I'm not here to talk about cars or the weather. Mum noticed your convoy loading up. So I was on my way down here anyway, to check if you needed someone to keep an eye on him while you're gone?'

'You were?' I blinked in disbelief. After all I'd put him through... Maybe he just wanted me alone to wring my neck? 'Umm, yeah. I mean, yes, please. I really would appreciate that, but the vet says you should get boosters urgently too. That's why I .. you know... phone.'

'You sound like you need a break first. Tell them to go, and I'll take you in after they get back.'

'But you've definitely been exposed to the same mud as Lucky... You would have walked the bacteria home on your shoes. On your clothing.'

'And it's probably been here in the soil forever anyway. An hour more won't make that much difference.'

'You haven't seen how fast it can work.'

'I had my shots only three years ago and they can last up to ten, so tell everyone else to go, then take a shower and nap. I'll hold the fort until they get back.'

He turned me around to face the stairs, leaving me wondering how many eyes had seen him come inside with me, alone. I didn't want any of them getting the wrong idea. So that became one of the rare moments that I ever did as I was told, and went upstairs alone to clean myself up a bit.

Two hours later, Jim led me into the doctor's office, turned around and unashamedly dropped his pants to offer his butt first.

I spun away embarrassed. I hadn't expected the doctor to call us both in at once, but he'd been inoculating kids and adults in batches or pairs all afternoon, and apparently he'd mistaken us for a real couple.

'This isn't how I pictured our next date,' Jim teased.

The doctor grinned, joining him in the good humour. 'If this is how you get along, you may not survive until your next anniversary.'

'I fear you may be right, Doc.' Jim buckled up and took his second shot in the arm, while smiling at me. 'Maybe we should go out for drinks and celebrate sooner, rather than later?'

'Sorry, but I can't celebrate anything now,' I replied. 'Besides, I'm under eighteen, remember?'

Yet another reminder that he was out of my league.

'Milkshake then, with a meal?'

'Okay, but it has to be fast food on the way home, and I'm paying.' I rolled up my own sleeve and my stomach growled, reminding me I hadn't eaten all day. 'After going through this, you deserve it.'

Jim winked knowingly at the doctor, so I knew he was only stirring me up for an argument. And since we'd come in his car, our destination was beyond my control, which risked putting me in greater debt to him.

It was raining again as Jim pulled into my driveway. I thanked him for the ride, the burger and shake, and apologised for the needles, weather and road muck all over his lovely car, then turned tail and jogged straight for the backyard – only partially registering that I didn't hear him leave yet. Instead, the purr of his engine cut to silence.

I spotted Lucky on the ground and my heart stopped. No sign of mum or dad anywhere. Just Penny, watching over him.

I couldn't run to him, no matter how much I wanted to. I didn't want to scare him or wake him if he'd only fallen asleep. But as I crept swiftly nearer, my stomach twisted up, warning me to expect something far more serious.

On his side, with his neck buckled awkwardly over a garden edge and his legs sticking out from his body, it looked as if my "concrete foal" had simply fallen over. Or like the dead dog I'd seen years ago in the gutter on my way home from pre-school.

That thought scared me more than anything.

I crouched over him and saw that his eyes seemed to be frozen white with fear.

Did one of them move when he saw me? I didn't know if I was only kidding myself.

I used my hand on his side, on the thinnest skin behind his foreleg, trying to detect a heartbeat.

Jim skidded to his knees beside me in the mud, and plunged his ear to Lucky's side, listening. 'He's not breathing.'

Three words that signalled the end of the world to me.

'Do you know CPR?' I asked, because I didn't. Not something I'd ever had time for.

'On a horse?' he asked.

I saw Lucky's eye move again, ever so slightly, but this time he fixed on me as if pleading again to save him. His ear twitched too, and I wondered how long a horse could go without oxygen before brain damage. I'd seen Apache swim across the river with his nose submerged up to his eyes for three minutes before he figured out he could hold his nose up, but he had the lung capacity of a small elephant. 'Do you?' I demanded, feeling the tick of every second as if they were minutes.

'Sure. I'm an electrician. I have to do the course every year as part of my licence.'

'Then show me... please. Or tell me what to do and I'll do it. The book warned me of spasms. If his lungs have paralysed, we should only need to keep his air flowing until he relaxes.'

I stroked Lucky, spending vital seconds that coaxed him down from his frozen peak of terror. I spoke to him softly too, and held one of his nostrils closed, while Jim inflated the other. We swapped regularly; since our human lungs were only half the size of Lucky's. Jim cupped his hands to funnel air into one side, and then the other, figuring that a little air had to be better than nothing.

After a minute that seemed like an hour, the colt sucked in a breath finally, and relaxed. Still stiff, but not dead.

'How often will we have to do that?' Jim asked.

I could only shrug. 'The antibiotics and anti-toxins should be working now. So I guess it depends on how big a job they have to clean up inside him.'

Still on the ground, Lucky tried to nudge his muzzle deeper into my hand. If he hadn't been happy at what we'd done, he would have moved it the other way. Easier that way, too, where the downhill slope would have made it less painful. Instead he chose to strain against his own pain to be closer to me, and I knew I'd done the right thing. I'd done what he'd wanted or hoped me to do. Take his pain away. So I did again, as much as I could manage, by repositioning his neck to make him more comfortable.

Jim went to fetch my dad, and between us, we managed to stand him up like a garden statue. He felt so rigid, Dad asked if I'd been feeding him rocks. Lucky could no longer bend his legs easily by himself, but once standing, he seemed able to stay upright, albeit a bit wobbly. Either way, he seemed very much happier to be able to stand side by side with his mother again.

'Sorry, honey,' Dad said. 'Nature called me away, and he looked okay.'

'Get some sleep,' Jim suggested. 'Big day tomorrow.'

I nodded. Easter Saturday meant the shops would be open long enough to stock up on hay and grain for Penny, but for now I could only stay with my hand hovering over the colt's rump to catch him before he fell again. I only needed to nudge him slightly if he teetered a little too far one way or the other, and he'd be able to save himself before he leaned too far.

Jim left me, but returned a moment later with my mother.

'My shift,' Mum said. 'I'll watch him.'

I assumed she meant until I came back again in the morning.

'His meds are working,' she assured me. 'He'll be frolicking about again by tomorrow.'

Reluctantly, I let Jim lead me up to the house.

'You are some kind of girl,' he said as he pushed me inside and closed the door between us.

I didn't know what kind he meant. I'm not even sure how I got upstairs to my bed. I only know that I didn't sleep a wink, worrying.

I might as well have spent the whole night down in the yard with my little mate.

27. Emotional Rollercoaster (Day 2)

Goethe
(pronounced 'gerta')
the famous German Poet and Scientist,
(often quoted by my highschool German teacher),
once said;

*Life belongs to the living, and they who
live must be prepared for changes.*

Crikey! Talk about changes!
But on the brink between Life & Death,
did they need to be so scary or dramatic?

5.30am Up before the bird, I found the colt alone and down again. Motionless. His eyes seemed glazed and I thought he'd died again, but when I touched him, the skin on his shoulder flinched. Then his eye moved to look at me. His chest moved, breathing.

A neighbour from over the back fence noticed us and came over to sticky-beak. I'd never met him personally. I'd only spoken to his girlfriend for the first time when I'd let all the neighbours know what was going on in our yard. She'd mentioned that he was a baker, and when I'd commented on a lovely candle ornament, she'd told me that he was Jewish, but that's all I knew of him.

'I'm running late for work,' he said, 'but I had to see how you're going. Is that the foal everyone's talking about?'

I checked over my shoulder, wondering how many other

foals he saw in the neighbourhood. 'His name is Lucky.'

'Not looking very lucky at the moment.'

Captain Obvious, I thought, cheering up a bit. I massaged Lucky's legs and helped to bend them gently in preparation for getting him upright.

'What's up with him?'

'Down, actually. I don't suppose you'd have time to spare me a hand for a few seconds?'

I wondered if I should check first about his inoculations being up-to-date, but I figured his girlfriend would have mentioned that already, and I didn't want to nag. If he'd been worried about the risk, he wouldn't have come so close with a smile on his face.

'Sure, thing. Any excuse to avoid the next batch of hot cross buns. It's barely the second day of Easter and I'm sick of the sight of them.'

I grinned at the irony of a Jewish baker making treats for Christians.

He slapped his hands together keenly and leapt the fence before I realised I should have warned him about avoiding any sudden noise.

Lucky startled, went rigid – a reflexive response from the toxins, which showed he still had the disruption of normal muscle functions and reactions. I showed the baker how to stroke him all over and speak softly until he relaxed a little.

'Glad to meet you, Mister…?'

'Hotcross. Just call me Hotcross. Everyone else does this time of year.'

'Glad to meet you, Mr Hotcross.' I offered him a handshake over Lucky's back, while my spare hand continued to stroke and relax Lucky's neck.

Hotcross hesitated in taking my hand, looking at it with a worried expression.

'Not contagious,' I explained. 'Sorry, I should have

mentioned it anyway before I let you jump the fence. How long since your last tetanus shot?'

'Tetanus? Oh, oy. Jenny mentioned something about that. Let me think… not since primary school. I stood on a rusty nail. Went right through my shoe. Must be thirty five years ago. Funny how time slips by…. But those needles last for years, don't they?'

'Not that long.' I noticed a burn mark on his hand that looked recent and red, so I explained the situation properly. 'I strongly suggest you make time as soon as possible, Mr Hotcross.'

'Just Hotcross.'

'My vet suggests it needs to be urgently if you're injured.'

'Ha! Medical advice from a vet. Don't let the lads at work hear that. Now what are we doing here?'

I showed him where to put his hands, how to take the weight and how to help me lift, by explaining how I'd seen my dad and Norbert handling the colt. 'When I say go… we lift together, okay?'

I gave him the nod, and in no time, Lucky popped upright.

'That's my good deed for the day, done.' Hotcross dusted off his hands and jumped the fence again. 'Will he eat a few loaves of stale bread?'

'No, but she will.' I pointed to Penny, standing aside, watching over her baby as always.

'Excellent. Keep an eye out for the Easter Bunny dropping sacks over your fence.'

'You will remember to wash your hands before you cook anything?' I smiled grimly.

He winked and clicked his tongue at me, also making a friendly, funny hand signal as if he'd just fired a pistol at me.

Lucky's eyes cleared slowly, and I stayed with him - talking constantly, and all the while, steadying his rump to prevent him from falling over again.

7:26am My dog and three cats came down the yard, looking for me. Not all at once. They came wanting breakfast, no doubt, but stayed, surrounding me at various heights on the fence and swing, checking out the foal and providing us both with comfort – except Muffy, my little bed monster. She decided to feed me for a change, climbing the mulberry tree and hanging over us, swatting at mulberries – which fell and hit me like heavy rain drops.

'Cut that out, Muffy! Go find a mouse for breakfast.'

'You say something?' asked my dad. He walked down between two citrus trees, skinning the yellow fruit he'd just picked. 'Good grief! Are you sick?' he asked, staring at my face.

I wiped a purple splotch of mulberry off my cheek and forehead. 'New disease.' I pointed up the tree to Muffy. 'Kitten-itis.'

'Looks like a rash. Better rub a green berry over those blotches to vanish the stain before your mother sees you. She'll have a heart attack.'

I chuckled, knowing there'd be no chance of that. 'If anyone can take bizarre things in her stride, it's Mum.'

'How's the patient?' he asked.

'He had me worried when I first came down. What time did Mum leave him?'

'Around midnight. Her eyes were hanging out of her head.'

'No, that was me. I left at quarter to.'

'That was her too. She came up a few minutes after you.'

'A few *minutes*?' I could hardly believe it. 'So he could have been down all this time?' I clenched my fists, furious. Not at Mum really, since I knew how hard she worked. I just felt flustered at the whole situation. Yet I couldn't let myself utter a single sound of frustration. That initial deal to let me get a horse years ago laid responsibility entirely at my feet, and I still accepted it without question or hesitation. No regrets either, except for being talked into going to bed. I took it as a lesson, determined not to let it happen again. If the foal had to stay up, then I would too.

'Need another break?' Dad asked, unaware of my fresh resolve.

'Never again, I dare say.'

He watched me standing with my legs crossed, fidgeting and holding my tummy.

'You sure?' He grinned knowingly.

'I'm fine.' I crossed my legs tighter.

'So if I went over to that tap, and turned on the water… let it splash or drip… drip… drip… on the fruit trees, that wouldn't worry you?' His grin widened, wickedly, as if he might actually do it.

'Okay, so I'm busting for the little fillies' room,' I confessed. 'But I can't go.'

'At *all?*' he chuckled.

'Not yet. Not even for a second. He's wobbly, Dad. It's too soon since his last fall, and he's been down too long already. I just have to tough it out for another hour or so.'

'I'll stay with him.'

I chewed on my lip. 'The whole time?'

'Until you get back.'

'You'd need to keep your hand on his rump the whole time too, like this. No detours for more fruit,' I warned him.

Dad's hand went to Lucky's rump, mimicking me.

'Thanks, Dad.' I hugged him, barely able to get my arms around him. "Fuel tank for a love machine," he called his stomach, but really, at six-four, born and raised on a farm, he didn't have that much fat on him. He really was a big boy, and mostly muscle. He could lift the rear of a car around in our driveway until the car faced the opposite direction.

'Five minutes,' he said. 'I've got an engine to get back to.'

I checked my watch. 'Great. It's 9am. That gives me time to call the vet now as well, please. I'll be quick.' Easter weekend or not, if the sun was up, so was Dad, and always busy, so I had to work in with him.

'Do you have to bother the vet this early?'

Jogging away, I reached the back door and glanced back to check on them. 'He asked for a daily status report and he should be open by now.'

'Go. Do.' Dad offered the foal a sniff at his orange. 'We've got big boy's business down here anyway.'

The colt could barely react more than a slight bend of his nose — could hardly move at all really, and didn't seem to like the orange any more than his mother did, but any reaction at all told me something. Two things, in his case. He still had an innocent curiosity for life; and his senses of smell still worked, which also suggested that not every nerve in his throat could be malfunctioning.

I wished I'd tested him yesterday so I could compare any progress, one way or the other. Live and learn.

I made a mental note to discuss it with Norbert, right after the little fillies' room

'Keep him moving,' came Norbert's advice over the phone. 'Gently, slowly, patiently. Take him through everything, like slow motion. A horse isn't designed for confinement. Their body functions begin to shut down. That's part of the reason why race horses need exercise when they're confined to stables. Aside from logistics, it makes them need to run, as well as want it.'

I ran outside, skidding to a halt in bare feet on the concrete path and heard Dad talking. I crept the rest of the way, expecting to catch him talking over the fence to a neighbour while Lucky lay fallen, abandoned, behind him. Instead, I found them under the mulberry tree together – Dad offering the colt a sweet young leaf with juicy berries, and a pep talk.

'Mmmm, yummy, num-num,' Dad said, pretending to eat some of it too. 'Got to get you back to your old appetite, son. I can't eat all these by myself.'

The foal sniffed it. Tried to eat, but couldn't get his lips or teeth open enough to get it into his mouth, no matter how much Dad tried to help or inspire him.

10am Time for his daily needles. The first of many that I'd need to administer. Norbert had stocked me up with all the medications, syringes and know-how; all cold in my hands now from the kitchen fridge … but it wasn't the cold that made my hands shake. I hated needles myself, and yet I'd much rather receive than give.

Luckily for me, while calling around all the hospitals, I'd chanced across a medic from the flying doctor service in the outback whose father had been a bush stockman with a swag full of old bush remedies. He'd advised me, 'If it comes time for needles, rub a smooth salt stone or river pebble around the target zone a few times, before puncturing, to numb the area. A chunk of rock salt is better, because it also kills surface germs. Then watch to see if the horse prefers the shot, fast or slow, so you'll know for next time.'

From my own booster shots, I knew I preferred them dead slow, so that's how I tried it first with the biggest shot of 20mLs of Penicillin. Lucky needed this huge dose three times a day into his muscle, so I put it roughly a hand-span from his tail, avoiding the softest skin, and marked beside the spot with the dot of a thick black marking pen, keeping the ink away from the fresh puncture, so I'd be able to choose a slightly different spot tomorrow to avoid soreness.

Provided he survived that long.

I performed the same ritual for the smaller daily anti-tetanus shot for his neck or shoulder.

Lucky hardly seemed to notice any of them – mainly because my mum chose that moment to offer him a drink of water from a bucket that she'd warmed to skin temperature. Much easier on his tummy than cool water. He'd been sucking it up slowly, and that simple task consumed all his concentration until he could swallow it. He must have registered the pain of the needles soon after, however, because we never got away with that trick of distraction again.

All day, Mum, Dad and I took turns standing by his rump, helping him to keep balance. Minimum one hour each. The alternative: certain death. If we'd left him on the ground that day; there's no doubting it. He never would have made it up on his own, ever again.

2pm He needed a few hours' sleep, same as any baby, but pain seemed to be keeping the little guy from getting any. Each leg seemed to hurt equally, so he stood squarely, with his feet in a wider rectangle and his weight shared more evenly than usual.

His mother, like all adult horses, could doze on her feet for hours, often shifting her weight from one back leg to another, just for a change of muscle, but when Lucky tried that, he began teetering. His rump swayed from side to side, often bumping against her. She stayed close for a while as his leaning post. But if he leaned away from her, without a human hand to keep him balanced, every time he dozed, he fell over.

And he hated falling. It scared him literally rigid every time he felt himself going over, and it made him strain all the more, trying to stay upright, or get up again. Yet I knew he needed to sleep on the ground each day *on each side*, to help keep his stomach digesting properly and his bones growing normally, without the constant weight on them. Dad called it flipping the pancake, and Lucky hadn't flipped his cake in two days.

If he couldn't sleep, I wouldn't. It seemed the only way I could keep him moving, rearrange his environment, and, stimulate his skin by grooming him. Anything and everything to keep him interested in life and keen to keep breathing. The more often I grew dozy, the more resourceful I became to stay awake, without any noise or lights. I could only use my voice and grooming brushes. I soon learned that it was easier to stay awake long after exhaustion sank in, if I sang to him.

The goal: to keep him going long enough that his daily dose of anti-toxins could overwhelm the toxins. I was tired, but unlike him, my body wasn't being racked with waves of pain that often spasmed up to agony. In our loneliest moments, I wavered a few times, torturing myself over whether or not I was still doing the right thing, keeping him going.

Yet every time I weakened, every time that I thought it would be kinder to call for that final green syringe, I'd crouch down with my little mate and ask him eye-to-eye... and I'd look not just at his eyes, but his whole body language, and every time... *every* time... it was *his* strength and *his* courage... *his* fierce determination to get through it, which kept me going.

That also made the responsibility weigh so much heavier on my drooping shoulders. With each passing minute, I knew I'd have to think of something soon, so he could get some rest finally.

28. End of the Marathon (DAYS 3 & 4)

Mark Twain,
an American "humorist",
(which is like a literary comedian who
creates sight-gags using only words),
once said;

*It's not the size of the dog in the fight,
it's the size of the fight in the dog.*

... which also applied to horses, apparently.
My little guy was still smaller than a Shetland pony,
but he was fighting like a war horse on steroids.

By 2am on Easter Sunday Lucky was virtually dead on his feet, so to speak, and so was I. My voice had gone croaky from singing to him, and my parents gathered for the great debate.

'Foals need their sleep,' Dad reminded me, 'and Lucky isn't getting any standing up 20 hours a day --and the other four are therapy after he's fallen, so it hardly counts as rest.'

'A sleeping body is a healing body,' Mum added. 'So perhaps he's not healing on his feet as well as he could be? If we could lay him down, maybe...'

Except the only way to get him down, required a fall. And Lucky hated to fall.

Possible solution: to lay him down slowly and gently.

Dad seemed strong like a tank, even recovering from his cracked ribs, but Lucky was built like one; and top heavy.

An awkward shape for laying down manually, if we had to do it slowly and gently. We needed a strong blanket to use as a stretcher and another three strong men. One for each corner.

Mum and I could serve together as one, but that still left two strong helpers to find.

At two in the morning.

Crikey, was I going to be popular.

'The house down the back has a light on,' Dad said.

I looked that way too, and realised he meant Hotcross, no doubt preparing for another bakery shift. I noticed a sack of bread by the fence down there, that Penny had been hoeing into. Judging by the spread of crumby debris, apparently she'd entertained herself by playing football with the loaves first. I must have been so tired and focused on Lucky, that I hadn't noticed.

'I'll go talk to him,' Dad said.

I turned around twice, wondering which of our other neighbours would hate me the least for waking them. Then I realised there were three in the street who already expected trouble from me; Mrs Parker, a frail old woman. Mr Nosey, even frailer. And Jim.

No lights on at his place, I noticed.

Leaving Mum behind with Lucky, I vaulted over the fence into the darkened gardens next door on a beeline for his driveway, wondering how I could ever wake him without stirring the rest of his family.

I crossed a gravel path along the way, so I scooped up a handful of tiny pebbles, intending to toss one or two at Jim's window to wake him. Clichéd, but hopefully effective.

However, my legs overtook my brain along the way, and at his window, I tossed the lot of them by accident.

I dropped to my knees in horror, gasping and puffing. When he opened his window and saw me, I had no idea yet how to ask him. I only noticed he was shirtless, which also made me wonder if he was naked.

Stunned by how handsome he really was, I had to shake myself back to my senses.

Clasping my hands together, I opened my mouth to plead my case to him, but he cut me off with a roll of his eyes.

'Why am I not surprised to see you out there at this hour?'

'It's Lucky. He...'

Jim disappeared, pulling the window closed behind him, and I could hardly blame him. I spun around, reassessing my options, glancing to all the other houses down this end of the street, and trying to remember names for all the occupants. On the far side of the road; the new tenants at 48 were a florist and junior dentist. At 46, a truck driver... truck driver! *Ding!* What was his name? I tried to remember if I'd ever heard it.

I bolted back along Jim's driveway, trying to think more clearly through my own exhaustion, and already looking both ways for traffic. Brain not caught up yet. Two in the morning. Duh! No traffic for hours.

A light came on as I crossed the kerb. Not only in my head. I saw Jim's front porch light flickering... and his front door opening. Jim; shirtless in the halo of light that made him look like an angel in boxer shorts. Jim; naked from the waist up, and juggling two flashlights. He looked hilarious, fumbling to scramble into a pyjama shirt, not pausing for the buttons. He left it flapping open down his chest.

'Boots,' he said, in the same time it took for him to grab them, and running... hopping down the stairs and street, he somehow managed to get them on before we crossed the road together.

'I didn't think you were...'

'Coming?' he laughed. 'I wouldn't miss it if you paid me.

How often does a guy see a damsel in distress these days?'

'Hey! I'm no damsel!'

'Argue with distress, I dare you.'

He switched on a torch, also offering one to me as we passed beyond the reach of the nearest street light.

I snatched them *both* off him.

'Forget those,' I said, switching off his again.

'Hey, I wasn't going to use it anywhere near him.'

'Glad to hear it, but you'll see more if you let your eyes adjust naturally first.'

The deed itself took barely a minute. We used Penny's thick weatherproof horse rug as the stretcher to help lay him down. He still tensed up all the way to the ground, but we all crouched around him like campers around a bushfire, stroking and patting him – and Hotcross began to croon a lullaby to him in the most beautiful male voice I'd ever heard, aside from my father's.

Dad joined in too for the second run through, and then we all did until the colt's eyes closed.

Sleep tight, little laaady.
Sleep tight little man.
Sleep tight when it's suuunny.
Sleep tight in the rain.
Sleep tight in your bedroooom.
Sleep tight in your camp.
Sleep tight till it's morrrning
Sleep so we can sleep.

I'd never heard it before or since, but it worked a treat. We covered him over with extra rugs to keep him warm, as the chill set in ahead of the dawn.

On day four, I woke at 4:08am, well before the bird again,

and crept downstairs into the dew. I saw Penny at the back fence, nibbling again at fresh bread, while Lucky laid exactly as we'd left him, breathing, snuggled up. And then the rug moved.

I peeled it back to investigate, and found a brown snake! One of the most venomous snakes in the world. A big one, too, curled around his legs and against his tummy. I fell backwards in fright. It wasn't uncommon to see snakes at any time of year near the river. I'd just never seen one that big. It had to be four metres at least, and had a bulge in its belly as if it had swallowed a bird or small cat.

Scrambling to gather my wits and fighting my own fears, I ripped down a leafy branch from the far side of the mulberry tree and tried to encourage the snake away, hoping not to stir it up enough to make it mad at me.

Up and along Lucky's body it slithered on its way to the nearest fence... *Poor Lucky*! I saw his eyes, terrified. He took a fit, just as it slid over and away from his head. Worst spasm ever! At the height of it, even his eyes seemed to paralyze.

I had to redirect the snake and usher it away again as it tried to turn back on me, then I leapt back to Lucky's side, praying he hadn't been bitten anywhere before I'd arrived.

I checked his muzzle for any sign of his soft breath, and discovered something far worse.

No heartbeat.

29. Dead Again

Bugs Bunny
once danced and sang with Elmer Fudd;

The wabbit kicked the bucket...
The bucket kicked the wabbit...

That's exactly the kind of
dance-around-death days
we were having.

Lucky's body tensed up so rigidly, his breathing stopped as well as his heart.

I patted him, talking to him, trying not to cry and praying for him to go whichever direction he truly wanted or needed to go. Up towards the light, or back to my voice. Either way, I promised that his mum and I would keep him in our hearts, always.

His body relaxed, and let go of the air from his lungs.

I breathed back into them for him, first one and then the other. I already had been, but kept going twice more before I realised it.

After a time that felt like eternity, but couldn't have been more than a few seconds, he sucked in a small breath by himself.

His eye moved to look at me.

I burst into tears.

A miracle. I'd witnessed a first-hand miracle.

I thanked God and all the colt's lucky stars, and raved

how clever he was. Then it struck me. This was Easter; no time of the year more appropriate for resurrection.

'I'm going to get you up,' I promised. 'But I need help, little mate, so I have to go find somebody. That means I have to leave you for a minute, but I'll come straight back, okay? You know I will.' I stroked his head, repeating my promise. He looked at me pleadingly, so when I rose, I kept talking - calling back to him all the way to the house, thankful that he drew comfort enough from my voice.

I called louder than I needed to inside the house too, giving him something else to think about and know that I hadn't strayed too far from him. Making our time apart seem so much shorter, I hoped.

I ran around the square base of the stairs and nearly crashed face-first into my sister, Rae, dressed as a cute bunny rabbit. Gorgeous, as always, fresh home from her school's Easter party and sleepover in the gymnasium. Dropped off by her friend's parents, but still with her hair, make-up and heels no less shiny than she'd been at the start of the night, dancing. Bunny ears; a little crushed and wilted, but her rabbit tail, freakishly fluffy. To me, she still looked perfectly prim, yet she never hesitated in dashing down to muck in the mud with me. She didn't care about her best stockings or dress either. She didn't even bother taking off her Easter Rabbit ears. She simply kicked off her gold shoes and plucked off her earrings.

Then two minutes with me, and she looked like she'd been mugged by a cyclone.

Gotta love her. It's always like that between us.

My parents weren't far behind us, and nor was Jim, who'd heard me calling out for help.

Thankfully, lifting the colt wasn't nearly so difficult as laying him down. He wanted to get up more than anything -

and after that snake, I knew it would be a long time before he'd want to go down again. He'd have more seizures than ever that day, as if he couldn't put the memory of that snake out of his head.

I couldn't either. Every time I closed my eyes to rest on my feet, a nightmarish snake crawled up inside the leg of my jeans.

We stood him up and I stayed with him, steadying his rump and cuddling him, while my parents went back to bed. Reluctantly, Jim and my sister agreed to leave too, but only after I assured them I'd be okay on my own.

As they turned away, I noticed that one of my sister's rabbit ears had broken and flopped down comically – and I realised *Rabbit* would be the perfect nickname for her, given that she hated her real name so much she'd banned us all from using it. I started to wonder if Jim had a name that he might prefer too, since his parents also called him James or Jimmy.

Not that it mattered, I decided, as I watched him walk out of my life. He'd be crazy to answer another rock at his window, or any other plea from me. And even if he *had* been closer to my age, I knew I could never be as attractive as my sister or the other girls I'd seen with him.

I wiped dirt off my cheek and turned my whole attention back to Lucky, deciding that the only guy for me would have to be a big strong farmer's lad, with his own horse and a love for them already. I also resigned myself to the fact that I'd never get a chance to meet him until *after* I moved out of the city.

A few hours later, my sister returned with a smile to watch the sunrise with me. I startled at the sight of her. She always slept in on weekends and public holidays. So much so, that I doubt she'd ever seen the sun on the Eastern side of the sky on any day but a school day.

'I thought you were asleep?' I asked, brightening a little myself.

She still wore her Easter rabbit ears from the party, so it took me a few seconds longer to notice that she'd changed into casual jeans and my floppiest blue t-shirt, which swum on her. It always looked more fashionable on her, of course, so I never cared if she borrowed it. Or *any* of my clothes, for that matter. Instead, I took it as a compliment that someone as stylish as her could like some of my things. I also knew she would have asked first, except I'd already told her that anything in my closet was fair game. She never woke before me, so anything I needed, was already on me for the day anyway.

'I'm still wired,' she said. 'Plus I've got friends picking me up in a few hours to go water skiing.' She tugged out the shoulder strap of her black bikini to reveal it underneath. 'You should let me take over here until then and catch a break.'

I smiled, admiring her energy. Thirteen years old and she had a social life far more lively than mine, which was practically flat-lining.

I shrugged, not wanting to leave. 'Love the ears,' I said, hoping to change the subject. 'They make you look like a rebel rabbit.' I mentioned it might make an appropriate nickname, considering how fast and easily she seemed to breed friends.

She giggled, and broke the news that I hadn't been the first to suggest it, and the name stuck.

'Listen, if you're really going to stay,' she pleaded, 'at least have the good sense to sit down on the swings and take a load off your feet, for once. I'll stay with him. I promise.'

I peered around dad's little fruit grove and realised if I sat over there, I'd lose my clear line of sight to Lucky. Not that I didn't trust my sister with him. I'd trust her with just about anything. We didn't have any of that teenaged angst that every book and TV show loves to present as the stereotype. To be honest, I didn't even *know* anybody like that. I simply needed to keep my eyes on the foal to be sure he was okay.

My responsibility, I kept thinking, and I really didn't want to let him down again.

Rabbit shook her cute little fist at me, making her gold bangles jingle as she pointed to the nearby fence between us and the Vietnam refugees. That boundary, like the other three, was nearly two decades old and made of wire mesh with a timber rail at the top.

I used to walk along it when I was little, pretending to be a famous trapeze artist – until mum yelled at me from her office window; 'Get down before you break your neck!'

'Fence. Sit,' Rabbit ordered finally, and I gave in.

For all of ten seconds. Too tired to think straight, I dashed off to fetch a chair for her, so she could be more comfortable while staying close to Luck, but all the spare chairs in our house were lined up in the waiting room for customers, and would have been ruined if I'd brought them out into the muddy yard. It never occurred to me that I could have used it sooner, because I needed to keep up with him if he moved.

'You're bizarre,' Rabbit said when I returned empty handed. 'Don't you get it? *You're* the one who needs help down here.'

She fetched a stump from the front garden for me – a short cylindrical cross-section from another mulberry tree which had died years ago.

'Wet,' she said, brushing it off. 'Maybe when the sun's higher…?'

'She needs something better than that,' Mum said,

appearing with dad for an early visit.

Somewhere nearby, I heard a neighbour's grandfather clock chime 5am.

Dad veered over to his garage, unlocked a small fuel drum from a string of them on a chain, and came back to me with it.

'Try this,' he said, leaving it with me. 'Sit on it instead of the wet ground. Just put it back with the others when you're finished.'

I nodded, but Lucky needed me to keep him steady a while longer, so I didn't get a chance to try the drum as a seat for almost an hour.

Being empty and made of only thin metal, it began to crumple the moment I sat on it, so I filled it with tap water — not realising my mistake or the bizarre chain of events it would trigger.

My sister's friends never showed up, so she brought me a Vegemite sandwich about 10am, which for me was breakfast. For her too, actually.

I inspected it first, to make sure she'd buttered it right out to the edge. 'Hey, where's my cheese?'

'Hiding,' she grinned. 'In my tummy.' She stuck two fingers into her mouth and asked if I wanted it back in one piece, or many.

I laughed. First laugh in ages, and I really needed it. 'You're repulsive,' I teased. 'But at least you make repulsive look good.'

'Only when I stand close to you, sis. Need another break?' She mimed a boy hosing the garden from his groin.

'Nah, I'm fine. But thanks for asking.'

She hugged Lucky, then headed back to the house.

Alone again. A nasty butcher-bird swooped past us

screeching, chasing a baby pigeon. It triggered a fit for poor Lucky – the first of six in a row, followed by more every hour all morning until Norbert's visit, scheduled at 12:30pm.

He arrived with five minutes to spare, and I felt so grateful.

Considering the complication we'd had that morning with the snake, and that Lucky's tension levels didn't seem to recede as much between spasms, he recommended sedation using Acetyl Promazine to help prevent the fits which were coming every few minutes now. They didn't all take him to the brink of death, although they all threatened heart failure, or brain damage. But I'd also learned that if I noticed the onset of a spasm swiftly enough from the look in his eye, and began stroking and crooning to him straight away, I could calm him enough to prevent his heart stopping. Usually.

'How can you tell a fit's coming on?' Norbert asked.

'He shifts his weight a little, trying to catch my eye – sort of pleadingly, and then we work together trying to beat it.'

I explained how I suspected it was mainly due to that snake, but Norbert couldn't find any sign or symptoms of a bite. Instead he pointed out that the heavy clouds had begun to thin, allowing the sun to peek through for the first time in days, so the shade of the mulberry tree was no longer dark enough to prevent fits from his hypersensitivity to light. We needed a stable with increasing urgency. Somewhere much darker, quieter and 'safe-feeling'.

We also needed the ground to dry out faster than possible. Mud stank worse than manure, and made working in the backyard all the more miserable.

'Wouldn't it be nice if mud behaved more like a wet beach?' I said. 'It would be so much cleaner and easier to work on.'

So Dad contacted one of his customers, who owned the local landscaping and soil supplies, and called in a favour — which resulted in the instant delivery of a truckload of free beach sand.

My sister stayed by Lucky's rump, keeping him upright, while the rest of us shoveled the sand over all the dampest spots and walking tracks. It soaked up the water beautifully, evaporated much faster than soil, and seemed much healthier and cleaner to walk on. But I also knew from horse care books that sand can accumulate in an equine's stomach — and kill them with colic, a condition where their gut twists up in knots or telescopes over itself, trying to pass out the sandy grains. So now we had to watch Penny every minute of the day too, and make sure she never ate any grass near the sand.

'Can I borrow her for a few hours to eat the grass over at my place?' Donny asked. 'My mower is still sick anyway.'

'Oh, wow! She'd love it!' I said gratefully. 'As quiet and well behaved as she is, I can tell she's getting a bit grumpy at being fenced up in such a small area. I have to feed her the best quality hay and grain so her milk is as good as it can be, but it's also making her feel fit to get out and stretch her legs. What she really needs is exercise, but I can't spare the time away from Lucky.'

I couldn't even spare the time to drive across town and check on Apache and Snow, and that was killing me, even though Mum and Dad had volunteered to take turns checking them once a day for me.

'Perfect solution,' Donny suggested. 'If we take off the top rail of the fence, we can lay down a couple of panels of wire mesh so she can run over it and do laps of my house.'

'Genius,' I said. Being an old-style boundary fence with one strip of wire mesh that stretched down the whole boundary, removing a single panel wasn't an option. It was too much work to take down the fence completely, so Donny simply bumped off the timber rail for two sections with a hammer - pulling out all the nails from the posts to remove any chance of injuries. Then he laid down the wire, making it almost flat in the centre.

I covered the flat wire with Snowy's oldest winter horse rug, using it like a bridge to save Penny's hooves from getting snagged in the wire mesh as she walked over it.

Penny figured out what we were up to about halfway through the job, and hung close, keen to try it.

'Go ahead, girl,' I said, and stood back to let her past me in the safest spot.

She snorted at the strange arrangement, then stepped across cautiously, buried her nose in the fresh lawn and promptly rolled in it to celebrate.

I still had to change the place she ate hay every day along the shed or fence, and file her hooves smooth with my dad's metal rasp — the horse equivalent of a ruler-length nail file - to save her from churning up more mud, simply from the weight of her.

The bizarre weather had also brought on a flea and fly plague, so that day marked the beginning of a new ritual. Twice a day, I'd have to rub both horses down with pyrethrum leaves that mum grew near our rubbish bin to keep away flies — and lavender leaves from the front garden, to help repel the fleas.

Penny didn't like it much. She knocked the herbs out of my hands on my first attempt, and then she stomped on them. Accident or not, I smelled the crushed sap, which seemed to chase off the flies anyway. So then I scattered crushed leaves all over the sand — remembering from my old social studies at school that medieval housewives used to scatter fresh herbs on their kitchen floors for similar reasons —as a bonus, it also stopped Penny from eating off the loose sand. But sand, by itself, didn't work well enough as a barrier against fleas. I'd never seen or heard of a horse with fleas before. Something about their sweat makes them uninhabitable -usually - but Lucky couldn't run, so he couldn't sweat properly. I caught one flea on his white leg, and I couldn't imagine anything more annoying than having skin as sensitive as a horse – as sensitive as a human face - and not being able to scratch an itch, or even stamp his feet. But luckily, scattering lavender on the ground solved that problem too.

Before Norbert left, I seized the chance for a rare break off my feet, and rocked gently in my childhood swings, watching him do all the checks with Lucky's heart, lungs and temperature.

I felt a drip on my shoulder and glanced up at the top bar – the spine of the swing set - to where I'd slung one of Penny's rugs to dry... and realised the solution to the foal's stable had been sitting here all along.

With a metal A-shaped frame at each end as the legs, the old rusty swing set turned into a tent as soon as I spread out Penny's heavy weatherproof rug.

'Hey, Norbert, what do you think about this?' I opened the flap of the rug wider. 'If I unhook all these swings and chains from the top, and get a few ropes running from end to end to hold out the canvas walls from the inside —more like a tent - I might be able to make it really dark in here.'

'Looks a little too rusty.' He came over anyway and tested the strength of the top bar by swinging off it and watching it bend and spring back again under his weight. 'It might work. Let's try it with a sling.'

I recalled him mentioning that once before. 'What sling?'

From the rear of his muddy Landcruiser - which always got priority parking in the driveway - he produced a bright yellow canvas sheet, shaped a bit like a giant band-aid. Black ropes and hooks hung off every corner, and while he untangled it, like sorting out a tangled fishing line, my dad and brother came to dismantle the swings and remove them from the support frame.

Another young apprentice came from the garage to help too. He'd agreed to work the public holiday to help Dad with an urgent job on an old lady's Mercedes, but the curly haired kid was so hopeless, dad had relegated him to cleaning parts, so he stank of oil and grease, which only managed to upset Penny. I sent him away twice, but he never went far enough.

'This is a small cow sling,' Norbert explained to me, with a circle of intrigued customers and neighbours gathering - including Donny. 'Farmers rent them from me to help keep their best young beasts off the ground during three day sickness, tick fever, calving paralysis or whatever else they happen to go down with. It's not suitable if the animals are heavily pregnant, obviously, because all the weight rests on their stomach.'

This was all news to me. None of the books I'd read had ever mentioned a sling, much less provided a diagram or description.

I smiled, trying to cheer myself up. 'I doubt pregnancy will be a problem for him.'

'You never know when you might need to know that later for a pregnant animal in future, so it's worth mentioning. There's other slings designed with holes to let a swollen tummy hang through, and bigger ones for adult horses, but this size is about the only size I have that might fit him. Fingers crossed everyone… We're going to use it to help keep him on his feet, so he can't fall over again, and so he won't need someone with a hand to steady him every second.'

'Crikey, I could have used that three days ago.'

'Not unless you wanted to string him up like a chandelier. The roof in your Dad's spare shed is too high, or I would have tried it earlier. I also noticed the rafters are too thin to support his weight, and too far apart to let the sling hang properly. Same goes for the rafters on your back patio.'

'I could rig up some chains to set the proper height,' Dad suggested. 'The shed would certainly keep him a lot drier than a makeshift tent.'

'Concrete under hooves is still dangerous. Given the mulberry tree and the ability to stay near his mum, he's been better off so far there. It's not as if you had anywhere else more suitable until this.'

I thought about our three patios and BBQ area; no exposed rafters there either.

Dad offered to shift his mechanical work into the boatshed so I could use his work-space.

'Concrete floor there too,' Norbert said. 'It's too harsh on sore feet. And his hooves are small enough to fall through the metal grids over the grease traps. You could cover them with a sheet of timber or metal, I suppose, but that still leaves the problems of a hard floor with the smell of toxins.'

'I could hose it out, and bring in stacks of fresh bedding hay,' Dad suggested. 'Maybe buy in a thick layer of soft soil for him?'

'Your decision,' Norbert said. 'But even if you cleared out all the sharp tools, scrubbed the place down thoroughly and opened up all the windows to flush with fresh air, he'll still smell all the exhaust fumes and petrochemicals that have soaked into the walls and floor over the years. It may not bother him visibly, being as well handled and quiet as he is, but that environment is still likely to cause irritation and muscle reflexes. He's loaded up with enough toxins right now. He doesn't need to breathe more, even if it is in small doses.'

'Right,' Dad said. 'The swings it is. We'll need more blankets.'

'Don't set your hopes too high yet,' Norbert warned. 'Your biggest problem with the sling remains the same no matter where you hang it. Getting him in and out, and up and down for regular therapy sessions will involve a few falls and scrapes no matter how careful you try to be, and you'll still need to do it four to six times a day or his muscles will begin to... do you know what atrophy means?'

I nodded. 'Deteriorate. One of my favourite uncles had legs that atrophied after a car accident put him in a wheelchair. But if I'm only bending Lucky's legs, do I really have to lay him down first? Can't I just lift his legs and bend them while he's still in the sling?'

'If he was older, maybe, and well trained enough in lifting his legs co-operatively, but in a foal, his first natural reaction will be to tense up and fight.'

'This is Lucky,' I reminded him. 'How's this?' I demonstrated by running my hand down the colt's front leg, leaning slightly against him, my shoulder against his, and tapping his heel as a signal to relax his weight off it, and lift it into my hand.

He complied by shifting his weight off it a little, and he tried to lift it. He really did. He needed help, and allowed me to lift it for him, but the moment I saw him lean more onto his other leg, and heard him catch his breath in pain, I stroked his shoulder and set his foot down gently – careful not to drop or jar it too sharply.

'Sorry, boy,' I said, stroking all four of his legs. 'We won't try that again until you've got the sling to help take your weight.'

I glanced up in time to see Norbert shaking his head, still

amazed.

'You've certainly got a better chance than most,' he conceded. 'You'll still need to lay him down at least twice a day, and flip him gently for both sides. But at least, you won't need to keep holding him upright, so you should be able to catch some sleep, finally.' He caught my eye and winked, then cast his gaze wider around the small crowd of neighbours and customers. 'Volunteers, please? We need to get this stable over him, rather than making him walk to it.'

Stroke of genius. No shortage of volunteers, and no room left for hands on the swing set, anywhere. Not even for me.

Penny blinked at us, standing back and watching the giant canvas centipede with the metal spine march alongside her foal, then settle over him. Her head went up in alarm, and as I ducked in to check on Lucky and Norbert, she trotted over to poke her head in under the rug too. She sniffed all over her baby, then nudged him, as if reassuring him that she approved.

'You should leave that gap loose for her,' Norbert suggested. 'Make sure she can check on him whenever she wants to.'

'I wish I had some old blankets,' Mum said. 'We could make it a lot darker in here, but we lost all our old spares in the big flood of '74.'

'I'll go see if I can scrounge up a waterproof tarp from somewhere,' Dad said, just as Donny from next door came jogging down the driveway with Dudley, the painter from across the road. Between them, they carried a huge clear plastic drop-sheet, the size of a living room, all splattered with every colour of paint.

'It's got a few punctures here and there,' Dud said, apologetically. 'I tore it accidentally at the last job, so you'll need to patch it with duct tape. Or cut it to shape. Whatever you want. You can have it. I've got all I need for a while.'

Until then, I hadn't noticed the crowd of volunteers thinning, but I certainly noticed them returning - with arms full of old blankets. Mr Nosey had a tattered blanket he'd brought home from the Vietnam War; every bullet hole or stain with its own story. Mrs Parker brought the treasured rug that her old dog had slept on before he'd passed away. An old lady customer fetched a pretty picnic rug from the trunk of her Mercedes, each corner embroidered with the names of her children or grand-children.

Each gift or loaner seemed like a precious treasure. Each came without being requested and I made sure they all hung up out of the mud and stayed sheltered from the rain, as best as possible, under the huge clear painter's tarpaulin. It looked like a colourful, pop-art tent.

Inside it seemed like the perfect temperature, and soothingly dark for Lucky's sore eyes. In fact it was so dark, we had to fold up a flap to provide us with enough light before we could rig up the sling to support him. Then we had to fold up *two* flaps, because the first gap in the tarps crowded in with faces, making it dark again inside, thanks to our growing circle of friends.

30. The Sling

Horace;
that rather insightful Roman poet,
also said;

Prosperity conceals genius.
Adversity reveals it.

I would have settled for clever, or simply functional, but this weird contraption was truly amazing.

Norbert rolled out the widest strip of the sling on the ground under the foal's belly, then raised each corner, until the wide strip of yellow canvas curved around the barrel of Lucky's tummy, like a U, with the corners hooked up to the swing set. He started gradually raising and adjusting the straps, working towards the perfect height to take the weight off Lucky's hooves, slightly, so it would support him without actually lifting him.

'The pain he's been going through so far,' Norbert explained, 'is akin to standing on four broken legs. His ribs and spine have felt broken and bruised too, which is why he's hated falling down so much.'

'And turning over or getting up?'

'Exactly. It also explains any resistance he might have been giving you during therapy, when you've been bending each leg, slowly. It doesn't matter how well-behaved he tries to be, or how careful or gentle you are, he can't physically strain against his own muscles when they tighten up on him so much during a fit. So we need to find the precise point between easing the weight and strain off his feet, and putting too much on his ribs and spine from underneath. Ideally, I'd like to let him swing for a minute, but the surprise of such an unusual sensation is likely to bring on another fit. Remember, it doesn't need to be a sudden fright that triggers them – it can be any form of muscle reaction - even salivation at the smell of his mother's milk. So we need to remain extremely vigilant, quiet and slow-moving.' He cast his gaze to the crowd until he received subtle nods from each of them. They all backed out of sight, quietly.

All the while, Norbert kept adjusting each corner cautiously, also keeping a constant watch on Lucky's reaction.

Outside, I heard voices of three newcomers to the audience, and I recognised them as the toddling twin girls and their mother, who'd moved in recently, five doors down. Part of me wanted to hunt them *all* away - well wishers included - in case they made a sudden noise that could make the colt's hypersensitive reflexes jam up on him, and trigger a fit. But arguing with them could cause it anyway.

'Mummy, can we get a pony too?' called one of the little girls as they came closer down the driveway.

'Shush, sweetie,' whispered the old lady customer who'd loaned me her picnic rug. 'The baby horse is very sick.'

'Don't tell my children to be quiet!' said the mother. 'The city is no place for a horse at all, let alone two of them.'

'Mummy, I want I pony... yeah, can we pat it?' the girls began to chime together, and tried to squeeze through to us.

Lucky caught my eye in that way that told me he felt a fit coming on.

'Oh, no. Here we go.' I cuddled his neck and head,

covered his eyes and began stroking and soothing him, as his body went rigid and began shuddering.

A bad one.

'Ew!' What's it doing?' shrieked the mother, making it worse. 'Don't touch it, girls. Get back here!' She grabbed her kids by their clothes and dragged them back with a warning about catching some kind of rare horrible horse disease.

'And that would be your fault for trespassing down here,' Dad said to her in a low voice. 'What kind of mother brings her little kids closer to a situation she suspects to be dangerous?'

'Oh, what was I supposed to do, Farmer Joe? Chain them up to the front fence like a hitching rail?'

'I'm shocked you'd even consider that as an option,' Dad said. 'You could have simply phoned us to discuss it. Now you'll also need to check with your doctor first thing tomorrow and make sure you're all up to date with your vaccinations.'

'Not going to happen. I'm only here because of the smell. The breeze is sending all the stink of manure down to my place. Get rid of it or I'll have the cops in here so fast…'

I wanted to shout for her to shut up, open her eyes and switch on her brain. The smell wasn't coming from our yard. I'd been collecting Penny's manure as fast as she dropped it and digging it in around mum's roses. The woman lived on the other side of Mr Nosey's place, where he fertilized his lawn and six veggie patches once a month with a foul mix of pulverized blood and bone from the meatworks. The smell usually hung around for three days to a week, and smelled many times worse than fresh horse manure.

'You're making it worse,' whispered Mr Nosey to her, leading her away. 'In this neighbourhood, we watch out for each other.'

I'd never thought of it that way. Most of the time, it felt like he was a watcher and I was a watchee, but with so many concerned faces around me, I could see his perspective now too. Yet my guts twisted up, fearing that this wouldn't be the last I'd hear from that woman.

Lucky relaxed finally, and while I continued to calm and soothe him with my hands and voice, Norbert kept at the painstaking task of winding up the sling. At last, the canvas rose enough to touch the colt's tummy, and I caught my breath.

Another three twitches of each ratchet and the weight lifted off his legs a little. Not enough to raise his hooves off the ground yet. Just enough to replicate floating him in water, but the result took us all by surprise.

He buckled at the knees, collapsing in the sling as his entire body fell limp.

'Oh, no!' I caught his head, just as his nose bumped the ground – and heard the crowd gasp. Supporting his head, I stroked his neck, calling him softly, but no response this time. None at all. I couldn't feel any breath from his nose, and with the canvas in the way now, I couldn't get my ear close enough against his chest by his heart.

He looked dead.

I glanced to Norbert, who seemed just as stunned at Lucky's reaction as me. But then he sprang to action.

'I've never seen anything like this,' he confessed as he checked all of the colt's vital signs.

'Heartbeat and breathing are weak but steady,' he reported. 'Temperature is... holding.' He stepped back for the full picture. 'I think he passed out.'

'You mean he's only sleeping?' asked Dud, the painter. 'Or is that what a coma looks like for a horse?'

'He fell asleep,' Norbert said. 'He *literally* fell... to sleep.

Totally exhausted, poor little guy, but this is how relieved he is to be off his feet. This is day four for him. It's been a real marathon.'

All around, we breathed a sigh of relief. I noticed that even some of the biggest men had damp eyes.

'Try letting his head go now,' Norbert suggested. 'Slowly and gently. It shouldn't worry him if he wakes up later with his nose on the ground.'

I tried, but his legs had relaxed and buckled enough that his muzzle rested on the ground too much for my liking. 'His neck's hanging over the plastic chest support,' I reported from my lower perspective, looking up. 'I think maybe it's constricting his air. Can we lift him a little higher please?'

'Not without raising his hooves to hang in mid-air,' Norbert said, 'and then he's virtually guaranteed to take a fit as he wakes up and realizes he needs to put his feet down to stand up. A strange concept for a horse. The fright could kill him.'

'I've got an idea.' I rushed to fetch the little halter I'd made for him out of macramé twine, fastened it around his head, and used two lead ropes to tie his head up to the spine of the swing set - one lead taking the strain on each side of his cheeks - to help support his head up at a more naturally level position.

Norbert checked his vitals again. 'That worked. He's breathing easier.'

As one, the whole crowd let go another sigh of relief with me.

I shifted my hand up to his rump as I checked him over myself, I didn't want to wake him. But considering how fast he'd passed out, I couldn't help worrying. 'Is it possible that the pressure around his stomach somehow ruptured something internally?'

'I doubt it, but it's worth double-checking.' Norbert grabbed for his stethoscope to listen inside again, this time more thoroughly around Lucky's legs and his little "stallion's tacklebox." He double-checked Lucky's heart, every hand-span across his chest and stomach cavity, and from every angle. He also worked his way around the colt's chest and rump, prodding and poking firmly but gently - all the while watching for the slightest reaction from Lucky.

'What's the difference between this and a coma?' I asked, and pushed my fists into my pockets to stop my hands from shaking.

'Not much. He's not far above borderline. The next few hours will be make or break.'

Easter Monday.

I hadn't been to church in more than a decade, but that was no measure of my faith in the big guy upstairs. As a lover of science and all things mysterious, I spoke to Him every day. Always had, but all this weekend I'd been praying like a minister. I'd been rewarded with my first miracle too, so now I had faith with a capital F.

I also knew Lucky, and trusted him to fight harder than humanly possible. It spawned a new saying at our place. He could *fight like a horse in hell*.

'I wish I could stay,' Norbert said as he stroked the colt's back. 'But I've got another emergency.'

I glanced up and saw him switching off his beeper. He must have had a vibration mode, because I hadn't heard it.

'Please call me the moment there's any change. Good or bad. It should be roughly an hour from now. If you can't get away, get someone else to call me.'

At the end of the first hour, long after the crowd dispersed, I called him anyway. And after the second hour... and the third. I didn't want to pester him that much, but being such a great vet, he really wanted to know... Lucky slept for four hours, fourteen minutes.

Actually, it was four hours, thirteen minutes, but I was so sick of that number, and so wary of "jinxing" him - even though I didn't really buy into that whole good luck/bad luck scene any more – I wasn't taking any chances so I mentally changed it.

'Wow, four hours?' Norbert agreed when I called him. 'So how is he now? Good news or bad?'

I sighed, taking a deep breath. 'Both, I'm afraid...'

Lucky woke abruptly at 5pm, and took a fit. The worst yet. He bucked uncontrollably so much that the entire spine of the swing set buckled. The top support beam bowed down about a foot and now it couldn't keep him off the ground. In fact, the sling hung so loosely under his tummy now that it annoyed him far more than it helped. Once again he seemed better off under the mulberry tree, so I set him "free" while keeping my arm around his rump to help keep him from falling over.

He staggered to the darkest shade under the mulberry tree, where Penny met him, keen to be milked. Instinct probably, since they both seemed to need the reminder that he couldn't twist his neck up enough to feed himself. The shade from the tree no longer satisfied him either, and turning around stiffly, he headed back to the darker shade of his makeshift stable. He made it all the way in to the sling, and tried to stand over it, as if he could somehow make it work again by himself.

I tried calling out for help from Mum or Dad, but they must have been inside having dinner with the TV on. Nobody else seemed to be within earshot either.

Except Mr Nosey, who had his nose glued to his window as usual, bless him.

He came to our rescue, along with Dud, the painter – this time carrying a plank which reinforced the swing's bent metal spine.

Dad must have seen them come in and he emerged with an even better idea. Soon they had rigged up our "dog and chain" from the truck to pull up the support bar and re-secure it to the plank. He also borrowed another two chains from the truck driver down the street.

I seized the chance of having others handy to whisk around and do all my chores for the mare and foal. I tossed Penny a fresh biscuit of hay and gave her a cup of crushed pollard, bran and mixed grain, and used the time that she stood still contentedly to milk her into an ice-cream container. Mixing that with some bran flakes and pollard mash, I made the runny porridge for Lucky's next syringe-feeding session.

Lucky tried to slurp and suck it up from the bucket faster by himself, but he could barely move his tongue enough now to swallow. It took me nearly half an hour to get half a cup into him, but it was enough to trigger his internal functioning. He managed to hang out his little fire hose and give me time to catch the splash in a spare bucket, in case Norbert needed to see a urine sample during his next visit.

Then Lucky fell straight back to sleep.

I hooked up his halter, supporting his head, and checked my watch to ensure my next report to Norbert would be accurate.

'Did you get any sleep yet yourself?' asked Dud, the painter.

'She won't leave him,' Dad replied for me. 'The most rest she's had so far is when I brought her an empty fuel drum to sit on beside him at three this morning.'

'Oh, that reminds me,' I said. 'I had to fill it with water so it wouldn't crumple.'

'You did *what?*' asked the truck driver. 'You can't mix fuel with water.'

'Never mind,' Dad said, patient as always. 'I'll get an apprentice to clean it out. The point is, she needs better rest than she's getting.'

'I'm fine,' I argued. 'It's not like I can't lean against a tree or sit on the fence or stump occasionally. It's a lot easier now that we can keep a patch of ground dry around him. I can squat right here.'

'Four days, and she's been on her feet nearly the whole time,' said Mr Nosey. 'Except for four hours, and only three of those were to sleep.'

I blinked at him, noticing only then that he'd returned with a wheelbarrow and shovel, which he used to collect Penny's latest horse "apples." [A polite term for manure.]

'For my garden,' he said to the others. 'I told that young woman I'd be collecting it twice a day, and digging it into my garden to minimise the smell.'

'Wow, thanks,' I said, 'but I can bring it down to your place during a break, if you really want it.' I didn't need him keeping any closer watch on me.

'It's all arranged. You've got enough on your hands.'

'Time for sleep then,' Dad suggested.

'I can't leave him now,' I complained. 'This late in the day, he could sleep for five minutes or five hours. If he's going to take a fit each time he wakes up, I need to be here.'

'The sand in there is still too damp to rest on,' Donny argued. 'I've got an old bar stool you can have. A bit rickety, but it's a lot more comfortable than a stump or fuel drum.'

'She can have an old leather sofa from the office,' Dad said. 'There's enough room in the corner beside the colt's head.' He went to fetch it down to the makeshift tent for me, which surprised me, because that white leather chair had once been his favourite and I feared for it surviving outside under the rough shelter.

We shifted it into place, waking Lucky briefly by accident, but within minutes, he seemed to love it as much as me. He wanted to nap with his head on my lap, or hooked over my shoulder.

'You should try power napping,' suggested the truck driver. 'My wife does it every night the baby won't sleep.' He explained how to use my wrist watch with an alarm to help teach myself. 'Just set it for five to fifteen minutes at a time, stick it in your back pocket so you feel it more than hear it, then wake up when it goes off, do whatever you need to do, and re-set it again. Do it a few times, exhausted, and you'll soon see how fast you can train your body-clock to cope.'

'Thanks,' I said, grateful as they all left me to it.

By the third alarm, those little naps began to feel like hours of sleep.

Midnight, Day 4 I realised the foal's bowels hadn't moved all day. I worried that he might be shutting down inside. However, he'd urinated twice, so I hoped he was just using up all the food I could get into him, leaving nothing as solid waste.

I made a note to mention it to Norbert anyway.

31. Dawn of the Prowler (Day 5)

Plautus,
a Roman playwright of comedies around 200BCE,
allegedly said;

*Good courage in a bad matter
is half of the evil overcome.*

Yeah, I wish.
If the mathematics had been that simple,
I would have quadrupled my courage
and overcome the whole dang thing by midnight.

By **1am** It grew chilly that early Tuesday morning – *icy chilly* – and I worried that the cold would make Lucky's legs ache even more. I dashed up to the laundry for a pile of old towels, and wrapped them around his body and neck on top of the rug I'd already made for him. A woolly beanie worked well as a hat with holes cut out for his ears. I also sleeved some old thin socks up his legs and tugged them up past his knees.

They kept falling down on him, and bandages were too scarce to waste on anything but wounds, so it took a bit of experimenting, but I finally managed to get his legs warm by cutting the legs off two old pairs of jeans, pulling them up around his legs like trousers, and then securing them over his shoulder using a line of string over his back to tie them together; one trouser leg to the other.

Mutual support. Two great words, I thought.

I shifted the sofa until he could hang his head over my shoulder so we could use each other's heads for a pillow as we slept together. Dog at my feet, cat on my lap; the full set of us napping.

It wasn't the wrist watch that woke me at 2am. I heard movement in the yard behind Donny's place. A dog barked in the next yard over. Just a poodle in a pen, but then I heard running – and something scrambling over the fence and thudding into our place.

I leapt to my feet in time to glimpse the shadow of a man skidding to a halt, in his dark clothes and sneakers. Almost without thinking I braced my stance for a fight, as I'd learned in basic high school self defence, but he didn't seem to care about me. He'd been stopped by a fearsome sight that startled me too.

It was Penny, as I'd never seen her before or since. As vicious as any stallion, she protected her baby by rearing up at the prowler – the first and only time I'd ever seen her rear up at anything. But with a black stocking pulled down over his face and his pale hair flattened, to her he wouldn't have looked entirely human.

He darted towards us and grabbed the fuel drum that I'd been using for a seat and forgotten to put away. He tried to dash further our way, but Penny cut him off, lashing and gnashing at him with hooves and teeth. She hunted him out over the back fence – jumping over it too and chasing him all the way out through the baker's place, into *his* street.

'Penny!' I called, fearing he might turn on her and whack her in the head with that fuel drum full of water. 'Come back here, girl.' She spun on her heel and came straight back towards me. But now she was on the other side of the fence, walking up and down, as if searching for a gate to come home – as if she had no idea how she got on the wrong side of the fence in the heat of the moment.

Hotcross noticed her in his yard when he came down to unlock his car for work. I explained what happened but he only grinned — moreso when he spotted a patch of bloodied denim jeans on his grass.

'Looks like she's been horsing around,' he joked. 'And like most women, she's got bad taste in men.'

'It's not funny,' I complained. 'The ground's too soft for her to jump safely home with me, if I tried to ride her over it. She could break a leg landing in mud with my extra weight, and I can't leave Lucky to ride her around the long way until after dawn, when my dad comes down.'

'So leave her in here,' he suggested. 'I'll be glad for it. She can eat as much as she wants. No gardens to worry about. I'll shut the gate on my way out, and our shadowy prowler won't be too keen to come back.'

'Wow, really?' I could hardly believe it. Aside from Donny's yard, the baker had the only other yard with absolutely nothing in it to worry about. No poisonous plants. No ceramic garden gnomes to break if she bumped them. Nothing within reach of her long neck into his neighbors' yards either, aside from their concrete driveways. 'I know she'll be very glad for the extra room and grass.'

'Settled then. When I get home, I'll grab your Dad, and he can help me lay down the fence like that one into Donny's place, so she can come and go as she pleases.'

That gave Penny over half an acre, all up. Plus another three yards in various directions by the end of the next day, after word spread about what she'd done to the prowler. One of the neighbours even joked they'd have to fire their dog and buy a pony.

3am I woke again to the sound of footsteps. This time, behind me. I grabbed a broken syringe out of a little bucket for rubbish preparing to defend myself. It struck me as bizarre for a quiet girl like me to be threatening anyone with a bent needle for penicillin, of all things, but it's all I had.

'Come on out,' I dared them. 'I'll take care of you.'

'Oh, that's a terrible play on words,' said a familiar voice.

It took me a second longer for my brain to click into gear.

'Relax, Neet,' he said. 'It's only me.'

His shadowy familiar shape emerged from the morning fog, yet I could hardly believe my eyes and ears.

'Jim?' I scratched my head, nearly poking myself with the needle by accident. 'What are you doing here?'

'Hour of the wolf.' He came past the security light at our back door, fully dressed in his uniform for the power station. I'd never seen grey look so good on anyone before, but with his dark curly hair and tanned skin, he made it look so good.

He took the needle from me, and tossed it back into the little rubbish bin, reaching past me a little too near and causing my heart to beat faster. The way he looked at me, I suspect he did it deliberately to unsettle me. 'That's what ancient hunters used to call the prowling hour before dawn.'

'I'm not following,' I said, stumbling back a step.

'That's because you haven't taken my hand yet.' He took mine instead and led me out towards the house, and that's when I noticed a glass jar in his other hand.

'What's that?'

'An apple a day keeps the vet away.' Holding it up to the light, I could see the yellowish pulp inside. 'He can't eat chunks yet, but I figured; maybe pureed?'

'Crushed apple? It's brilliant! Thank you!' I couldn't get my mouth to confess how wonderfully sweet and considerate it was as a gift. All I could do was smile and state the obvious. 'But it's 5am.'

'Which puts it well past your bedtime.' He tugged me nearer to the back door of my house.

'I can't...' I planted my feet, glancing over my shoulder at Lucky, awake again and watching us.

'You can't keep hogging him to yourself. There's a full roster of people who want turns now. I'm here for my 3am shift.'

'Your *what?*'

'Every day on my way to work, I'll be here until six, when your Dad relieves me for the breakfast shift until nine...' He started to lead me away again, and me; I was too tired and bewildered to argue. 'Then after your sister's at school, your mum takes over until noon. That's nine hours sleep for you, and not a minute less, or there'll be a blockade to stop you from getting back down here.'

He mentioned something about dropping in for another shift on his way home, but by then he'd already led me inside to the downstairs bathroom.

'Shower time.' He turned me around, pushed me in and tossed a clean towel at me from the rack.

I spun back to argue, but by the time I opened my mouth, he had a hand up to my lips, already expecting it.

'You smell like a horse. Don't be a nag too, or you'll never live it down.'

'My horses aren't nags.'

'Joking, Neet.' He grinned and winked. 'Now do I have to coax you with that cute little tapping thing you do when you're teaching your horses a new trick, or must I scrub you down myself and tuck you in bed?'

My mouth hung open, with my brain still hung up on the word Neet. Short for Anita, sort of, but the only people who ever called me that were my family.

'Good girl.' He kissed me on the nose - the only clean spot I had, and closed the door in my face. 'See you tonight then.'

3:30am-ish I don't recall what really happened, but Jim tells me he remembers it vividly;

I sleep-walked out of the house, wrapped in a bath towel, with my hair wringing wet and my eyes glazed.

'Oh, no you don't,' he said, and swept me up over his shoulder with a spank that failed to wake me. He carried me all the way upstairs to my room, and tucked me in tightly.

No teddy bears anywhere in sight. My kid brother had burned their backs warming them in front of the heater years ago, when he'd thought they were feeling chilly. So the only stuffed toy in my room was a large horse, designed as a pillow. It usually laid across the end of my bed, but Jim shifted it up under my arm, and that's how I woke the next day at eight.

Cuddling it.

32. Resignation
(DAYS 4 to 6)

Okay, this is a weird one;

Publilius Syrus,
a Syrian from Antioch...
who was taken as a slave to Rome...
where he wrote MIMES...
in Old Latin...
and became most famous for sayings such as
'the end justifies the means'
and 'a rolling stone gathers no moss'...
which in turn inspired the name of Mick Jagger's band...
who wrote many songs that I hummed to the foal...
also once "mimed";

Prosperity makes friends.
Adversity tries them.

Honestly, I have no idea how anybody could mime that.
I suck at playing Charades.
In any case, for me, it was Adversity which would soon attract my best friends and allies, not Prosperity.

I'd reached the end of the long weekend, finally, and woke to the horrific realization that I was due to start in the office at eight.
    Five minutes ago.
    I hate that feeling of running late. It makes my stomach

twist up. And I really loved my new job. Loved it. The privilege of flexible working hours meant it was okay if I didn't turn up until 9:30am – and the same went for the senior manager and my office supervisor. I'd also worked up enough extra time before Easter that I could take off the whole morning, and start as late as 2pm provided all my seniors agreed. But I couldn't go to work at all. Not at 2pm, or 10pm. Lucky needed me, and that was that. In one hand, I held his life. In the other, my job, my car; my first block of land and all the repayments that my parents had guaranteed but relied on me to make. Also at risk, my reputation as an employee, and my self-respect for letting down all my new workmates.

I'd only been working a month and I was still on probation, which meant they could sack me any time. So I'd been dreading this call every minute of the long weekend.

I ducked down to check on Lucky first and found Dad inside, giving him another pep talk.

'... brave lad,' he said, patting him and calling him Plucky instead of Lucky.

He didn't hear me coming, so this time I managed to hear most of his speech.

'... and I've seen Thoroughbreds and Arabians throw in the towel over a lot less than this. First sign of a bloody nose, the most pampered ones can just lie down and die. But you've got Aussie stock horse in you too, lad, and tougher horses never faced up to a battle. So you'll do fine, as long as you don't give up... Which brings me to determination; reminds me of a black pony stallion I had as a kid... Winston... Nothing like your sweet nature when it came to temperament. I had to ride him to school every day, and being a stallion, I had to lock him away from the other kids' mares. So the cranky little mongrel hated school even more than me. He used to crawl down into the lantana bushes on the creek every morning, and hide… '

I backed up quietly, and approached again with heavier footfalls.

'Hey, Dad.' Opening the flap interrupted him. 'How's the patient?'

'Damn fine little animal. If he lives, you'll never wish for a better horse.'

'Can you watch him another five minutes? I need to call work.'

'Batter up,' he replied, resuming his place at Lucky's side. 'Go see which way Fate's going to pitch your next ball.'

I trudged up to the house, past my kid brother, who was hanging upside down by his toes from a rafter. A normal sight in our house. He claimed it helped to stretch his back, but I think he just liked showing off what a fit little grease monkey he was.

Slumping into the big black chair in mum's office, I sucked in a long breath for courage and dialed my highest senior manager.

Ring, ring…

'Hello, boss? It's Anita, the new girl. How are you?'

He replied cheerfully about having a quiet weekend camping with his daughters, and hoping that I'd enjoyed my four-day weekend too.

'Not exactly. I'm sorry, sir, but I need to resign,' I replied, unable to soften the blow any further. 'Or maybe it's easier for you to replace me if you sack me for failing to turn up to work? At least then you can cut through a lot of red tape.'

That grabbed his attention long enough for me to explain myself. He reminded me that my office had crushing deadlines to meet for the payroll, and even though I had twenty days holiday accruing for the end of the year, I'd barely worked a month so far, so I had only 1/12th of it up my sleeve, which equated to just a day.'

'You realise I can't approve *any* time off *now*,' he said. 'Your team is already needing overtime to catch up work after public holidays.'

'I understand. I suppose what I'm really asking is how to hand in my resignation without any notice. I mean, to make it easiest for you, will this phone call be enough? Or do you need someone to hand in a letter from me?'

'Is it really that serious?'

'Honestly, it's life or death. No exaggeration, I can get my vet to call and verify for you if you don't believe me, or you can call his surgery. You'd even be welcome to come here to see for yourself, if you wish?'

'You do realise it's just an animal?'

'Animal or not, he's my responsibility. As much as your kids are for you. I know it's not really the same, but if one of your girls was fighting off an illness that's normally fatal, what would you do?'

'Can't you just leave it at an animal hospital?'

'I tried, but the only vet I could get isn't equipped with his own stable yet. Everyone else would have put him down four days ago. I know it must sound silly to you, but this is all new territory for us too. He seems to be responding and holding his own now, even though nobody's ever survived a case this bad. Or if they have, there's no records or medical case studies. Not even for humans yet.'

'Are you sure this is what you want?'

'No. I really enjoy working there with your team. I took a big pay cut just to get this job, and it's nearly all mathematics, my favorite subject. So this is a really tough decision for me. But I also understand that I can't mess you around. So if I don't resign, you'll be forced to sack me anyway for failing to show up.'

'Then it's probably best to terminate your services today.'

'Okay,' I said with a sigh. 'I know that means sacking me. I'm so sorry to let you down.'

'Wait,' he said, as if he'd only meant to bluff me. 'Do you really understand how bad this will look on your next resume?'

'I do, and that isn't the half of it. I just bought a property that I can't afford any more, unless there's a miracle and I secure another job before settlement date.'

'At *your* age?' He sounded dumbfounded. 'You bought a house at *your* age?'

'No, just the land. A small farm, hopefully, after I clean out all the thorny scrub and weeds. If I grow something, like flowers or pumpkins, it can help pay for itself. That was my pipe-dream, anyway.'

'Isn't that impossible? To buy land as a minor, I mean?'

I shrugged to myself. 'Where there's a will, there's a way... for me to get into trouble,' I added tiredly.

The line stayed silent for a long time. 'Wait one second. Let me double check the situation with your office supervisor.' He promptly hung up on me.

I stared at the receiver for a long moment, wondering if it was deliberate or if he'd pressed the wrong button. I swallowed my pride and reached to call him back, but the phone rang before I could.

'Sorry about that,' he said. 'I didn't realise your super would have such a glowing report on your work after such a short time. He wants to keep you if he can, so how does LWOP sound?'

'Leave without pay? I thought I needed to work a whole year and be on permanent staff before I'd be eligible?'

'At manager's discretion, and that's me. So we can take it a day at a time up to a fortnight for starters, but you'll need to call your supervisor each morning with an update, and if you can come back sooner; all the better… with a happy ending, preferably.'

'Thanks isn't enough, but thank you! Thank you!' I couldn't help but choke up. I still had my job! 'Same time tomorrow,' I promised.

I hung up, called Pizza Hut and arranged delivery of three big ones to the office that night during their scheduled overtime, as thanks to everyone who pitched in to cover for me, and at a time when they were already so busy.

Bursting with fresh faith in the Big Guy upstairs and in mankind generally, I called Norbert with his morning update. He supported my theory about the lack of bowel movements, but advised me to keep a careful watch.

'Try increasing the porridge you're feeding him by syringe, but be careful not to put too much in his mouth at once. Also make sure you do it yourself, or use only people you trust, or the food could get down into his lungs and then we'd lose him for sure.'

I raced down the yard – careful to steady my pace and be calm by the time I came within earshot of Lucky.

I spotted Dad, holding a fresh sprig of lawn up to his own mouth, pretending to eat it and make it sound delicious before offering it to Lucky.

'Great idea, Dad. His tummy must be keen for some solid nibbles by now.'

The foal showed interest but when I put two small juicy leaves of grass gently into the soft natural gap between his front and back teeth, he couldn't move his tongue or jaw enough to chew, swallow or even shift them around in his mouth. So I gave him a minute or so to absorb as many nutrients as possible from them through his saliva, and tugged them out. Then I milked his mum, while I still had Dad to watch over him.

Alone again, I began another long day of trickle-feeding

him over the back of his tongue.

'We've got a deadline,' I whispered, even though I knew he didn't have a hope of understanding. It seemed impossible for him to try any harder than he was already anyhow. But talking to him seemed to keep him calm and interested, no matter what I said to him, so I explained the concept of counting sleeps, and how my boss had given him a deadline of fourteen.

Thirteen, considering it was already Tuesday. The very latest Lucky could leave any last minute recovery would be 9am a week from next Monday, so I could still make it to work by 9:30. Even with a swarm of volunteer helpers at home, I'd never be able to concentrate at work if he wasn't able to stand on his own feet to feed himself by then.

I stroked his throat all the way down, helping him swallow, and praying yet again for another miracle.

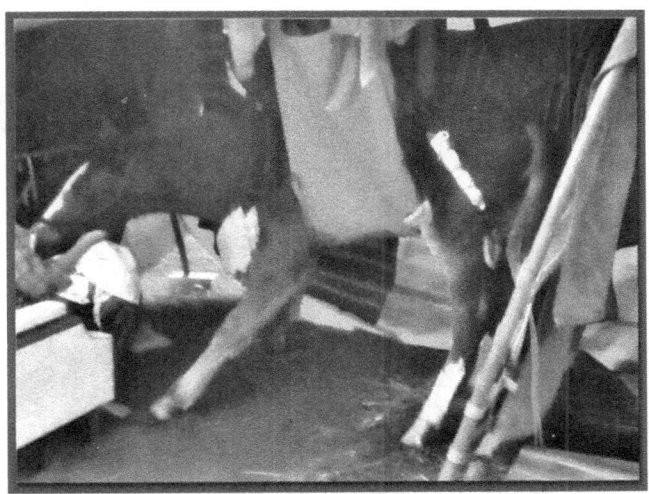

Lucky napping in his sling with his head in my lap and soft towels to help prevent the straps from rubbing. This makeshift 'stable' was normally quite dark inside, but the flap is up for dad to take this photo (the only photo we ever took between the diagnosis until he was better).

33. Day Five

Virgil
another famous Roman poet
from the Augustan period,
in the final century BCE,
once said;
*Come what may, all bad fortune
is to be conquered by endurance*

Yet another way of saying;
*Suck it up, Buttercup.
I'd get through it*

... but it was never me I'd been worried about.

Penny spent most of Tuesday morning standing patiently with her head stuck through an opening in the tarp, watching over her baby - with Muffy sitting on her back and Doggo laying sprawled between her front legs.

I fed her a biscuit of hay, but her manure was beginning to become too green and runny, so I knew it wouldn't be long before she began to get sick too unless she could get more fresh grass into her tummy and a little exercise. The neighbors' lawns simply weren't enough to sustain her. I mentioned it to Donny briefly next time I saw him, but I wasn't complaining. I merely acknowledged that I knew in my heart, there'd be no fast or easy solution. The weather and time were both against us.

Mum relieved me for an hour around lunchtime and sent me up for a nap, but I couldn't sleep. Instead I baked a double batch of Anzac Cookies and two large chocolate cakes. Then with a full oven, I set about whipping up a nice thick coffee icing.

My little brother came up, covered in grease, as usual, and set about making himself a sandwich beside me.

'Aren't you going to clean your hands first?' I asked as he plunged his filthy little fist into the fresh bread packet.

'Why?' he chuckled. 'It's clean grease.' Slapping six slices down, he splashed one with strawberry jam, one with peanut butter, and one with a huge chunk of roast lamb, then grabbed the last piece of yesterday's chocolate cake from the fridge and squashed it all down into one fat hamburger.

I gaped at him, horrified as he tried to squash the first bite into his mouth. 'You're eating chocolate cake on a sandwich with meat, jam and peanut butter?'

'Yeah, so?' he grinned. 'It all ends up the same in my gut.'

'Delightful.' I pouted, wondering why Fate chose me to be the pudgy one. Three kids in our family, we all ate virtually the same thing every day, yet we were all so different. An athlete, a super-model and me.

'Are those eggs boiled?' he asked, pointing to the ones I'd laid out as ingredients for the chocolate cakes, but apparently forgotten to include. Too worried about Lucky.

'Oh, crap.'

I grabbed the nearest damp dish towel – another mistake, since damp cloth conducts heat better than dry cloth, apparently – and wrenched out the cakes, burning my fingers. Thin crusts had already begun to form around the circumference, but I didn't let that bother me. I poured both cakes back into the huge mixing bowl and whipped them again, crusts, eggs and all. I confess; with a chip of shell that fell in and disappeared.

Best cakes ever. The recipe really earned its nickname

that day: The Never Fail Chocolate Cake. (For this fun family recipe, see *A Sweet Finale* in *Appendix I*.)

3pm Mr Nosey collected Penny's smelly piles of "horse-apples" into his barrow, and poked his nose around the painters tarp to check on the back end of the foal.

'Did you shift his manure already?' he asked.

'He hasn't made any yet. We think he's using up everything he's eating, so it could be another day or two. I just have to keep feeding and massaging his tummy as much as I can.'

'My grandfather had a horse that split its hoof. They bandaged it and slung him up like that so he couldn't walk on it until it re-grew – but he died in the meantime because his guts fouled up without exercise.'

'Out!' I whispered harshly, and grabbed him by the sleeve. I led him away, trying not to shout in any way that might upset the foal. 'Don't talk about dying around him.'

'Why? It's not like he can understand us.'

'Maybe not the words, but your tone and body language tell half the story, and that's too much as well, so please… Look, I really appreciate your help with the manure, and keeping the lady down the street happy, but if you can't stay positive when you're here, I'll have to ask you to stay away please?'

'Fair enough,' Nosey said. 'I was only saying…'

'Nothing I haven't worried about already, I guarantee it.'

By 5pm I was exhausted again. My neighbours and family had helped me get enough breaks to grab another two hours of power-napping time, but even so, I couldn't sleep. I'd hear the swing-set squeak from my bedroom, and know that he'd taken another fit. I'd have to go down each time and make sure he was still alive. I switched to sleeping downstairs on a couch, so at least it wouldn't be as far to go.

6pm Jim arrived after a full day working at the power station – freshly showered and changed into warm clothes for the night.

'Your other two are fine,' he said. 'I checked in on them on my way home with a fresh pack of bread.'

'You didn't need to,' I said, grateful anyway. 'But thank you.'

'Eaten yet?' he asked.

I nodded. 'I just finished feeding him another cup of porridge, but I think the paralysis is still creeping into every muscle and joint in his body.'

'Not him, for once. I meant you.' From behind his back, he produced a large bucket of fried chicken and chips, and fetched a laundry basket to use, upturned, as a dinner table.

Lucky showed interest in the bizarre smell so Jim offered him a sniff at a chip, but he couldn't open his mouth enough to taste it – and wouldn't have anyway. He turned up his nose at it, as we embarked on our first dinner date, *under* the embroidered picnic blanket that formed part of Lucky's tent.

On dusk, Jim checked his watch, then tidied up our meal scraps and took me by the hand.

'Time for the show,' he said, leading me out into the fading light. 'It's this way.'

He led me out to the driveway where I saw the young single mother headed towards me with a wheelbarrow and her twin girls toddling either side of her.

'What's she doing now?' I whispered to him.

'It's called an apology. Turns out it wasn't your horses she could smell, it was that lawn with the blood and bone.'

As they drew nearer, I noticed the barrow seemed to be

full of fresh cut grass clippings. Not minced from a lawn mower. Every blade looked to be freshly plucked or trimmed. The smallest of the twins grabbed a tiny handful and offered it up to me.

'It's for the sick baby horsey.'

'We can't afford a mower yet,' explained their mother, 'so we took inspiration from our new neighbour and cut it with scissors.'

I glanced back at the small pile, and realised how long it must have taken them. Such hard work for tiny hands, which now seemed to glow red from the effort – as did their mother's.

'Oh, girls,' I dropped to my knees, hardly knowing what to say. 'Thank you soooo much. That's very nice… but the baby horsey is too sick to eat. Would it be okay if I fed it to his mummy, so she can turn it into milk for him? She gets all her favourite food every day, but she's really hungry for ordinary grass right now.'

'Not a problem,' Jim said. He turned me around by the shoulders, and I saw a whole street full of children appear, all plucking handfuls of grass from their lawns and footpaths. A small army marched towards me with wheelbarrows, buckets, salad bowls, and empty cereal boxes, all stuffed with fresh grass for the sick baby horse and his mother. It looked like a dream, despite seeing it with my own eyes, I could hardly believe it. I turned around to call Penny so the kids could feed her themselves - but she was gone from Donny's yard.

The gate hung wide open!

My heart rate shot up but then I heard the familiar tap of her hooves from a driveway three houses down. She appeared, contentedly being led by a small gang of punk-haired girls I'd never seen before. They waved at Jim and broke into a jog, while Penny trotted keenly, keeping up with them.

'We put out the word for horse-loving girls,' Jim explained, 'and they've come from all over the city. Your mum has the schedule, so Penny will be exercised, fed, groomed and cuddled at least twice a day.'

Blown away, I wiped my eyes, trying not to cry. So many strangers. So many new friends. And my whole community pulling together to help one little foal and his mother.

34. The Littlest Soldier

Virgil again
(also spelled Vergil)
once wrote a poem with the expression;

Love conquers all.

It was uttered by a love-sick man,
as he lay dying from a broken heart.
Three Gods tried to save him,
until he gave up on death and chose life.

Yet Lucky was striving so hard to live,
he never stopped choosing Life.
Everybody kept telling him the same thing;

Love conquers all, little man...

I truly hoped so,
and I didn't dare to give voice to my doubts.

By 10am on Anzac Day, Wednesday the 25th, the paralysis seemed complete.

Every muscle, every ligament. Even his eyes and ears.

For two hours.

All morning, I kept grooming the colt, softly soothing him with my hands and voice – until 11 minutes past 11. National Remembrance. We heard the bugle calling out from all the radios and TVs around the neighbourhood, in honour of all the fallen soldiers.

Following my own tradition, I spent an extra minute in honour of all the animals who'd died in battle too. Not only horses who'd served in harness, against their greater instinct to run, but also trained bullocks, donkeys, camels and dogs. The forgotten fallen.

The rest of the time, I spent in prayer for my own little soldier. Then as the neighbour's clock chimed a perfect high noon, the colt's eye finally turned to find me, cheek to cheek, eye to eye, softly stroking him.

A sweet expression of relief seemed to sweep over him. I felt him relax under my hand; his whole body slowly sliding out of the paralysis, and I took it as a good sign. I didn't dare to say it aloud, but I felt sure that we'd reached and passed over the worst of it.

'Six days,' I said, hugging him around the neck. 'What a good little warrior.'

I couldn't help but hope that half our battles were won. Except his jaw and lips had clenched tighter, so now in order to keep his fluids up, we had to reduce the thick 20ml syringe down to a narrower 3ml syringe before we could squeeze the runny milk-bran mix over the back of his tongue towards his throat. And because we could only do two or three mLs at a time, it became a constant process. All day. All night.

Warm muggy days made the porridge sour quickly, so to keep it fresh Penny now had to be milked more often for less volume – once every hour, instead of three or four times a day. I'd take a full cup each time and send half up to the refrigerator. Then at night, I'd give her a break and use some of the reserve from the fridge, which had to be warmed gently first, until it reached skin temperature – or a little warmer as the night grew chillier.

We had a microwave that would have made heating faster

and easier with less containers to clean, but I chose not to use it because I didn't want to overheat any of the natural healthy bacteria that Lucky needed for his stomach. Bad enough that I had to chill their fuzzy little butts down to dormancy first.

After milking her hourly through the day, her body kept producing at that rate through the night, even when I needed to let her rest for a few hours. So by morning, if I used surplus milk while giving her a little peace, her udder would be really full - producing far more than the foal could use in his weakened condition. However, I knew he'd need a high daily volume from her once he started to get better. So I'd have to empty her each morning, not only to give her proper relief, but also to keep her milk production high enough for a normal hungry foal.

We soon had so much milk in the fridge, Dad started using it on his breakfast cereal and Mum in her coffee. No wonder Lucky had been growing so fast and so strong, so swiftly. Mare's milk was rich, and yet not nearly as creamy as I'd expected. It tasted sweet, and yet surprisingly watery, like skim-milk, rather than full-cream, and also tasted as if three full teaspoons of sugar had also been dissolved in each cup.

Milking her more often meant that I also had to be far more careful that her udder and teats didn't get sore, cracked, bruised or flaky with dried milk. Saliva from the foal's mouth usually solved all those problems, so as gross as it sounded, I had to clean my hands thoroughly first, and spit on them for lubricant each time before milking her. Then after taking all I needed, I'd have to rinse her udder with a splash of warm water – perfect skin temperature each time, so she wouldn't get sick of it. Then I'd finish off with a final spit to serve her as moisturizer without leaving any chemical residues. An ad in a horse magazine promised that a new antiseptic cream would do the job for me, but at this stage, I didn't want to risk any more contaminants.

Therapy for the colt had to be done entirely in the sling now, since the process of lying him down on the ground was guaranteed to bring on a fit; each one still risking instant death.

I made a point of lowering the canvas sling three times through the warmest parts of the day, to relieve the constant pressure of it on his intestines and internal organs, and to give his skin time to breathe long enough for his sweat to dry. Salt on a horse can cause burn-like sores, so I also had to take the time to brush it off, along with any mud to help keep him clean.

Amazingly, he continued to grow, and his coat shone like a healthy foal's - so much so that Norbert made comment about it during his next visit. I took these as promising signs because I'd heard so many stories about sick animals "shrinking" or their coats thinning and dulling or standing up and becoming wiry when they are terminally ill. At school, one of the comprehension exams had been a short story about an old mare who'd run away from her stable to die. The only sign that she'd been sick had been the dullness of her coat and the patches of hair she'd begun to lose.

Despite the havoc going on in the colt's flesh and muscles, his head had already grown so much in our back yard that I had to let his halter out by an extra hole on each of the three buckles around his ears, nose and chin. That sounds far-fetched even for a healthy foal to have so much growth in under a week, let alone a foal whose bloodstream was full of poison. But in years to come, I'd learn that it was just a normal growth spurt for his age. At the time, however, it seemed like just another "impossibility".

3:13pm I lowered the sling for the third time that day, and Lucky winced as the canvas fell away from his chest. I bent down to check how much sweat had built up this time between his front legs, and in the soft turn of skin – right at the edge of his "armpits" where each of his front legs joined onto his chest – I found two of the longest, deepest cuts I'd ever seen in my life. Each slice looked to be clean and fresh as if cut by a knife! Each looked to be longer than my hand and deeper than my thumb!

I fell back, horrified... not yet registering that there wasn't any blood. For a long moment, I could only stare and wonder how anyone got past me to mutilate him like that. And who would want to? How much pain he must be in. How much longer they'd take to heal. How far they'd set back his recovery... It wasn't fair on him. It just wasn't fair! He kept trying so hard and life kept cutting him down again and again!

This time, literally.

I couldn't take it anymore. I burst into tears.

My poor little colt not only walked like a mini-Frankenstein on his stiff legs, now he also looked like one with his flesh falling apart.

He bent his nose down to sniff me, straining in pain against his own aching muscles – *him* worried about *me*! I felt totally pathetic in comparison.

I slapped my own face, disgusted with myself; wiped my eyes and hugged him with all the love I could muster. Fighting back tears, I cried out for Dad, who came straight away from the garage.

'Did you see anyone run through here?' I asked urgently.

I showed him the problem, and saw my dad morph from mild-mannered mechanic into warrior. He tore off his greasy overalls, shedding them as he ran around each side of the garage and house, hot to find the perpetrator.

I'd never seen that side of him before, or since.

'I'll call the police,' he said, coming back to me.

'First let me use the phone to call Norbert,' I pleaded. 'Lucky needs painkillers.' I couldn't say it, but I knew the time had also come to reconsider a lethal injection.

I measured the injuries against my arm by marking my skin at the appropriate distances from the end of my longest finger. Then I hooked up the sling loosely around the colt - leaving the chest section down so it wouldn't hurt, yet still keep him from falling - and ran straight inside to the office desk. Mum's ruler confirmed my estimates. The cuts were seven inches long and three inches deep; 17.8cms by 7.6cms.

'Hold your call to police,' Norbert said. 'I'll be right there.'

Fifteen minutes later, he pulled in and confirmed his suspicions.

'They're pressure wounds.'

'They're *what?*'

'A foal's flesh between their front legs is very soft, and this foal's chest has been supporting his entire body weight for almost a week in stifling, muggy wet weather - something it was never designed to do. He wasn't attacked. His flesh has simply split under pressure. That's why there's no blood. The meat has opened up by giving way along a mucous membrane or in the natural gaps between cells on a molecular level.

I'd never heard of such a thing. 'Will the splits heal?'

'It's too early to tell, but they should. As bad as they look, they're still the least of his problems. He's already on the top dose of antibiotics, but I'll give him a boost on painkillers and you'll need to clean them every two hours around the clock.'

I shuddered to think of all that extra work when my schedule was already packed with feeding, cleaning, stimulating, grooming… I barely had time to scratch myself. Literally.

Norbert gave me an extra-large tub of prednoderm with instructions to coat the wounds each time after flushing them clean with pressurized hose water – leading Lucky over to the tap as often as possible to avoid muddying the ground around the sling.

Ordinarily, I would have used a little silver water and aloe vera leaf too, but these cuts were deeper and different to anything I'd ever treated before and I didn't dare to stray from Norbert's advice. I obeyed him to the letter, setting my alarm and waking for the task, even while others took their shift with him.

The plucky little colt took it all in his stride, but he started to get a little shy of needles – and who could blame him? Norbert extended his penicillin course by another three days, so he'd still be getting five needles a day - three of them still a whopping 20ml each, as thick as my thumb, and twice as long.

At least his fits seemed to ease up, coming less often and mainly when a neighbour's dog barked or when he sensed a needle coming.

I kept drawing dots for every needle to avoid injecting the painful fluid into the same tender skin twice by accident, but he was swiftly running out of places I hadn't used yet.

He'd begun to resemble a spotted horse, a different breed known as Appaloosa, made famous by American Indians.

My little guy, every bit as tough and brave.

35. Warm Horse Tea (Days 7 & 8)

Bugs Bunny
once said;

*The way I run this thing you'd think
I knew something about it.*

I felt the same way.
I could work through Lucky's nursing ritual with
the efficiency of a pro by now,
but the gaps in my knowledge were gaping.

Despite flushing both chest wounds with salty water every two hours around the clock and applying a thick glob of prednoderm each time, flies managed to sneak in to lay eggs in his wounds – at least twice a day. I couldn't believe it. Pyrethrum leaves had been keeping them away so well. I'd been scattering a fresh layer of leaves every day, so the scent rose with every step, but the blowflies must have been crawling down between the sling and his body. So now we needed fly shoo-ing duty as well.

'Spray him with fly repellent,' suggested the youngest of Dad's apprentices. 'Or *surface spray* the canvas.'

'If he wasn't so sick already with toxins, I would. But I can't risk it. His fits are only five times a day now - each time he tenses up for a needle.'

'Hey that's better than yesterday, right?'

'I sure hope so. I've watched him so closely for so long and hoped so hard, I don't think I can trust my own eyes any more. I keep seeing the tiniest of improvements in his attitude, but then I'll refocus on the big picture of his wounds, and wonder if it's only my imagination.'

My private fear: that I'm only torturing him by delaying the inevitable. We all die anyway, so I kept thinking 'a hundred years from now, what difference would it make?'

The whole neighbourhood must have had similar doubts, but around us they donned brave faces, staying hopeful, while we continued our round-the-clock vigil throughout the seventh and eight days.

I kept reminding myself that we owed our progress so far to the pioneers who'd forged the way for Pottie's Horse Dictionary, and I drew comfort, not only from Lucky's own fierce determination, but also from knowing that others who'd lived more than a century before me had put in no less effort, trying to save for their own horses, without the benefit of modern medicines.

When Norbert came on the eighth morning, he had the same concerns.

'I think we've reached a plateau,' he said. Yet he couldn't give us any clue as to whether we might be winning the battle or not. He'd spent hours researching professional journals, but still couldn't find any practical case studies to help or advise us. Librarians in three capital cities and several universities were now also searching their records, with no more clues on how to beat tetanus.

The nights turned cold. Downright freezing for April. Some nights down to five degrees Celsius.

The foal's legs became the hardest to keep warm. I cut off the legs from two more pairs of old jeans and used wider but light-weight string and a plait of baling twine over his shoulders to hold them up. Note: I made the plait wide and soft so it wouldn't cut or rub into him.

While singing songs of summer heat and the beach, I

looked at his four little white socks, wishing I could do more, and realised I could – with real woolly socks. So I raided the laundry basket for orphaned footy socks of every color. It looked like rival teams uniting for the same battle.

Extra blankets over his back and neck also helped, along with regular sessions of vigorous grooming with soft and stiff brushes to help stimulate better blood flow. A constant therapy requirement anyway – and one the colt seemed to enjoy more and more. Each small measure of pleasure, we treated as treasures. So much so, that I often sang that to him as a rhyme.

Stifling hot days chased off the freezing nights, and it became annoyingly hot and muggy for a few hours either side of midday, so Mr Nosey timed his visits with the most pleasant parts of the day, mid-morning and late afternoon.

Mid-morning of the eighth day, he came a little later and caught me singing songs of winter snow as the sun began to steam up the day. He paused outside the makeshift stable with his shovel and barrow for the first of his twice-daily checks on the foal.

'Still no apples?' he asked, looking worried.

'Still no apples.' Maxed out with worry already, my expression must have been grim because Nosey left without slipping in the final word, for the first time ever.

Staying busy helped me maintain a sense of progress, even when there didn't seem to be any, one way or the other. I lacked the heart of a horse, but I kept striving to find joy in the smallest moments - which felt a whole lot better than sitting back, feeling powerless and sorry for myself – although I had to leave occasionally to do that too, before I could pick myself up and get back into it.

I kept working down through my hectic schedule, annoyed to see Nosey interrupt us again a few minutes later

— until I realised it wasn't a few minutes. The sun had flipped sides in the sky, and begun to set already on the seventh day.

Nosey glanced to the ground under Lucky's tail, and then to me. He didn't bother to say anything. He didn't need to any more. We both knew the foal should have made a contribution to his garden by now.

That night, despite the growth I'd noticed previously, Lucky looked to be losing weight. Not much, but enough to make me redouble my efforts at getting runny porridge into him all night as well as all day — all the while, holding onto the positive observation that his coat remained shiny. Yet I couldn't help but worry that he wasn't getting enough fluids.

Until midnight.

An icy chill crept over us along with a mist.

Mum brought me a cup of hot tea, and the foal showed interest in it. His eyes perked and his nose moved a little to sniff it, even though he still couldn't open his lips.

We wondered if he could suck in enough to drink by himself, so I ran and fetched a bucket. Into the bottom, I poured about half a cup of thick, dark molasses syrup, and dissolved it with double the volume of hot water, then topped it up with cooler water to make a horse version of warm tea. Full of sweet goodness and energy, but I also hoped it would act a little like prune juice and get his bowels moving.

'That's not how you make a horse drink,' my sister teased as she joined us. 'You can't lead him to water. You have to lead him to a blender, and then make a horse drink.'

Mum chuckled, but it took me longer to get the joke.

'Oh, that's sick...' I couldn't help grinning anyway.

My clever little lad got the idea at first sniff - and loved the concoction.

36. Power Naps, Power Nightmares

I never could have made it through
without a sense of humor.

Bugs Bunny
also reminded me;

*I know this defies the law of gravity,
but I never studied law*

It was the same with my foal.
Don't tell me it can't be done,
and I won't mention the supernatural...

Saturday morning, day nine, I woke with a start. After running from lava monsters in the fiery bowels of the earth all night, I'd plummeted to the climax of my latest nightmare, landing neck deep in manure like black tar, which set like concrete and kept me stuck rigid like a statue, while all my demons swelled up around me.

Waking from that horror into reality, I wondered if my subconscious was trying to warn me that something might be wrong, very wrong, with Lucky's digestive system or intestines.

I mentioned it to mum, and she grimly reminded me of the little mantra she'd been teaching me, ever since I'd first refused to eat up all my greens as a baby. 'If you don't eat, you don't poop, and if you don't poop, you die.'

I called Norbert.

'He's still managing to hang out his little fire hose at least once a day into a bucket. The movement seems to hurt and the volume has dropped. The fluid is also darker and smells stronger, but at least his kidneys still work. I've been getting more food into him. Between one and two liters of runny porridge a day, but still nothing solid out of his tailpipe in six days.'

'When you pinch his skin, does it snap back into place, or return slowly?'

I blinked, mystified. 'I don't know. I've never pinched him. Why would I do that?'

'It's a test for dehydration. It won't hurt him. Try it on the side of his neck where the skin moves most as he bends, and count how many seconds it takes to snap or slide back into place. I'll wait.'

'Okay, sure.' I dashed out to Lucky, careful to approach calmly and not startle him, but also mindful that Norbert's work and time with other pets was too valuable to waste, waiting for me at the end of a phone.

Surprisingly, Lucky's skin pinched up easily and didn't seem to bother him at all. Even more surprisingly, it slid back into place in less than five seconds, like slow motion.

I dashed back to the house and reported my findings.

'Okay, that's not too bad. Keeping him hydrated like that with such hot days and cold nights is a battle all by itself.'

Norbert suggested he might only need an enema. I'd never heard that word before, so he had to explain it meant dosing him up the tail end with a special tablet and a small volume of mildly medicated water, made to feel soapy or oily, to help lubricate Lucky's intestines and flush out any blockages.

'The risk is considerable under the circumstances,' Norbert warned me over the phone. 'So far I haven't been able to feel any blockages inside him, hence forcing his bowels to work when there's nothing in them can cause the intestinal tubes to telescope, like one pipe rolling over a smaller pipe – and then you'll have even bigger problems.'

'Like what can happen sometimes with colic?'

'Exactly.'

I weighed the risks against the terrible gut feeling I had. 'I think we need to try one this morning.'

'I can be there in ten minutes.'

Revelation; the first adult to respect my opinion on life or death issues – aside from my parents - was a vet.

It took two oil enemas to get Lucky's bowels going again. The blockage turned out to be barely half the size of my fist, hard, black, dry ... and deadly if it hadn't come out that day.

After that, Lucky seemed far more comfortable in the sling, and the molasses water proved to be imperative for keeping his bowels working, also re-hydrating him until his urine volume increased to normal.

The relief to me personally, however, had a bizarre side effect. Depression. Despite the apparent advances, we still seemed to have so far to go. I had to keep telling myself we'd saved him yet again. That it couldn't be much longer now. That I needed to stay positive for his sake, if not my own. But I kept looking into his eye and wondering how such a young animal could keep finding the strength to fight so hard, while I sensed myself approaching breaking point.

Lucky leaned forward to sip his warm tea, and I realised I had a new chore for my list. Keeping it fresh. Warm by night, cool by day.

'Hey, hey!' Nosey cheered when he poked in for his next visit. 'Pipes are working again?'

'So far so good.'

He shoveled up the little pile, and the spindly old pirate made off with it, like treasure for his garden.

10am Despite all the help and support, I could still barely cope. So I gave in to the keen pleas from two of the city girls, and showed them how to milk Penny.

'Don't forget to rinse and spit, in that order, when you're done. And make sure you use warm clean water from the laundry. Not too hot. Just lukewarm when you drip it on the tender side of your forearm, so you know it's the perfect temperature *before* using it on her.'

They assured me they'd be fine, and proudly produced a cupful after half an hour, so when they pleaded for the next two milkings as well, I relented, since I still had my hands full with Lucky anyway.

1pm I went to milk Penny after the girls left, and discovered a dry crust of milk and cracked skin – which meant they'd failed to rinse her udder properly, and failed to re-lubricate with any spit. So two of Penny's teats cracked from the dried milk - to the point of bleeding.

This would not only make the next few days of milking painful for her, it would also halve the amount of milk I could get for Lucky because she couldn't stand still for me to get at the two sore teats. It also meant I had to start moisturizing that part of her udder with a special ointment – which also meant extra cleaning every hour to ensure it didn't get into Lucky's milk. And then half her udder swelled up so tight it went lumpy, so by dark, I had to start milking her out of that side anyway, at least once a day no matter how much it hurt, to prevent mastitis – a disease that can be almost as deadly as tetanus.

Diagnosis; if it didn't kill her within a week or month, it could cause her milk to dry up completely. She could also lose a teat or two permanently – and any milk I drew from that half had to be discarded for risk of infection.

By sunset, Penny also became annoyed and touchy around her back legs. She no longer trusted strangers so much near her tail, because of the constant pain in her udder – so she also refused to stand still for anyone but me to milk her - and even then, she stayed grumpy, blaming me. The situation would take three days to heal physically and another three weeks emotionally, before Penny would trust me thoroughly again with that part of her, but in the meantime, I still had to cope. On that day in particular, I also had much to learn about finding good times in bad.

3pm Time for the third needle of the day. I came down from an hour's nap in my room to find Lucky alone. I'd passed Mum, who was rostered to be down with the colt, but instead she was in her office, busy on the phone. I couldn't be mad at her. She had paperwork for five other businesses to do, aside from Dad's, so I'd already been amazed and grateful that she'd been able to spare any time at all. But I panicked and hurried down to check Lucky.

To my great relief, he was fine and didn't seem to worry about being left alone. It probably did him good to be alone for a while, with only his mum and the other animals hanging out with him.

He heard me coming and tensed, smart enough to tell the time by now from all the signals around the neighbourhood, and know that it was time for his needles. Signals like a neighbor's grandfather clock, which chimed hourly nearby, and the radio news theme that began a few seconds later in the garage. The coming and going of staff for their breaks. And every afternoon at five, an episode of *Lassie* on a neighbouring TV. Sound only. Lucky seemed to prefer the mid-day matinees when he heard other horses in western movies, but for an episode of Lassie, Muffy and Doggo always joined him to listen too.

Golden moments.

I'd seen every episode so I could narrate for them, even

though the whole script contained little more than barking, whimpering, meowing and whatever other sounds were needed from guest-starring animals.

That day, a kitten trapped on a rocky beach with the tide coming in, needed rescuing, so without my narration, they could only hear; mew, mew… splash, splash.. mew… splash… woof, woof… mew… splash…

An episode of Skippy the Kangaroo seemed just as fun and surreal.

'Tsk, tsk, tsk…' Skippy would go with her tongue.

'What's that Skip?' I'd narrate for my own pets. 'Sonny's stuck down a well?'

'Tsk, tsk, tsk – tsk, tsk, tsk…'

'Oh, no! And he's broken both legs and all his ribs, and he wants us to bring a… what did you say?'

'Tsk, tsk, tsk….'

No wonder my pets looked at me so weirdly.

More than once, I'd tried to use distractions like this to give Lucky his needle.

Norbert confirmed that five to twenty minutes one way or the other in the timing of each dose shouldn't make much of a difference, but each day for the last week, I'd tried a new tactic, trying to find one that didn't seem to worry him so much.

I tried injecting it fast, injecting it slow. In new places and old. At one time I had the idea that using the same hole I'd used last time might make it easier, but nothing helped. I even tried sneaking up on him a few times, but he'd always stiffened up with worry for longer.

Fifty five spots for fifty six needles so far, and counting.

4pm The Vietnamese family next door cooked their dinner at precisely the same time every day - torturing me with their delicious scents of subtle herbs and spices. Talk about mouth watering. Then two grandmas emerged with a plate of home-made spring rolls and dipping sauce just for me. Oh my sweet mother of pearl! I had to get that recipe.

'Thank you!' I said, making all kinds of weird sounds and signs of appreciation. Luckily for me, my sister came down to save me. She pulled a Vietnamese dictionary out of her pocket and I caught sight of a library sticker as she thumbed through it.

She offered them weekly lessons in Aussie English, and as she hopped the fence to start there and then, I decided I'd make them a plate of Anzac biscuits and chocolate cake as a peace offering for any distress or inconvenience I might have been causing them, because their house and back door were barely two metres from the fence where Lucky spent most of his time.

5pm Time for the last needle of the day.
How I did it:
Keeping to my strict schedule, I'd measure each dose of milky white penicillin upstairs in the kitchen, out of sight from the colt. I had to keep the serum bottle in the fridge anyway, so I opened a new needle and fitted it to the syringe upstairs too.

Serum for the antibiotic came fitted with a clever little rubber cap, which meant no lid to remove. I'd simply shake well first, then upturn the bottle, push the needle up through the rubber, and suck out the 20ml dose using the syringe. Keeping the needle upturned also made the task of bumping and squeezing out any air bubbles much easier and more efficient. Less loss of precious serum droplets that way too, but I'd still check it again, behind his back, in the last seconds before plunging it, since this was only the first part of our ritual.

I also took care to numb the area first with five fast

circles with a smooth river pebble – which seemed to help more than anything, then I simply produced the dose, plunged it gently, squeezed it in as slowly and cautiously as I could manage, while tickling the area around it, which also seemed to help. Then to complete the ritual, I showed Lucky the empty syringe, so he could finally calm down while watching me bend the needle and toss it into our rubbish bin.

One dose, one needle, even though I needed to spend the next few minutes back in the kitchen, rinsing, boiling and chilling the cleaned plastic syringe for reuse.

That time, the needle went in, and came out and still he hadn't suffered a fit. In fact, he'd barely tensed.

I should have been euphoric. And I was for a few minutes... until I peeled down the sling to clean Lucky's chest wounds.

I found maggots and pus in a patch of soft, rotting flesh.

Grief overwhelmed me.

I tried to scrape out the maggots with my bare fingers, feeling horrible at how much extra pain I must be causing him. My eyes welled up until I could barely see. I felt sick at the sight of the squirming mass, but for Lucky's sake, I had to get them out of him. I'd never felt so desperate and despairing as I did at that moment.

Lucky turned his nose to check if I was okay – him, worried about me, and straining against his own pain to check on me... and it broke me.

I had to get away. I ran off apologizing, promising to come back, but I was such a mess I could hardly understand myself.

37. Dark Moment of the Soul

Technically speaking, I know I shouldn't be
pulling you aside like this for brief
interludes from Lucky's story.

He deserved my full attention, but
I often needed to step back to catch my
breath, and seek a fresh perspective.
So I hope this helps you to feel some small sense of
frustration or need to get back to him, as I did.

In this case,
Novalis, the German poet,
also chided me;

A hero is one who knows how
to hang on one minute longer.

Sure, but Lucky was the hero, not me.

I ran inside, keeping my head down. Quietly enough to avoid everyone – except Jim. I ran into him by accident, just as he'd arrived yet again to share dinner with me in the makeshift stable. But shame devastated me and I couldn't stand to look at him.

Chasing me down the hall, he swept me around a corner into the bathroom, which was normally reserved and kept clean for staff and customers.

He pushed my hair back from my eyes and tried to look at me, tried to say something. Something sweet, about me, I think. He looked so worried, but all I could hear was my own voice inside me screaming; *What the hell is wrong with you? Get your ass back down there. He needs you. You don't run when a friend needs you!*

'Neet,' Jim said, forcing me to look at him. 'Are you okay?'

'Can you go down to him?' I pleaded. 'He needs...' I shook my head, wishing I didn't have to confess it. '...someone better than me.'

I promised myself over and over that I only needed a few minutes rest. That I'd pull myself together somehow and go back down, hiding my whole mess behind a fake brave face. I don't know how much came out aloud. I only knew I was babbling and making no sense to Jim, because he kept asking the same question. 'Are you okay?'

'Don't ask me. Ask *him*! That poor little horse is down there... so brave! And look at me. I'm a mess. You'd better go quick...' I clutched my stomach, trying not to degrade myself any worse in front of him. 'I'm gonna be sick!'

I swung around to the toilet, preparing to drop to my knees, but Jim swung me around further, into the shower for employees. The water hit me hard, drenching my hair and my clothes. I didn't care that it was cold. I didn't care about myself at all anymore.

Jim washed off the worst of the mud and muck from my clothes, stroked the wet hair from my eyes, and hugged me against his chest.

'I'm so sorry!' I sobbed. 'Now I've soaked your shirt!'

'I'll dry.' He chuckled and wrapped a large soft towel around my shoulders. 'I've never met anyone who could shower, and still be a mess.'

'Oh?' I smiled grimly. 'With me, it's a daily occurrence.'

I straightened my shoulders, took another breath for

courage, and headed for the door.

'I guess I'd better go back and finish cleaning him up.'

'Oh, no you don't,' Mum said, appearing in the door and pushing me back towards the shower. 'You're not going out again today, young lady.' She tossed a clean set of pyjamas at me. 'You're going to take a long soaking bath, and get twelve hours sleep, *at least*, or else you won't be going out tomorrow either.'

'Twelve hours? Mum, that's impossible. He's still got maggots dripping out of his armpits!'

'And we've opened up the sling so more can get in.'

'You did *what?*' I flushed hot with fear and rage.

'Trust us, honey. Maggots will eat the rotten flesh.'

'Let them clean out the wound,' Dad agreed. His deep, molten voice had a way of pouring cool syrup over my fires. 'I know it sounds bad, but they can get in further than you can - and they'll fall out when they're finished. Doctors and nurses used to use them like that deliberately during medical supply shortages in the second world war.'

I shuddered, repulsed by the idea. 'What about Penny?' I persisted. 'I still need to milk her, and moisturise...'

'I'll handle it,' Dad said. 'Penny has always co-operated with me.'

'And me,' Jim said. 'Unless you'd rather me to help with your bath?'

He winked at me, but Mum tugged him out of there. She sent him outside, then tugged me out too and shunted me further down the hall to the stairs. 'Go... do...' She smacked me on the butt - first time I could ever remember - and sent me upstairs with a final warning to take care of myself first for a change, instead of my pets.

Emerging from the bathroom half an hour later, I found Mum and my sister in the kitchen, serving dinner.

I tried to sneak past them to check on Lucky, but my

sister blocked my path.

'He's asleep,' Mum reported without turning away from the stove. 'Quit trying to fight the world and hit the sack. Or can you eat first?'

My sister pushed a hot plate of lamb roast and vegetables at me, but I couldn't stomach it.

'Drink this then,' Mum insisted. 'It's vitamins in warm orange juice.'

I screwed up my nose, refusing that too, but she glared at me until I swallowed it in one long horrible gulp. Then as she turned away, I bolted for the stairs — where my sister cut me off again.

'Oh, come on!' I pleaded. 'I need to check him one last time, or I'll never sleep.'

'You'll sleep once that orange drink kicks in. Mum just slipped you a sleeping pill amongst all the vitamins.'

'*Please?* I promise I'll hurry.'

'Oh, mother dear,' Rabbit called calmly. 'I win our bet. Pay up. I told you she'd be keen to get back to him.'

Mum laughed and waved a long wooden spoon at my sister, as if it was a magic wand casting a spell. 'You are hereby appointed big sister for the night. Now put your little sister to bed.'

Younger than me, but taller, Rabbit spun me around and marched me straight to my bedroom. She shoved me into my bed, but then goaded me to try to get past her again.

'I get an extra five bucks each time you try the door. Or ten if you try the window. Easy money. I'll be rich by morning.'

'Can't have that on my conscience.' I slammed the door, feeling powerless and frustrated all over again — but far too exhausted and washed out to fight any more.

Whatever Mum had put in that glass worked fast.

I fell asleep, hoping I hadn't worried Lucky too much when I'd run away from him, but if I'd known then, what I knew by morning, it would have taken a whole army of sisters to hold me, or a full bottle of sleepers.

I would have been up all night, partying.

When I woke, I thought I was still dreaming. I heard squeaking; like the whole swing set, rocking. It sounded like the biggest, longest fit so far.

Then a whinny, shrill and bright.

At first I thought it must be Penny, calling me for help. I'd never heard her call like that. She had a much deeper, rolling nickering, similar to Snowy's.

Whinnneyyy, I heard again, and the truth dawned on me.

My little mate had found his voice.

38. The Sound of Joy

>   Bugs Bunny,
> Bless his furry little tail,
>   once said;

> *Well, what did you expect in an opera?*
>   *A happy ending?*

>   He was joking about epic tragic musicals,
>   but Lucky's shrill little crescendo
>   sounded far from tragic.
> It was something else that I needed to check...

I ran downstairs, crashing into Jim as he came out from the staff bathroom, and then into Dad as he ran out from the laundry wearing only long fleecy pyjama pants.

'Did you hear that?' Dad asked.

'Did I ever.' I glanced over my shoulder at Jim, wondering why he'd come inside the house so early, while Dad only glared at him.

'Hey, nature called,' Jim said, raising his hands. 'I've been up all night, and he was sleeping when I left him, honestly. Not two minutes ago.'

'He must have heard you leaving.' I made it to the back door, barefoot, and didn't stop for my slippers or yard shoes. Not angry at Jim. I could only be grateful for the night he'd put in, and yet as I raced for the makeshift, blanket-covered stable, I saw the whole thing rocking and squeaking.

I skidded to a halt in the frosty grass, the short icy blades as painful as shattered glass, and yet I barely felt them.

My heart stopped and I couldn't breathe. The canvas frame shook, warning me to expect the worst. Penny, such a good mother, had her head in already, watching over him.

'Steady mare,' I said to avoid startling her. Nudging Penny aside, I ducked through the flap, careful not to let in the first sharp rays of dawn.

In the dim shadows as my eyes adjusted, the sight of Lucky stopped me in my tracks again. He stopped too, and turned his head slightly to look at me – with a cheeky expression; *look what I did!*

In front of him, his bucket of warm horse tea had been knocked off its timber stump and been splashed all around. His fault, obviously. Both of his front hooves were now resting up on the stump where the bucket had been.

Stuck, by the looks of him. His front legs were hooked up at such an odd angle. I couldn't understand how he'd managed it. If this had been a fit, he'd recovered faster than ever, and all by himself.

Inspecting him closer, I saw that both wounds in his armpits seemed to be completely clean. No maggots anywhere, except for a few on the ground, being carried away by ants.

Lucky snorted for the first time in a fortnight.

I'm so clever, he seemed to say as he tossed his nose at his busted bucket.

'Oh, yes, very clever, naughty boy. Now we have to mix up a new drink for you! Now hold steady,' I said, still thinking he must be stuck. I reached for his nearest front hoof but he lifted his back legs too, and pushed back with his front. He set the whole frame to rocking, swinging himself back and forwards.

Look at me! He whinnied happily.

Around me the metal swings creaked, just as I'd heard from my room.

'What's wrong?' Dad called from outside.

'What's happening?' asked Jim.

I clasped my hand over my mouth, hardly daring to believe my eyes.

Lost for words, I threw back the flap.

'He's playing!' I cheered.

Jim dropped my old shoes at my feet. His jaw dropped too, in time with my father's.

We laughed and cried and hugged Lucky, and he hammed it up, as if thinking he was so clever. Deliberately swinging himself back and forward with all his feet tucked up, he looked happier than I'd ever seen him.

How great is this? he seemed to say. *I can move again!*

Dad shifted the old sofa to give him more room, and revealed the only patch of grass that Penny hadn't been able to eat yet. Pale from lack of sun, but soft and juicy.

'Try this,' Dad said to the colt, as he plucked a small handful.

Lucky took it into his mouth, his jaws still stiff, but finally able to chew and swallow all by himself.

'No disputing it now,' Dad said. 'This is progress.'

The colt played for the next three hours in his sling, working his muscles, and with every passing hour, he grew stronger. And happier. And cheekier.

Word spread fast, and a constant stream of visitors began to pop in to cheer and congratulate him.

Hotcross came over, straight after his shift finished at ten at the bakery.

'Jewish,' he reminded me, and offered me a candle. 'Today is Yom HaShoah: Holocaust and Heroism Remembrance Day.'

I'd never heard of it before, even though I'd learned about many religions at school, so he sat with me to explain the tradition of sharing stories. He had no family, aside from his Christian girlfriend, so he shared the special gift of a story from his grandparents and their old grey gelding, Jablko, which meant Apple. Jablko had escaped confiscation by German soldiers and braved crossfire to run home. Then with nearly no food or rest possible, he'd carried his owners and their newborn daughter through neck-deep snow for seven days to escape over the Czech border into Switzerland.

Hugging Lucky before he left, Hotcross was a big man with tattoos, and a tear in his eye.

1pm A police car pulled into our driveway. The same two officers.

Sergeant Cook went straight to the garage to greet my dad, while his sidekick went to the trunk of their car and retrieved a familiar fuel drum. Sloshing it, he made it sound almost empty.

'This yours?' Cook asked, pointing to it. 'There's a service sticker stuck underneath, looks like your name on it.'

Dad shrugged. 'No good to me anymore. My daughter filled it with water.'

Cook laughed. 'That explains why we found your prowler broken down on the highway. Local lad, by the nickname of Donkey. He had a car load of stolen gear – and so much bad luck he came clean as soon as we collared him. He's also the guy who messed with your car jack when he tried to steal it. So if you want to press charges for your broken ribs, we'll take your statement.'

'Kismet,' agreed his partner, using another word for luck. 'For better or worse, he won't be bothering anyone around here for a few years.'

2pm My little chestnut colt could bend his neck enough to chew and tug at the sling. And stamp his foot. He wanted out. Impatient as he was, I didn't think his legs could hold him yet. Every time he tried to stand up in his sling, taking his whole weight on his hooves, his front knees seemed to bend grotesquely the wrong way, as if his tendons and bones had grown without the muscle strength to hold his own legs straight. Or maybe his tendons had contracted too tightly in the wrong direction. Either way it looked as if his knees now bent the wrong way. So I rang Norbert, who promised to come as soon as he'd stabilised a cat suffering from snake bite.

While we waited, Lucky began pawing the ground in earnest, pleading to be set free. So Dad and Jim each took a side, ready to catch him, while I lowered the sling.

As soon as he sensed himself free, Lucky didn't hesitate. He stuck out his nose determinedly, and Frankenstein-walked straight to his mother. He sidled up to her in the way foals do when they're hungry and tried to tip his neck up to help himself to her milk bar.

Ten gold stars for trying, and another ten to Penny for standing up on tip toes on her hind legs, trying to raise her udder high enough for him, but he simply couldn't twist his neck down and around enough yet to reach. So I milked her out into a salad bowl, while he pestered me the whole time to hurry, and then slurped the bowl dry.

No more syringe feeding! Yay!

Half an hour on his feet began to tire him, or so it seemed, so I turned him around to head back for the sling. He stopped at first sight of it, and who could blame him? He'd had so many hours of pain cooped up in that thing, but I couldn't have him learning to disobey me when we seemed so close to winning. So I pretended I was only turning him to look at an edible plant in Mum's garden.

'He hasn't done therapy in a while,' Dad suggested. 'I mean, aside from all the leg exercises you've done with him in the sling, a foal's intestines are designed to spend a couple of hours a day spread out on their sides, remember? Perhaps he could get some rest that way for a change, while you work on him?'

'Worth a try.' I had my doubts, though. I remembered the episode with the snake – and so did Lucky. As we stepped into position to lay him down, he went rigid, totally terrified. 'Stop,' I decided 'He wants to stay up, so he stays up. He's been such a good little patient. He already knows all his options, so let's just let him go at his own pace until Norbert gets here.'

The colt appeared determined to stay on his feet a good while longer, despite teetering from lack of muscle control and coordination. He seemed top-heavy, as he had on the first day; his front legs splayed and stiff, needing to swing out sideways to take each step. It took so much of his concentration to control the front half of him that he seemed to forget his hind legs, often teetering a little too far with his heavy rump – to the brink of tipping over. So I stayed alongside his tail, keeping one hand on him lightly to help keep his balance.

Penny grazed away in the opposite direction, content to leave him in my care. By the time Norbert drove in, we'd made it halfway down the driveway, exploring the garden and playing hide and seek in the daisies with Muffy.

'Wow!' Norbert climbed out with his stethoscope. 'Whose foal is this?'

I patted him proudly. 'He's got the heart of a horse. I'm only worried for his knees now. Can you tell if he'll be crippled like this permanently?'

'Hard to say. If it was any other animal, the prognosis wouldn't look promising. His tendons may have deformed or been damaged permanently during paralysis, or it may be a form of wastage from being immobilised so long during a burst of development. We'll have a better idea in two or three days.'

'I had to expand his halter a few days ago. And I think he's grown about five centimetres in height. So if it's only wastage, then careful exercise and the right mix of feed should fix it anyway, right?'

'Possibly. I've never seen anything like this before. Knees aren't supposed to bend that way.' He continued with his usual checks for heart, temperature, lungs, stomach and so on, while I kept asking questions about how long it would normally take for each of his remaining symptoms to clear up, if they weren't necessarily associated with tetanus.

Norbert didn't want to raise my hopes too high too soon. Yet I couldn't help noticing the prognosis had improved from impossible to possible, and he had begun to talk about what might happen in two or three days, instead of one or two.

'He hasn't had a fit since yesterday morning,' I said. 'Nearly thirty hours ago.'

Norbert replied by resupplying me with needles and medications for another five days. 'Whatever you're doing,' he said. 'Keep doing it. There's light at the end of the tunnel now.'

By noon of the ninth day, we enticed Lucky back into the sling, making a game of it, with a spoonful of "porridge paste" as a reward for each step. He slept for an hour, then asked to be set free again. A fair request, so we let him out and with each step he seemed to grow stronger and more determined to stay upright on his own.

At dusk, he seemed so happy standing by his mother and resisted returning to the sling, without actually refusing that I relented and let him stay up for the night. I couldn't imagine a better reward for all his hard work that day.

10pm Lucky could stand by himself without teetering. I still worried about him tiring and falling over, so Jim and I stayed up with him until midnight, watching over him. Sitting on the fence together, we spent hours talking about nothing. Gossiping about the gossips, mostly, until I finally worked up the courage to ask him about his latest girlfriend. But instead of asking who she was, my stupid nerves kicked in and my tongue twisted up, and it came out as:

'How's your girlfriend?'

'Not sure.' He smiled and stroked a straggle of hair from my eyes. 'You tell me.'

'Don't tease.' I slapped his hand away. 'You know who I mean.'

'Actually, I don't. I work all day at the power station and my nights have been consumed by studying for my engineering degree. I just finished after six years, so it's been impossible to establish any kind of relationship. The only girls I know all hang out with my mates at the pubs on weekends.'

'What about that pretty blonde in your car last week? She looked nice.'

'Oh, her? Yeah, she is nice. She likes horses too, so next time she's around, maybe I should bring her in? She'd love to meet you.'

'Sure. Great,' I said, lacking enthusiasm. 'Any friend of yours, is welcome here too I guess…'

Jim laughed. 'Don't tell me you haven't heard who she is yet?'

I shrugged.

'Circle the date,' he teased. 'The gossips finally missed something.'

I jumped off the fence and slapped my hands against his chest, threatening to shove him backwards into the muddy yard of our Vietnamese neighbours. 'I'm going to see how funny you look down there with the weeds.'

'Go right ahead. Shove me all the way to Vietnam, if it gets us another shower together, fully clothed again or not.'

'You wish.' I didn't shove him. I didn't want to risk hurting him, not even by accident - or upsetting our neighbours - so I turned to walk away.

He grabbed me, pulled me into his arms and brought his face nearer...

'Cut that out,' I said, dodging and struggling. 'I'm not that kind of girl.'

'Neither is she,' he said. 'She's my cousin.'

'She is?'

He pulled me closer and swept me away with a kiss that left no doubting his feelings.

When he let me go, finally, I noticed Lucky and Penny both watching us under the light of the smiling crescent moon.

'Hey, not in front of the kids,' I joked. 'The gossips will start rumours about us next.'

'Too late. That was last week's news. Mrs Parker is taking bets on which day we'll hook up. Shall I put I fiver down on tomorrow ? Or day after?'

I checked my watch, and grinned. 12:10am 'Make it today. Life's too short to waste.'

39. Frosty Road to Recovery
(Days 10, 11 and 12)

Abraham Lincoln,
the 16th American president
whose term ended with assassination,
once said;

The best thing about the future is it
[only] comes one day at a time.

He made it sound leisurely.
Something to be desired,
and yes, I was grateful to be less busy,
but things didn't end well for him.

It made me worry that I might have trouble ahead too.

Monday, April 30 and my small corner of the world seemed to be returning to normal, finally.

Another workday for Jim. He'd sent me up to bed finally at 2am, leaving both horses napping on their feet under the mulberry tree - but when I dashed down to check on Lucky at dawn, I found him and his mother dozing with their heads over the sofa, resting on Jim's shoulders.

'Help?' he whispered, grinning. He'd come back in uniform for the 3am shift, and now he'd be running late for the power station. 'I didn't want to disturb them.'

Throughout the day, Lucky showed me when he needed

his mother to be milked – every three or four hours, roughly - a litre each time, which I used as enticement back into the sling for a "time-out" of therapy to ensure he still progressed through his leg exercises and napped each time, for at least the next hour after each feed. He was still just a baby, after all.

Over the course of that day and the next, Lucky grew anxious at being 'cooped up' for so long. Even Penny's pleasant temperament began to flare. Yet by dusk of the twelfth day, the colt could finally feed himself from Penny's milk bar.

He swished his tail, triumphantly, suckling happily...

Watching him, I felt a tear trickle down my cheek. Salty, and yet so sweet.

Content at last, the colt curled up on the lawn to sleep at his mother's feet; his legs straight and strong enough now to get up and down by himself. I'd still need to clean the wounds in his armpits twice a day for a month, but his pain threshold had shot so high, he showed no further sign of discomfort.

Norbert came for one more visit and I told him I wanted to settle my account. He scratched up a bill for a mere two hundred dollars, which barely paid for the medical supplies.

'You did most of the work,' he told me kindly.

I thanked him with a hug.

That night, we held a street party for the whole neighbourhood to celebrate Lucky's amazing survival.

At midnight, while people were still dancing in the street, Jim led me into our backyard under the mulberry tree, where Penny and the colt stood, dozing contentedly.

'It's about time somebody spoiled you, young lady.'

'Oh, don't call me that,' I pleaded. 'I'm so used to hearing it as an insult, often accompanied by *listen here*.'

'Listen here, young lady,' he teased. 'It's about time you

had a real date, with a dinner and a movie.'

'Oh, really?' I grinned cheekily. 'And who's good enough to make me do anything against my will?'

He stroked the wild curl from my brow, making my heart beat faster. Then he kissed me under a million stars.

Drifting back to earth an eon later, I rested my head against his warm chest, listening to his heart and watching the horses, so at peace.

40. One Final Turn of Fate

Socrates,
the legendary Greek philosopher,
once said;

*Wisdom is knowing
how little we know*

... like a polite slap in the face;
Hey, wake up! You don't know what you don't know!

I should have paid more attention.
I should have gone around and double checked
everything before heading to bed.

That night I slept blissfully unaware of anything.

Barely four hours sleep, and yet I woke fresher than ever. It was sunrise, day 13. I leapt up before the early blue bird again. I couldn't wait to check on the colt. My heart swelled, fit to burst with love and appreciation for the whole world.

Throwing back my bedcovers, I made the biggest leap yet for my door into the dining room. I beat Muffy past the large timber table for the first time, so she bolted under it – cutting a shortcut over the sleeping dog - to tackle me in the hallway.

'Grr-ow-ow-ow!' Doggo yowled, waking with a start and leaping after us. Dining chairs flew backwards and he took his turn at tripping me. I tumbled sideways against my parent's door.

'Anita's up,' Dad mumbled as he turned over.

I filled five pet bowls with fresh mince, feeling energised by the return to familiar routines. Racing downstairs, I forgot my shoes, as ever, and skidded to a halt in the icy grass.

The mare and foal; missing.

I couldn't believe it.

I dashed over each of the fences into neighbouring yards where Penny had permission to graze, and searched around their homes with no luck. . literally, no Lucky anywhere.

Jogging around Donny's house in bare feet again, I came to his stony driveway, headed back down his yard, past my own bedroom...

Splat!

Overhead, I saw Bruiser freshly crashed on the ledge to my bedroom window. Above him, high over our roof, circled a swarm of similar blue-winged birds that darted about, striving to dodge the deadly beak of a much bigger, meaner butcher bird. It explained the mystery, finally. Considering the size of the large flock, it seemed that Bruiser wasn't such a stupid bird after all. More likely he'd been several different birds, each learning about glass the hard way as they fled from the predator.

No time to waste watching them. I had to find Penny and Lucky.

The first clue was the forty-four gallon drum of old sump oil that blocked the narrow passage between Dad's workshop and our boundary fence with Donny. Somebody had moved it.

Dad's youngest apprentice had moved it, not bothering to think about any consequences.

A trail of hoof prints in the frost led me out alongside our driveway and through our front gate.

No dogs barked in any direction, and no hooves

thundered on bitumen, which made me worry how far away they could be. Frantic to find them before the trail melted, I didn't stop for shoes. I just grabbed an old damp towel from the clothes line – the only thing handy that could keep the chill from my shoulders, and long enough I could use it to lead Penny, if only I could find her.

I still had no idea how far ahead they could be. As much as four hours, perhaps, since I'd last seen them at 2am; both dozing contentedly under the mulberry tree.

How far could a sick foal run on still-stiff legs? Judging by his tracks, he'd recovered enough to progress from Frankenstein walking to Franken-trotting.

I bolted off down the icy footpath in bare feet, following their trail of hoofprints in the frost – a painful lesson! The ice felt so cold, ironically it seemed to burn my feet as hot as fire. It also made my feet swell and glow pink as if I'd really been walking on hot coals or shattered glass.

I tracked the hoofprints north towards the nearest bend in the river. But halfway down the street, the trail veered northeast through a set of newer homes, where nobody had any fences. Dogs barked inside their pens and garages, warning all of their owners that I was prowling. I saw lights switch on in a house beside me, so I ran faster just as a window slid open above me.

It didn't take long to notice I'd turned in a bee-line for the old river paddock. Puffing with relief, I found them, dozing outside the gate of their old home, under their own city-funded security light.

'Hello my little escapees.' I skipped across the road, already tearing the old towel into three long shreds – also noticing the bright street light no longer hurt the colt's eyes.

'You had me worried,' I said, mostly so they could hear that I wasn't mad at them. Having run away once, they might take it into their heads to run away when I tried to catch them. 'If you're ready to go back to the herd, you should have just asked me.'

I tied all three strips of towel together into one long rope, and tore a hole in the middle to use as a noose around the mare's nose, while the long ends served as reins.

Sliding up onto her damp back, I turned her head gently for home.

I called Lucky to follow, and as he turned, he stumbled and trotted after us, leaving the end of his misadventures as a trail of hoof prints in the melting frost behind us.

*3 weeks later: Happy to be healthy again.
His chest wounds are still healing
(the light patches on his chest)
but his front legs are nearly completely
straight again.*

Appendix I: Recipes for a Sweet Finale

Our 'Never Fail' Chocolate Cake

#1: Melt together in a saucepan:
    4 tablespoons of butter
    + 4 tablespoons of cocoa (or more if you like)
    + 1 tablespoon of any berry jam (or apricot)
    + 1 cup of milk (usually full cream from a cow).

#2: Add to large bowl and beat with:
    4 eggs
    + 2 cups sugar (or half a cup of sugar substitute)
    + 2 cups of SR Flour (Self Raising)

3: Whip until it looks like cake mix.

#4: Bake until it looks like a cake. About 20 minutes if using a medium oven heat.

#5: Cool & smother in any of 3 icings:
    i) Light dusting of dry icing mix, or...
    ii) 2 cups icing sugar+ 2 tabs cocoa + drips of water and/or lemon juice/coffee, or...
    iii) 2 cups icing sugar+ 1 cup soft butter, whipped until it looks like icing, and flavoured with a few drops of lemon juice (+ either cocoa/coffee to suit taste).

Tip: Try not to forget the eggs, like I did.

Anzac Biscuits (or charred chunks)

#1: Into a big bowl, mix:
    About 2 cups of rolled oats
    + 1 cup of plain flour
    + 1 cup of SR flour (Self Raising)
    + 1 cup of sugar (or half a cup of sugar substitute)
    + 2 cups of shredded coconut

#2: Into a large saucepan, melt:
    1 cup butter
    + 4 tablespoons of golden syrup (or maple)
    + 4 tablespoons of water

#3: Add to saucepan:
    3 teaspoons of baking soda
    + be amazed as foam rises.

#4: Add yummy foam to dry mix, and stir until it looks like biscuit mix. If it's too runny, add more dry ingredients, in any proportions that taste great to you.

#5: Scrunch into ball shapes and squash onto a greased baking tray.

#6: Lick fingers often, coz it's so yummy.

#7: Bake in a slow oven for 20 minutes, or hot oven for 10.

Tip: Bake as long as you like, eg a short time until light golden soft... or get distracted and come back to find them burning, hard, crunchy, or totally black.
    It is nearly impossible to ruin this recipe. I've tried and failed many times, but the darn things are still edible... at least by Lucky. He adores them.

Appendix II: Extract from *Pottie's Horse Dictionary*
[1882/Reprint Edition 1983]:

Note: This is the entire entry for Tetanus, was the only hint of any prior case studies that I could find anywhere. Yet these three words; "most reliable treatment" gave me the glimmer of hope I needed;

Tetanus: An acute, highly febrile[1] disease of all animals, the horse being very susceptible[2].
Causes: Germ infection (clostridium tetani) of deep, punctured wounds, e.g. picked-up nails, injuries from the prongs of stable forks. Castrations, docking, unhygienic conditions during foaling. Causative germ lives in old manures and humus[3].
Symptoms: In the early stages, the symptoms are very slight and difficult to recognise. Later, the horse becomes slower, starts dragging toes along the ground, breathing becomes distressed and the ears are moved backwards and forwards continually. Eyes flicker, the muscles of the neck and back are rigid[4]. Head and neck slightly raised, the lips are stretched backwards, exposing the clenched teeth[5]. The ears are rigid and their points turned to each other, and the two jaws are 'locked'. The forelegs are splayed outwards the better to retain balance. If head is lifted up sharply, the third eyelid is seen to cover the eye. The spasm is caused by any sudden movement, daylight or unusual sound, e.g. slamming of doors.
Treatment and nursing: The site of the wound by which the germ has gained entrance should be found. Disinfect it with strong solution of condy's crystals, hydrogen peroxide. Place the horse in a dark loose-box and while attending, take all precautions not to frighten the animal. As long as the horse can swallow, plenty of green feed and fluids should be provided. After the jaws become locked, feed him on very thin bran mashes,

linseed or hay tea, gruels, milk etc. Keep the bowels open by adding Epsom salts to the food or water[6]. The ***most reliable treatment*** is injections of anti-tetanic serum, supplemented by antibiotics.

Prevention: In all cases of deep, penetrating wounds, an injection of tetanus anti-toxin should be given as soon as possible. Long term protection can be provided by an injection of tetanus toxoid.

My Personal Notes to this Extract:
1) febrile = feverish

2) In other sources, tetanus is also referred to as 'lockjaw'.

3) humus = partly decomposed organics, like garden mulch.

4) In my experience, his spine didn't become rigid until day 2, by which time most horses would have been dead naturally anyway. This symptom was at its worst by day 6, and lingered, even as he regained control of his legs.

5) This peeling back of the lips never happened in Lucky. Instead, his lips were clenched closed.

6) We used an enema to get things going again, and then drinks of warm molasses water.

7) Since my foal's puncture had scabbed over quickly and been almost fully healed by the end of the fortnight before first symptoms appeared, I would suggest that all puncture wounds should be treated as if the tetanus germ is inside, even if they seem to be healing well by themselves.

Dedications (& Pat-hooeeys)

To the old Blackwood Street neighbourhood. You know who you are. And where: in my heart forever.

To the Ipswich librarians, who let us borrow all the books with the word tetanus; far above our legal lending limit. And helped to gather them all so swiftly! Thank you sooooooo much!

To Ger Curly and Rob J Green for compelling me to try Photoshop for the first time, so I could breathe fresh life into Lucky's baby photos for publication in time for the first edition. Taken using a cheap disposable 12-shot camera that had no flash, most of the pixels were never captured properly in the first place, so even this level of modest restoration seemed almost impossible way back then. Thank you!

Special thanks also to my editor, Hazel Flynn, who believed in me from my very first book at Random House.

Pat-hooeey with spit on the "vet-o-matic" who dumped me as a client when he realised the symptoms I'd described indicated tetanus.

More pat-hooeys on all of the hospitals who hung up on me because my little fella was "only an animal."

But to the many other vets, doctors and nurses who tried to help or advise me from a distance (because the disease affects humans the same as for animals), a huge warm hug of thanks, with special thanks to those who went to extra lengths to research or ask around their more experienced staff at: The Royal Brisbane Hospital, Princess Alexandra Hospital, The Wesley Hospital, Ipswich General and St Andrews', all in Queensland... And interstate: St Vincents Hospital (Sydney), Prince of Wales (Randwick), Prince

Henry Teaching Hospital (since demolished with campus transferred to Randwick), Victoria's oldest hospital, The Alfred.

There was also the Royal Perth Hospital, plus a sister and 2 elderly patients at Mercy Hospital (Wembley aged care, where the sister found two retired farmers who'd owned animals who'd fought tetanus but lost).

In the Northern Territory, I can't forget the Royal Darwin Hospital, where I found a nurse with a father in the flying doctors' service and a grandfather who was a tough old "bushie" with a lifetime's experience in bush remedies, including the "stone rubbing" trick before an injection.

There were also the smaller country hospitals in: Laidley, Toowoomba, Warwick, Townsville, Mackay and Cairns, where I managed to find doctors who also owned their own farms and had an insight into the treatment of horses, generally speaking, all of whom tried to help by searching their records for anything that might help, albeit unsuccessfully.

And to the world class vet, Norbert Gaulton, our hero.
Thank you.

Lucky on his 13th & 26th Birthdays:

Age 13   Age 26

... at the home that Jim and I made together with our children. He grew into a fine strong fellow; brave, smart and loyal for 26 years and counting...

Published here in the hope that all of our dear fur-babies may also live on in these pages of History long after they have earned their Pegasus wings, [Vale Penny aged 32, Apache 36 and Snowy 42]

With Love,

Anita, Jim and family...

Thank you, dear reader,
for sharing these memories with us.

If you are blessed by a much beloved fur-baby too,
I hope you get to share many wonderful
moments together...
but without any bad luck or danger.

About the Author

Initially best known for her budgeting achievements on a low income, [after purchasing her first property as a minor at age 16 and paying it off before her 18th birthday], Anita Bell has since stretched her creative talents into comedy thrillers and animation, where she has won the NK Hemming Award for Excellence twice, and earned over 20 Laurels from International Film Festivals for her first two productions, most recent of which is "Grovely and The Big Fish".

With "Fortune's Foal," Anita shares the remarkable true story of this; her first year after graduating highschool as a 16 year old, meeting Lucky, and finding land to keep him in a river city, despite flooding.

When she is not immersed in her writing or animation, Anita can be found on her farm, surrounded by the beauty of nature and her beloved animals. Through her work, she continues to inspire others to pursue their passions and embrace the power of storytelling.

Other Series by this Author

Award Winning Sci-Fantasy by AA Bell:

For Budding Artists & Composers by Ani Bell:

& Ani's Happy Office Series:

www.ingramcontent.com/pod-product-compliance
Lightning Source LLC
Chambersburg PA
CBHW072148070526
44585CB00015B/1040